THE ASTONISH FACTORY

Presents:

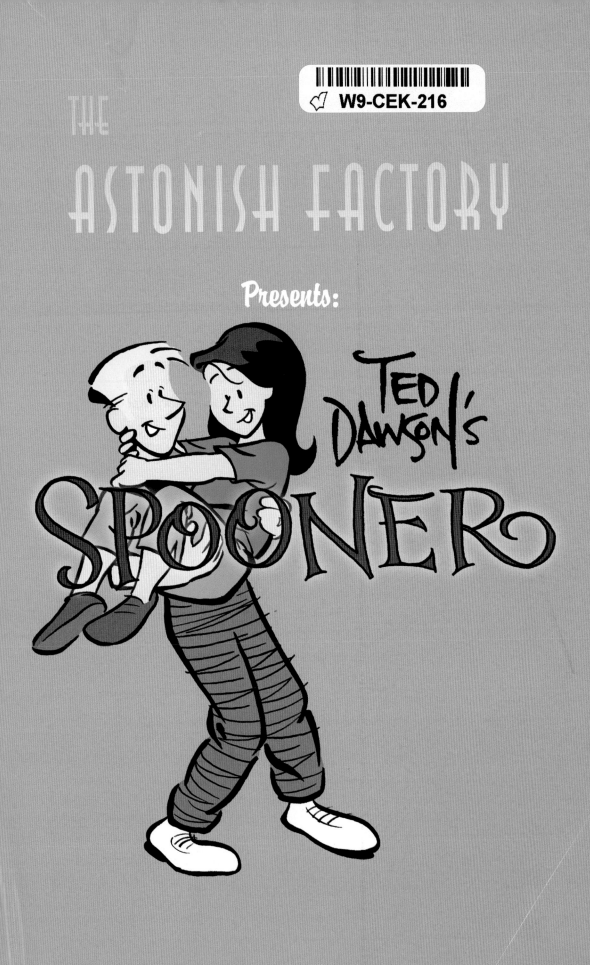

Ted Dawson's SPOONER

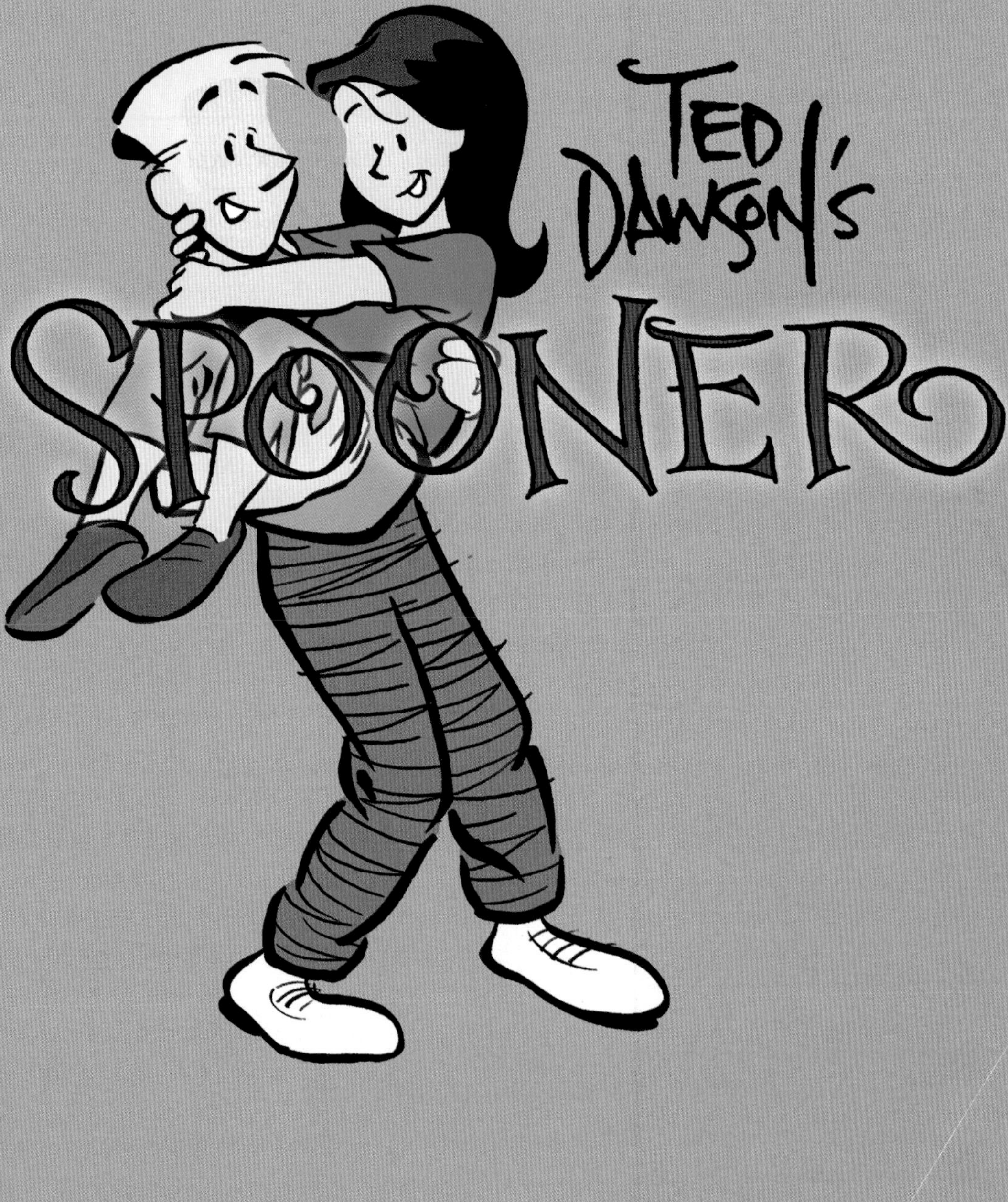

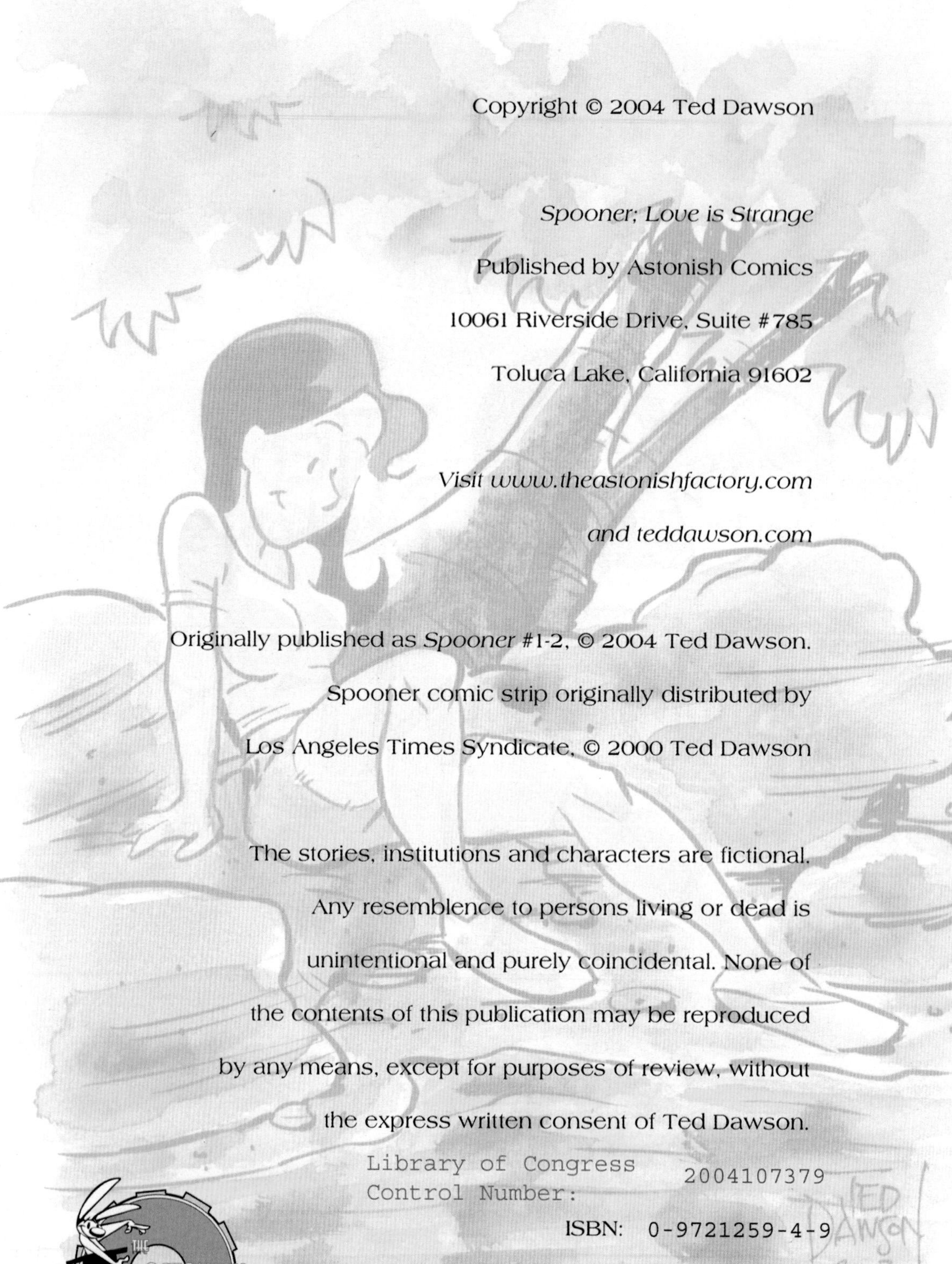
TED DAWSON 2003

Spooner; Love is Strange

Published by Astonish Comics
10061 Riverside Drive, Suite #785
Toluca Lake, California 91602

Visit www.theastonishfactory.com
and teddawson.com

Library of Congress Control Number: 2004107379
ISBN: 0-9721259-4-9

The Astonish Factory
Remember your childhood...and pass it on

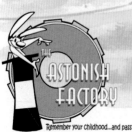

First printing July, 2004 Printed in Turkey.

To Robbin

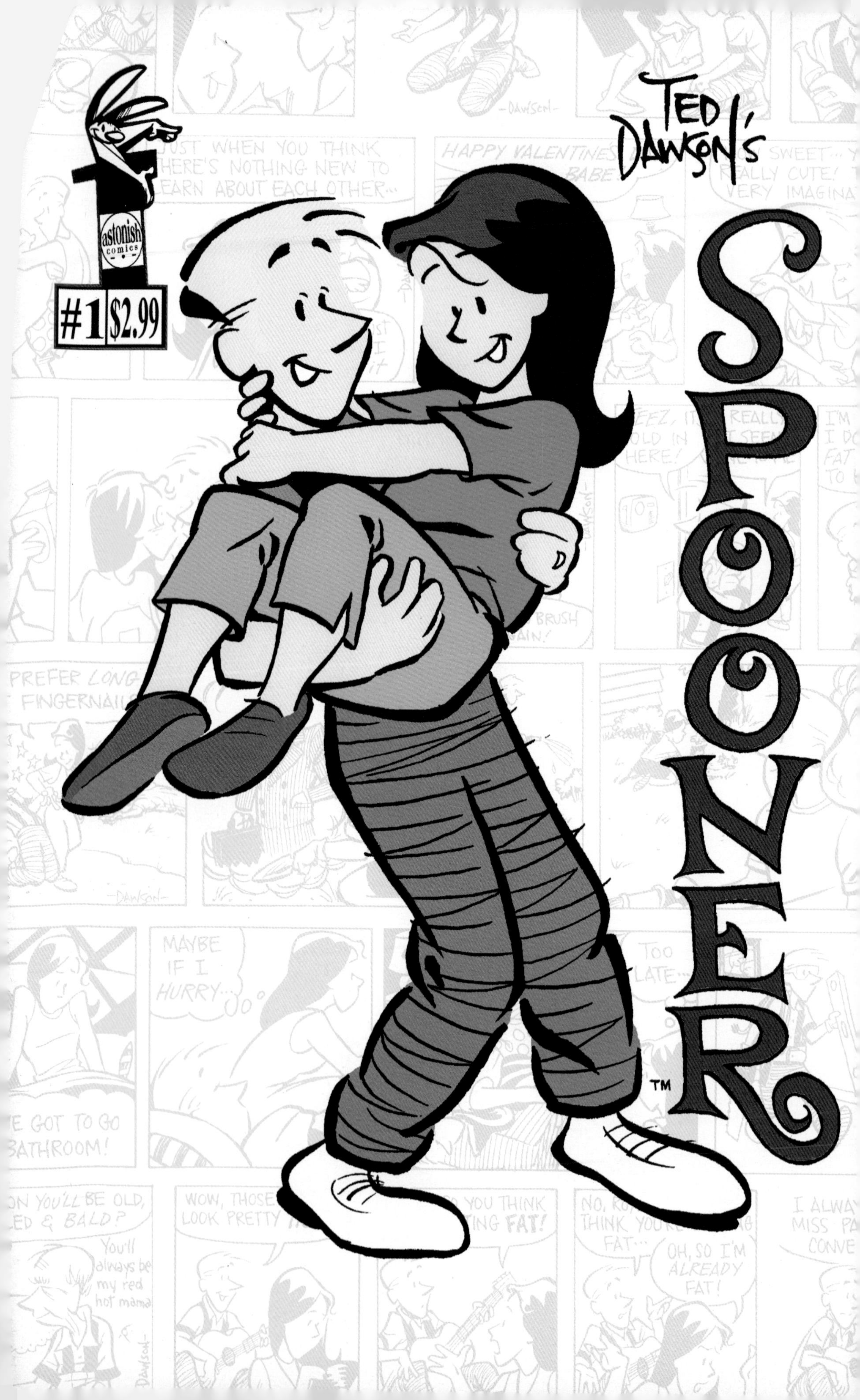
astonish comics
#1 $2.99
TED DAWSON'S
SPOONER™

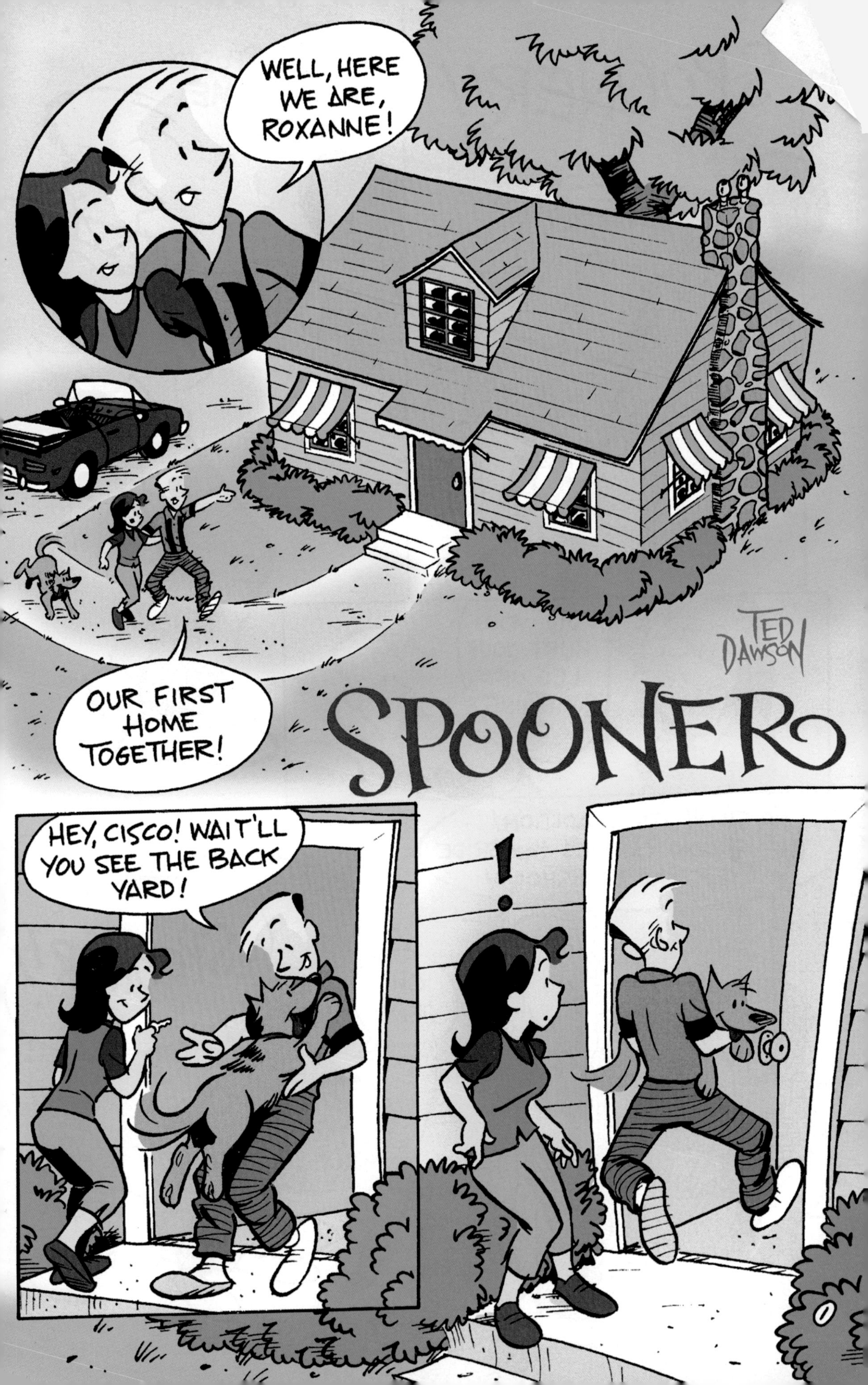
WELL, HERE WE ARE, ROXANNE!
OUR FIRST HOME TOGETHER!
TED DAWSON
SPOONER
HEY, CISCO! WAIT'LL YOU SEE THE BACK YARD!
!

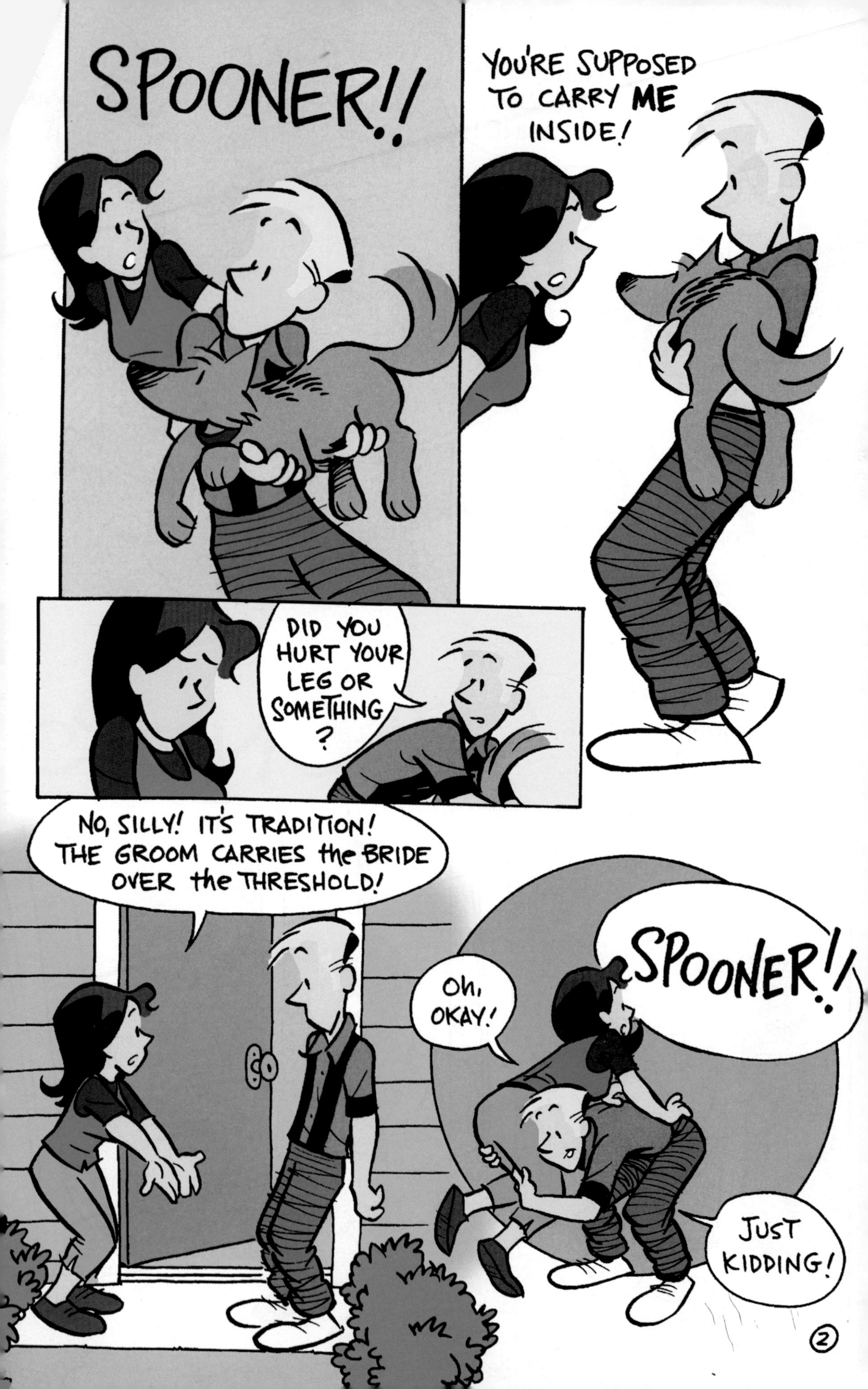
SPOONER!!
YOU'RE SUPPOSED TO CARRY **ME** INSIDE!
DID YOU HURT YOUR LEG OR SOMETHING?
NO, SILLY! IT'S TRADITION! THE GROOM CARRIES the BRIDE OVER the THRESHOLD!
Oh, OKAY!
SPOONER!!
JUST KIDDING!

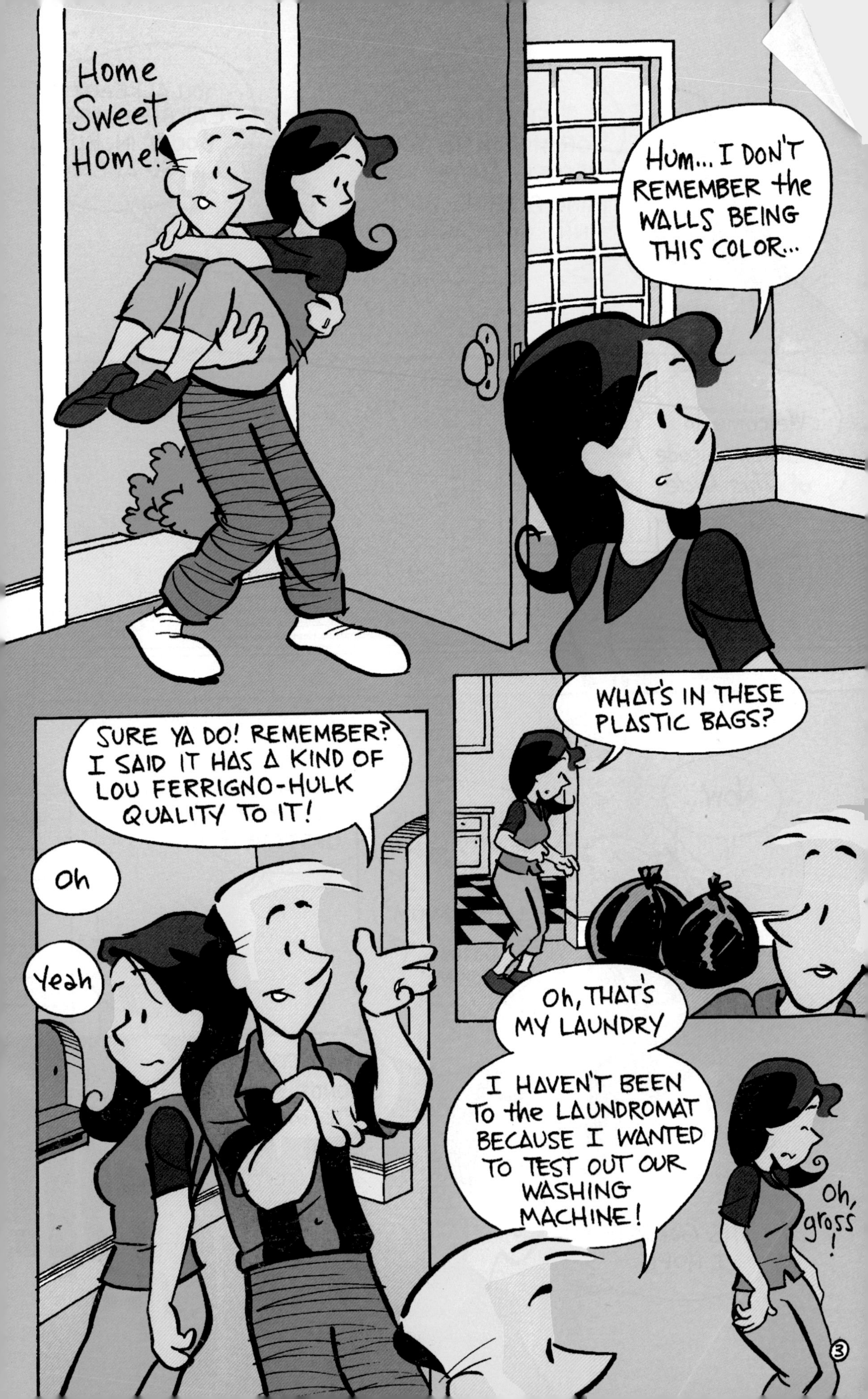
Home Sweet Home!
Hum... I DON'T REMEMBER the WALLS BEING THIS COLOR...
SURE YA DO! REMEMBER? I SAID IT HAS A KIND OF LOU FERRIGNO-HULK QUALITY TO IT!
Oh
Yeah
WHAT'S IN THESE PLASTIC BAGS?
Oh, THAT'S MY LAUNDRY
I HAVEN'T BEEN To the LAUNDROMAT BECAUSE I WANTED TO TEST OUT OUR WASHING MACHINE!
Oh, gross!
3

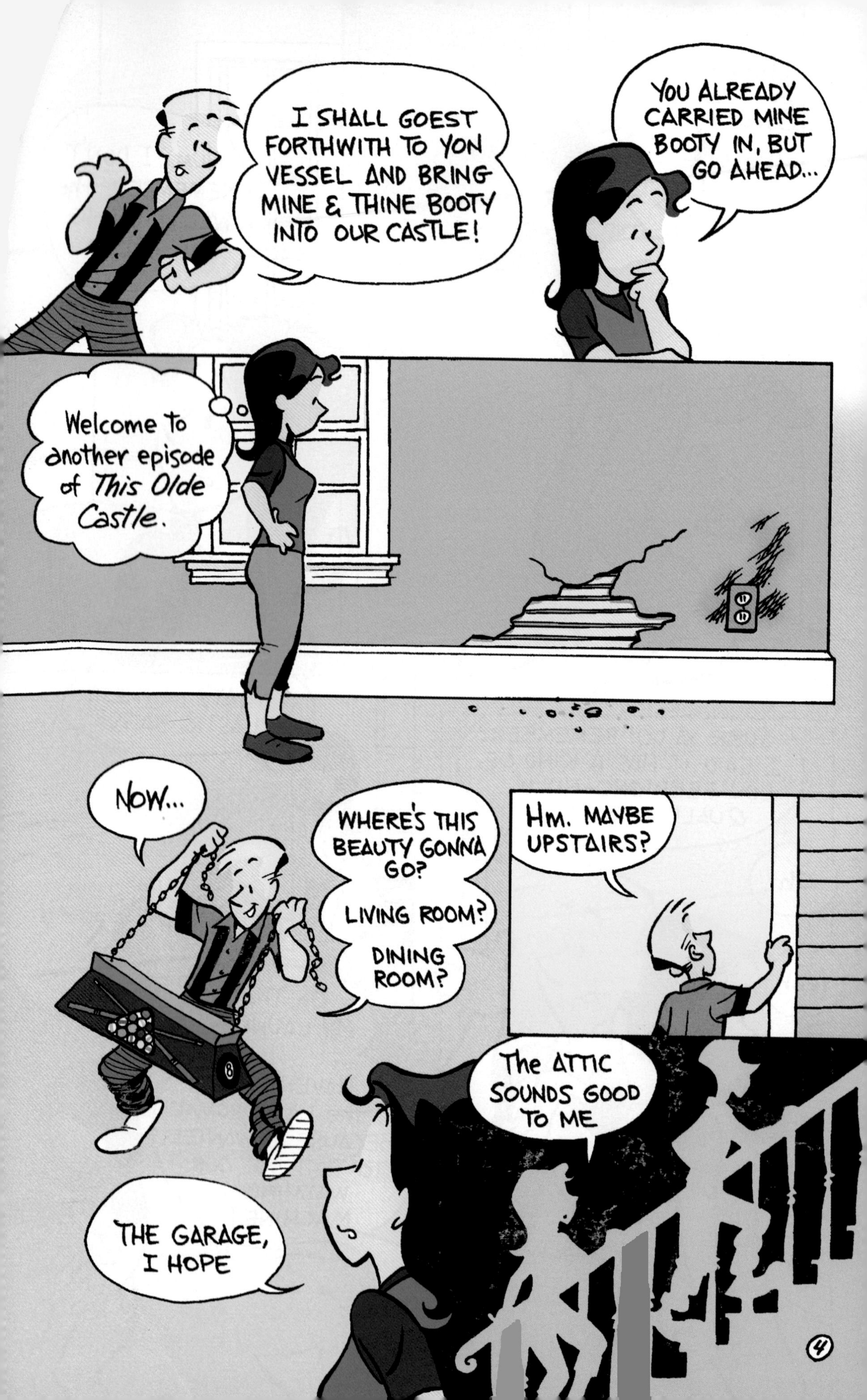
I SHALL GOEST FORTHWITH TO YON VESSEL AND BRING MINE & THINE BOOTY INTO OUR CASTLE!
YOU ALREADY CARRIED MINE BOOTY IN, BUT GO AHEAD...
Welcome to another episode of *This Olde Castle*.
NOW...
WHERE'S THIS BEAUTY GONNA GO?
LIVING ROOM?
DINING ROOM?
HM. MAYBE UPSTAIRS?
The ATTIC SOUNDS GOOD TO ME
THE GARAGE, I HOPE

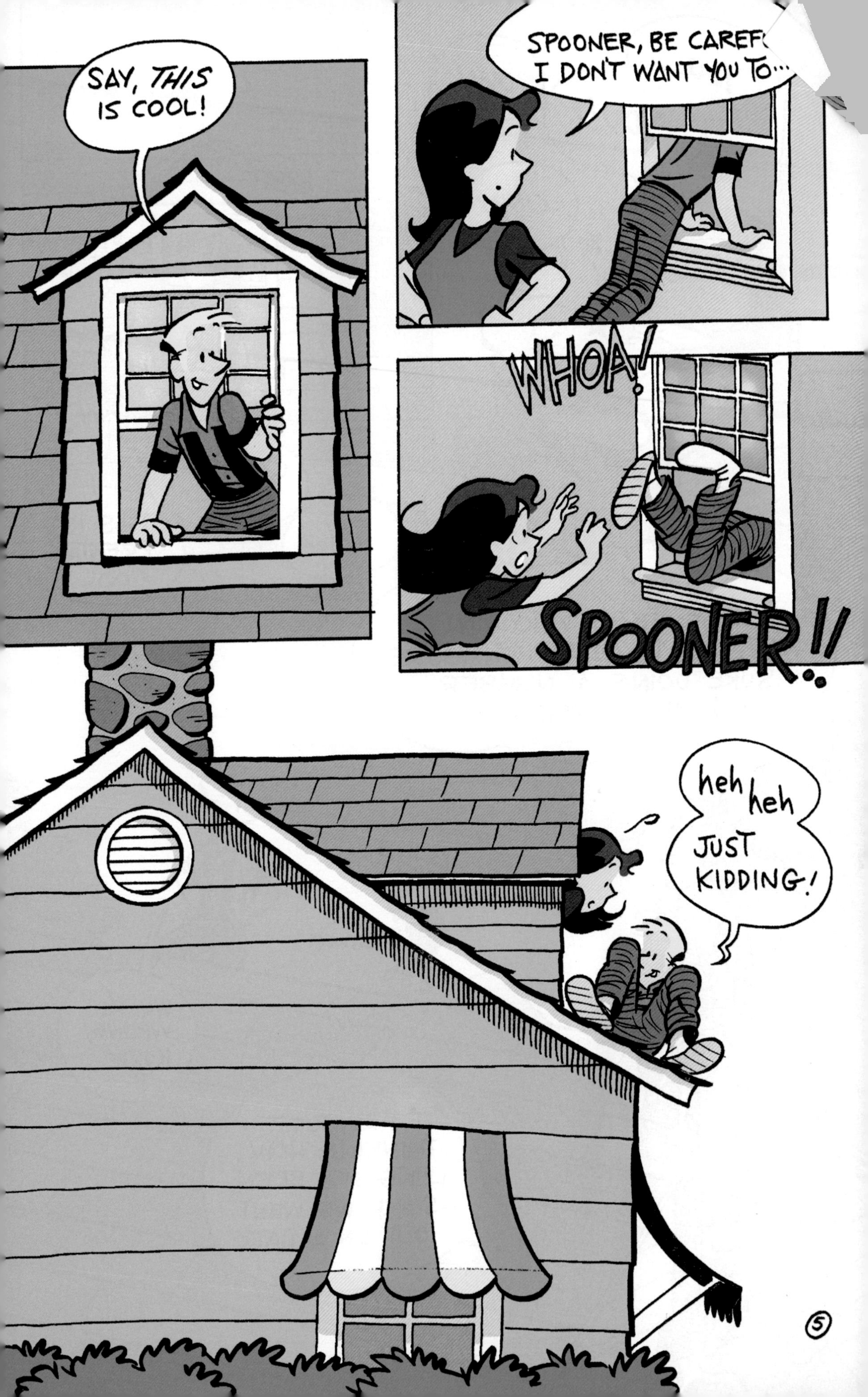
SAY, THIS IS COOL!
SPOONER, BE CAREF
I DON'T WANT YOU TO...
WHOA!
SPOONER!!
heh heh JUST KIDDING!
5

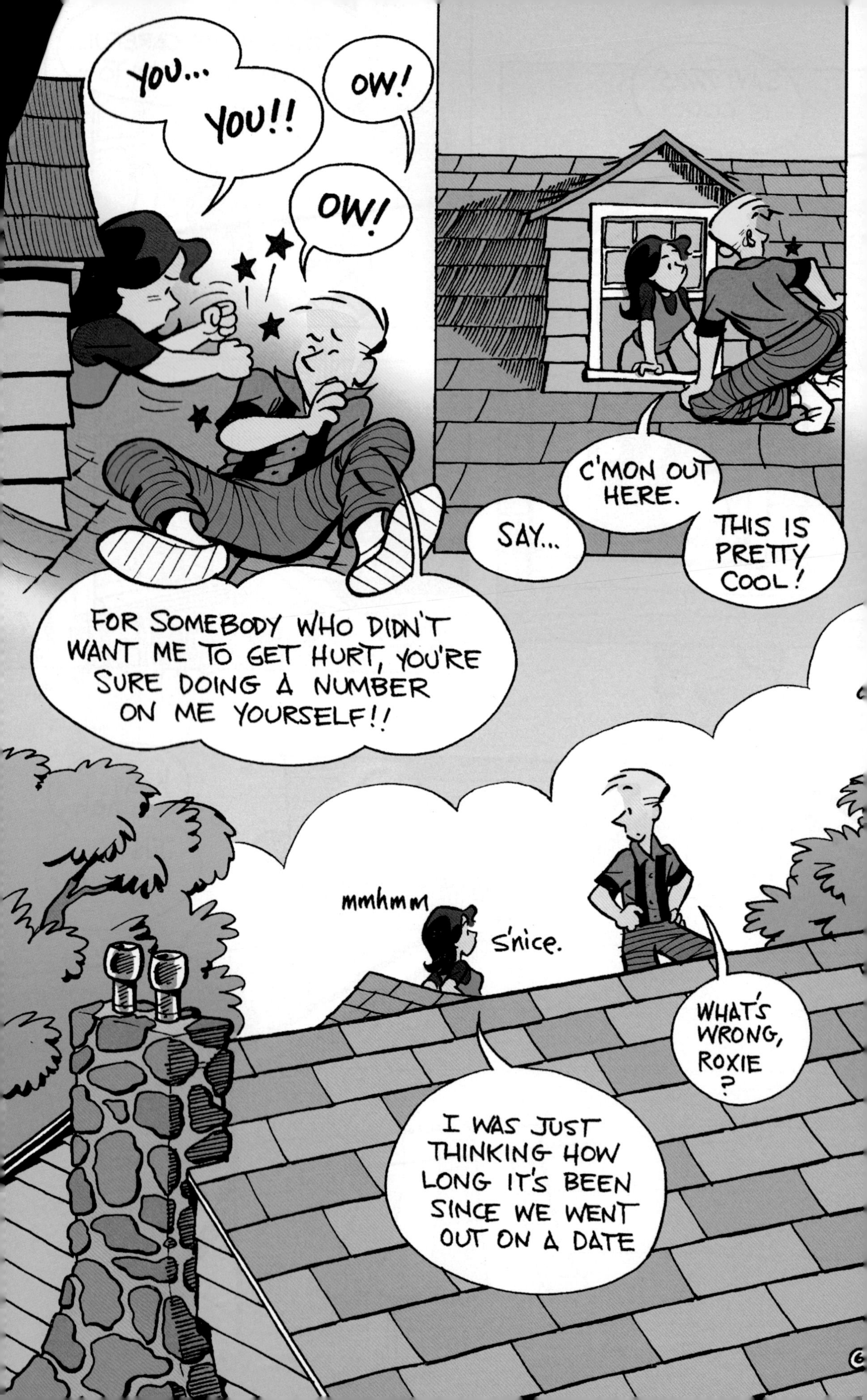

YOU...
YOU!!
OW!
OW!
FOR SOMEBODY WHO DIDN'T WANT ME TO GET HURT, YOU'RE SURE DOING A NUMBER ON ME YOURSELF!!
C'MON OUT HERE.
SAY...
THIS IS PRETTY COOL!
mmhmm
S'nice.
WHAT'S WRONG, ROXIE?
I WAS JUST THINKING HOW LONG IT'S BEEN SINCE WE WENT OUT ON A DATE

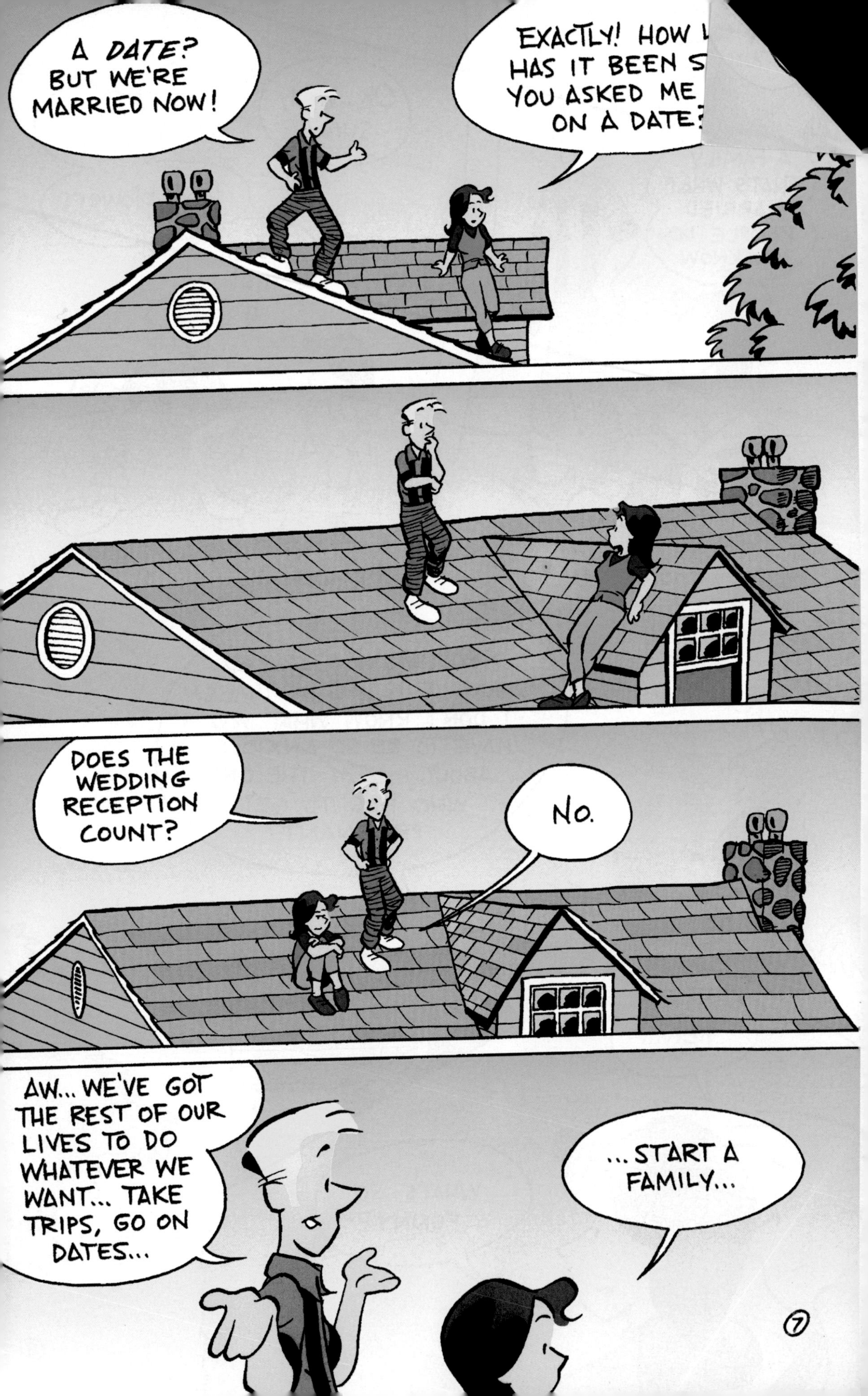
A *DATE*? BUT WE'RE MARRIED NOW!
EXACTLY! HOW HAS IT BEEN S YOU ASKED ME ON A DATE?
DOES THE WEDDING RECEPTION COUNT?
NO.
AW... WE'VE GOT THE REST OF OUR LIVES TO DO WHATEVER WE WANT... TAKE TRIPS, GO ON DATES...
...START A FAMILY...

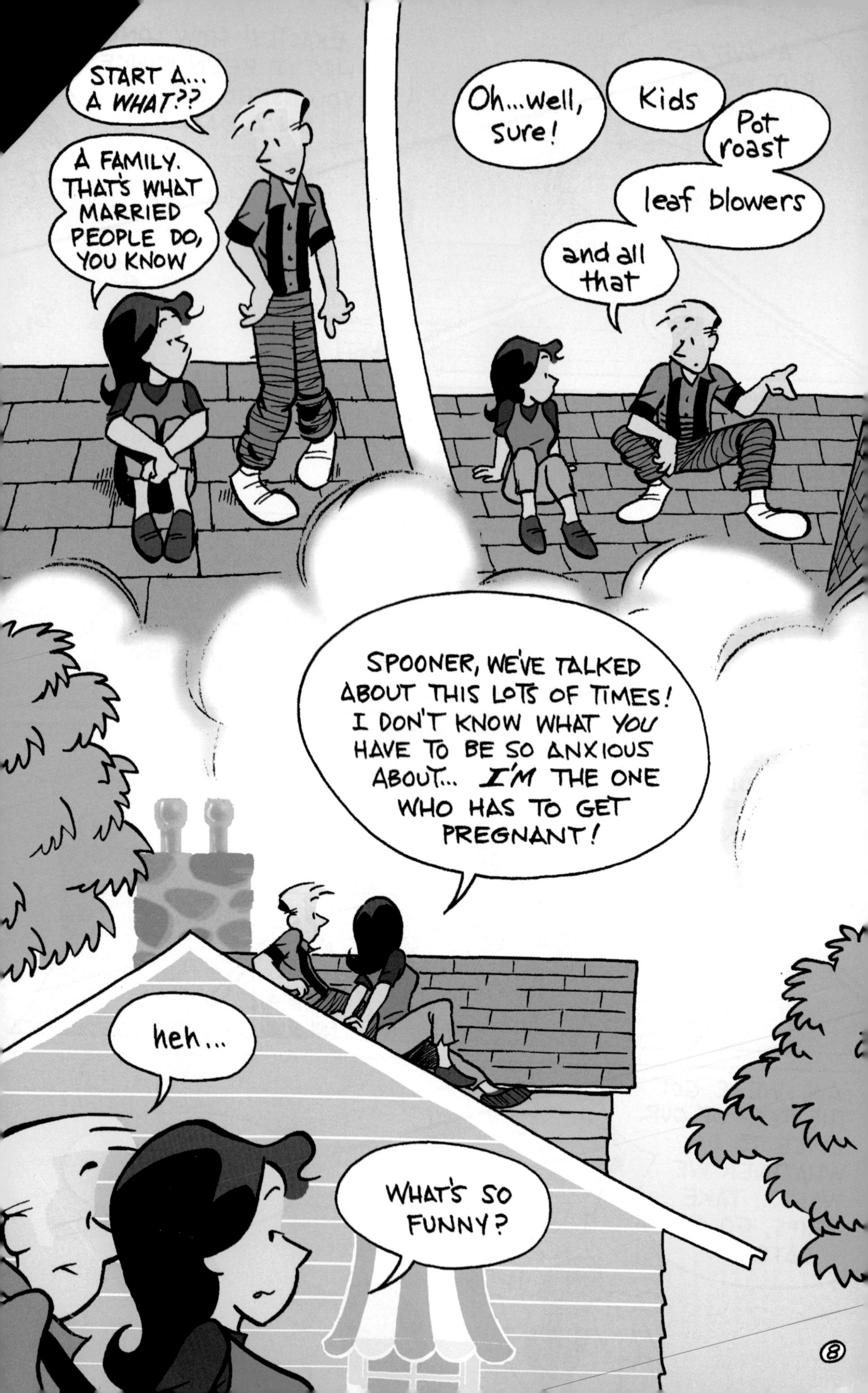
START A... A WHAT??
A FAMILY. THAT'S WHAT MARRIED PEOPLE DO, YOU KNOW
Oh...well, sure!
Kids
Pot roast
leaf blowers
and all that
SPOONER, WE'VE TALKED ABOUT THIS LOTS OF TIMES! I DON'T KNOW WHAT YOU HAVE TO BE SO ANXIOUS ABOUT... I'M THE ONE WHO HAS TO GET PREGNANT!
heh...
WHAT'S SO FUNNY?

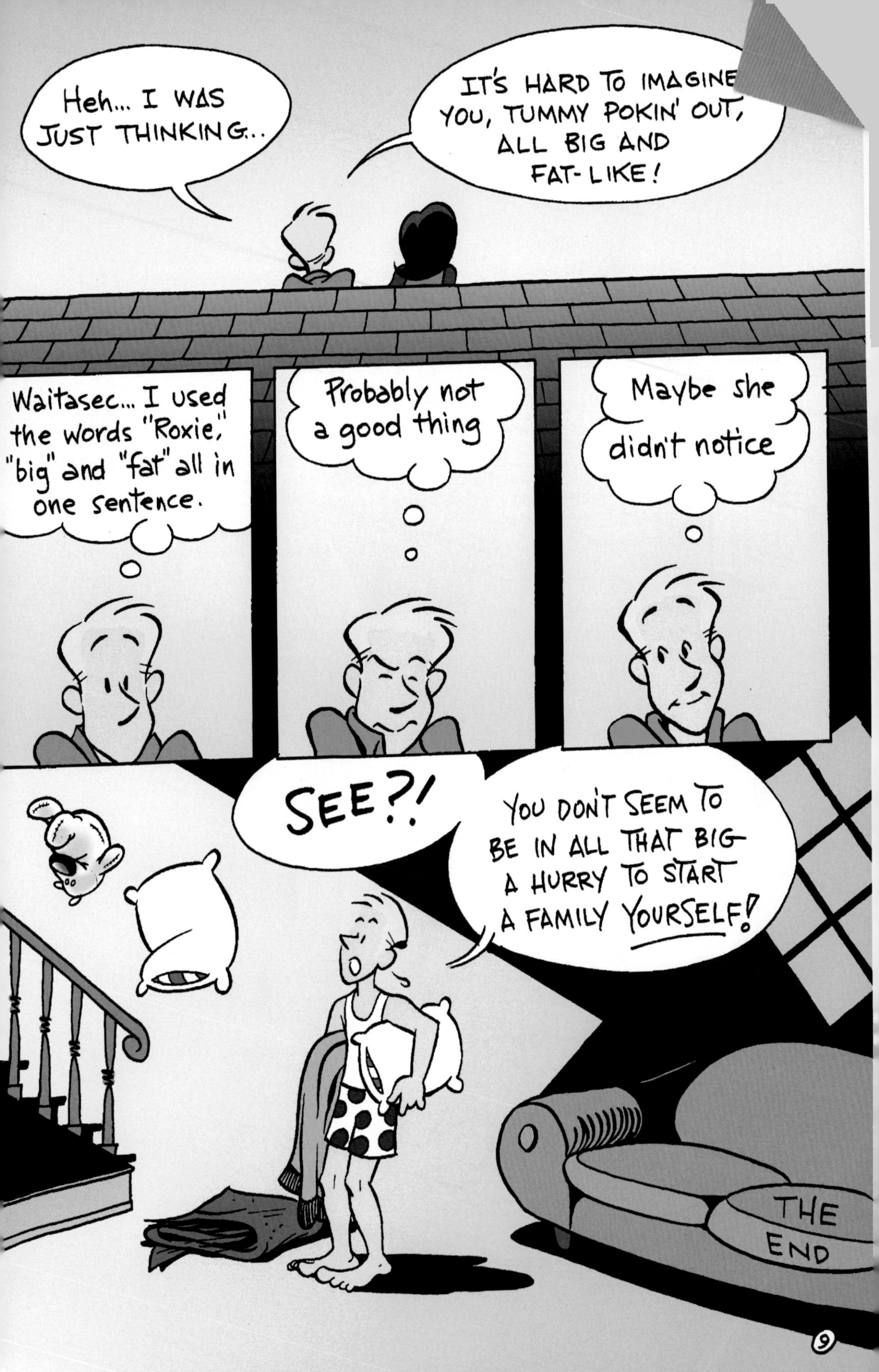

Heh... I WAS JUST THINKING..
IT'S HARD TO IMAGINE YOU, TUMMY POKIN' OUT, ALL BIG AND FAT-LIKE!
Waitasec... I used the words "Roxie," "big" and "fat" all in one sentence.
Probably not a good thing
Maybe she didn't notice
SEE?!
YOU DON'T SEEM TO BE IN ALL THAT BIG A HURRY TO START A FAMILY YOURSELF!
THE END

Spooner first appeared in newspapers on January 3, 2000. This was a bitter-sweet day for me because that was the last day of the Peanuts daily strips. Like most cartoonists, I count Charles Schulz as one of my influences.

The good folks at the Los Angeles Times Syndicate put Spooner on the comics pages, and I was fortunate to be able to work with Sarah Gillespie as my editor. Sarah had a positive influence on Spooner and myself.

Spooner and Roxanne were given life one evening over Shepherd Pie at an Irish Restaurant in Florida. My wife, Robbin, and I wrote several strips which appear on the following pages. These comics were part of my syndicate submission and were then used for the launch.

There's a lot of my wife & myself in these strips. And chances are you might see a little of yourself as well.

TED

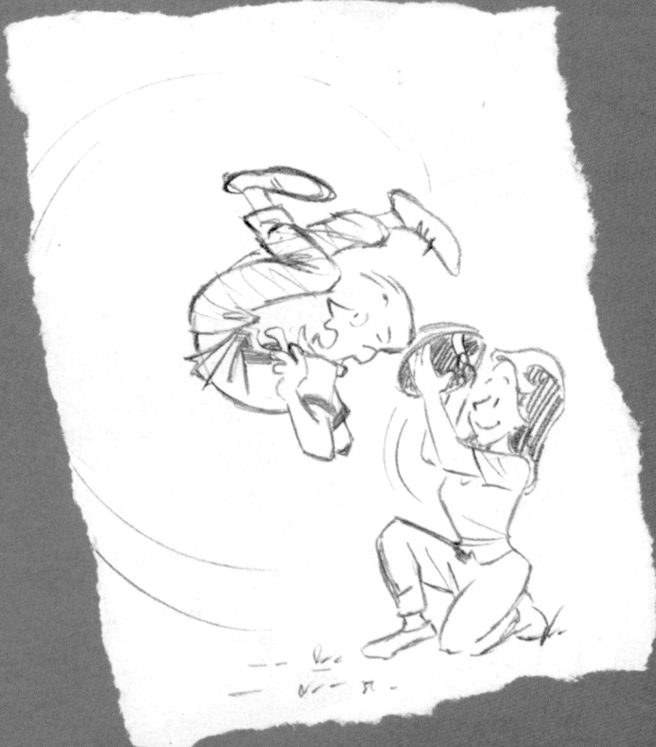

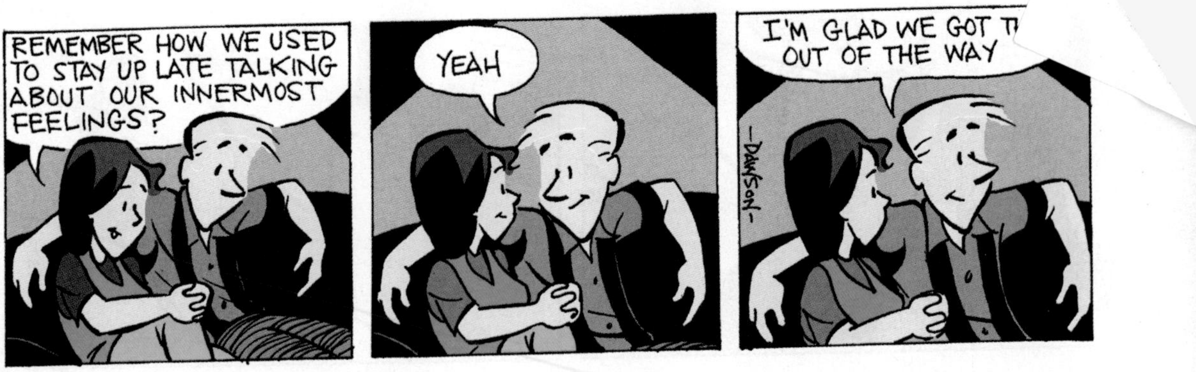
REMEMBER HOW WE USED TO STAY UP LATE TALKING ABOUT OUR INNERMOST FEELINGS?
YEAH
I'M GLAD WE GOT
OUT OF THE WAY
—DAWSON—

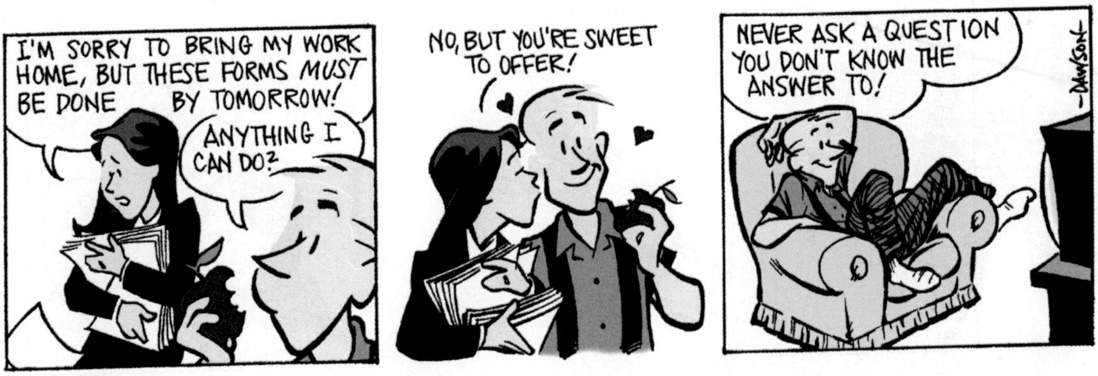
I'M SORRY TO BRING MY WORK HOME, BUT THESE FORMS *MUST* BE DONE BY TOMORROW!
ANYTHING I CAN DO?
NO, BUT YOU'RE SWEET TO OFFER!
NEVER ASK A QUESTION YOU DON'T KNOW THE ANSWER TO!
—DAWSON—

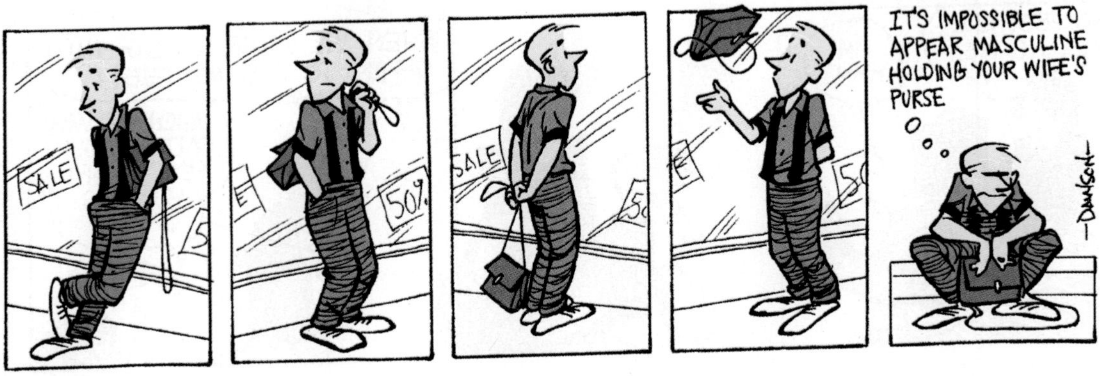
SALE
50%
SALE
IT'S IMPOSSIBLE TO APPEAR MASCULINE HOLDING YOUR WIFE'S PURSE
—DAWSON—

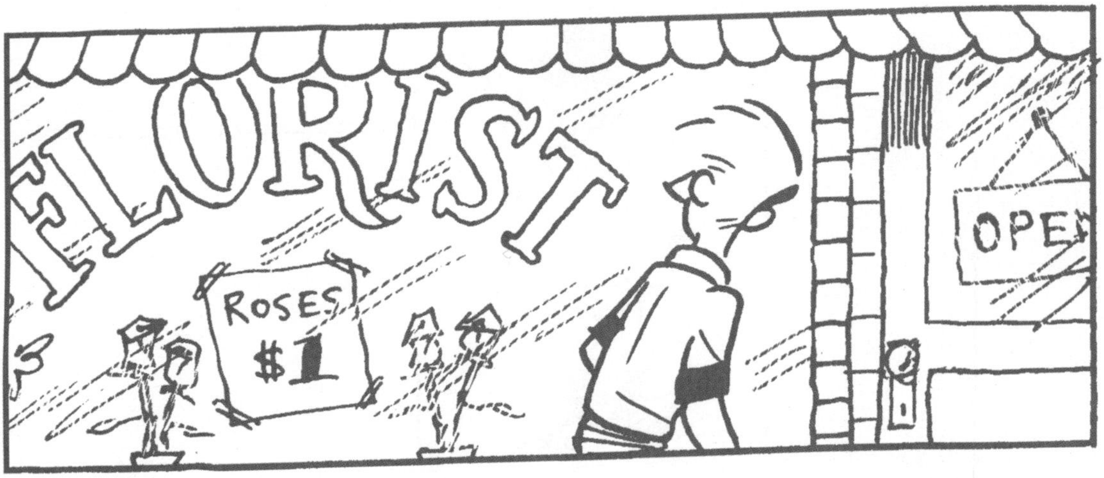
FLORIST
ROSES $1

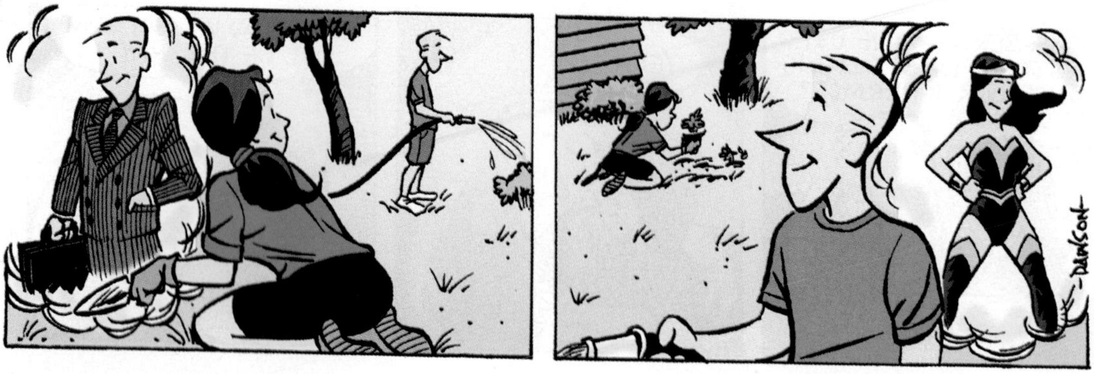

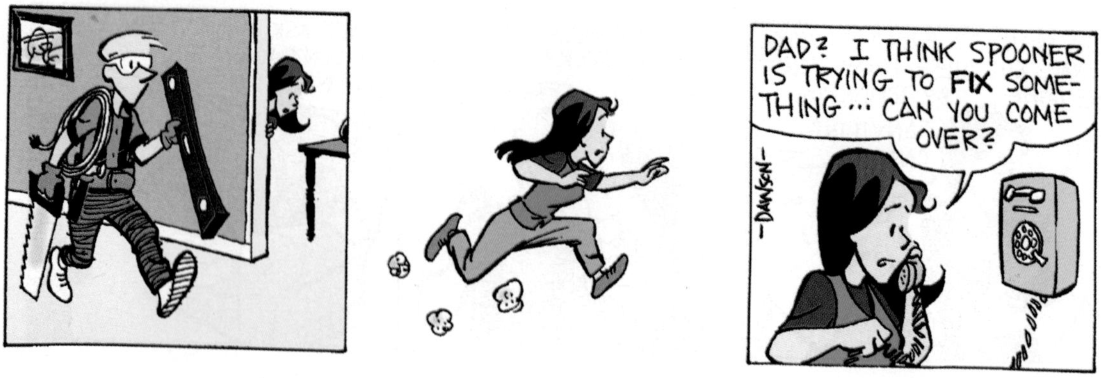
DAD? I THINK SPOONER IS TRYING TO **FIX** SOMETHING... CAN YOU COME OVER?
-DAWSON-

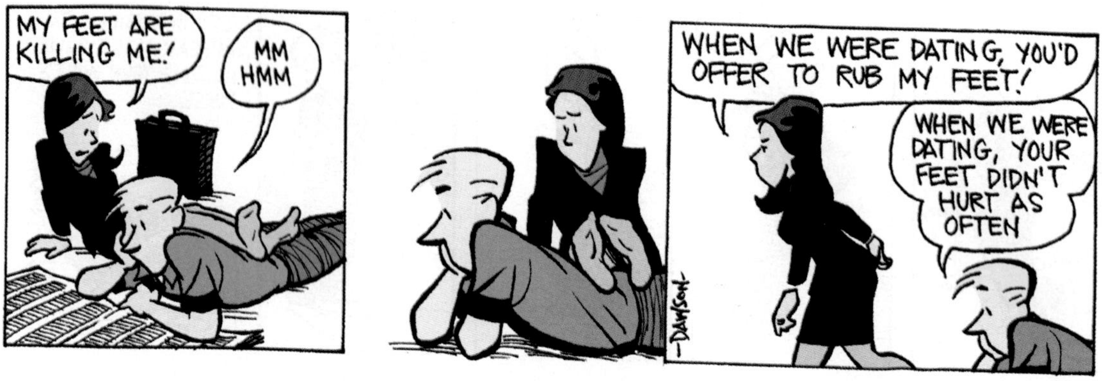
MY FEET ARE KILLING ME!
MM HMM
WHEN WE WERE DATING, YOU'D OFFER TO RUB MY FEET!
WHEN WE WERE DATING, YOUR FEET DIDN'T HURT AS OFTEN
-DAWSON-

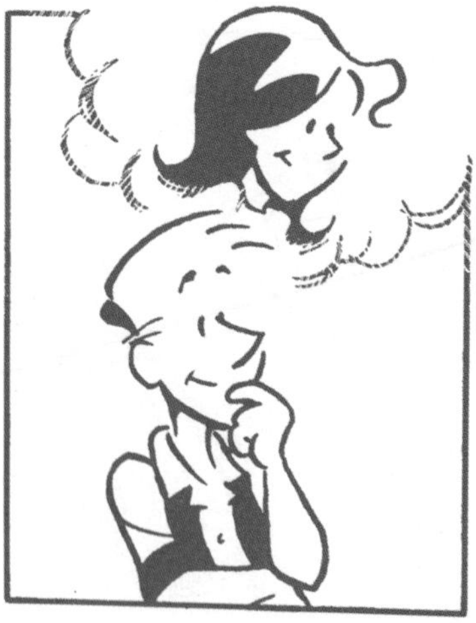

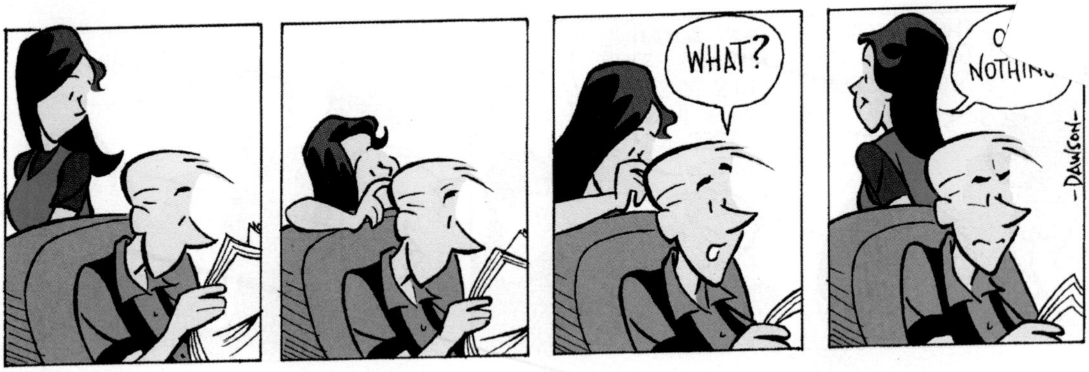
WHAT?
O
NOTHIN
-DAWSON-

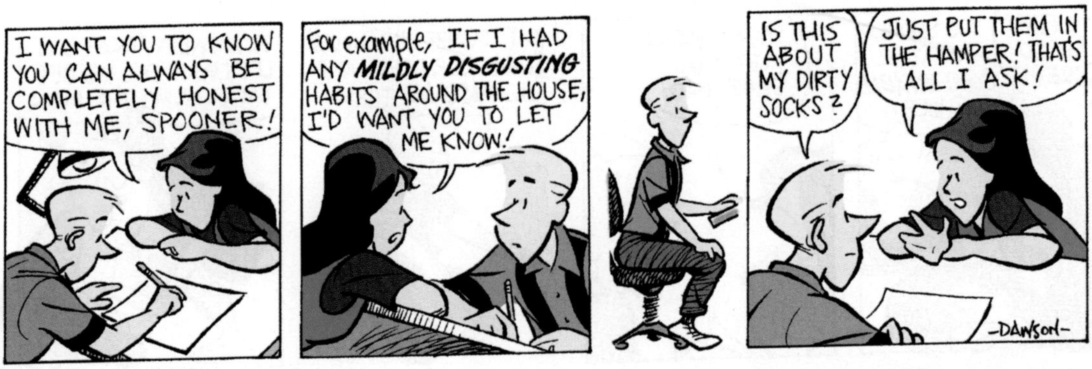
I WANT YOU TO KNOW YOU CAN ALWAYS BE COMPLETELY HONEST WITH ME, SPOONER!
For example, IF I HAD ANY MILDLY DISGUSTING HABITS AROUND THE HOUSE, I'D WANT YOU TO LET ME KNOW!
IS THIS ABOUT MY DIRTY SOCKS?
JUST PUT THEM IN THE HAMPER! THAT'S ALL I ASK!
-DAWSON-

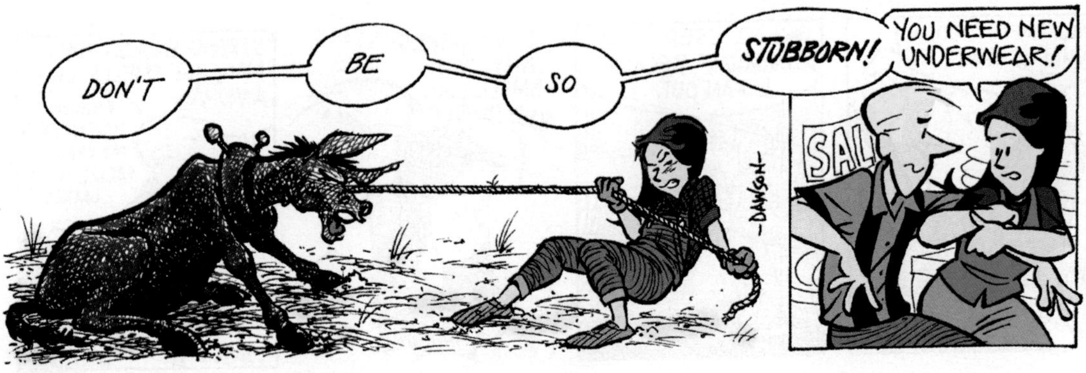
DON'T
BE
SO
STUBBORN!
-DAWSON-
YOU NEED NEW UNDERWEAR!

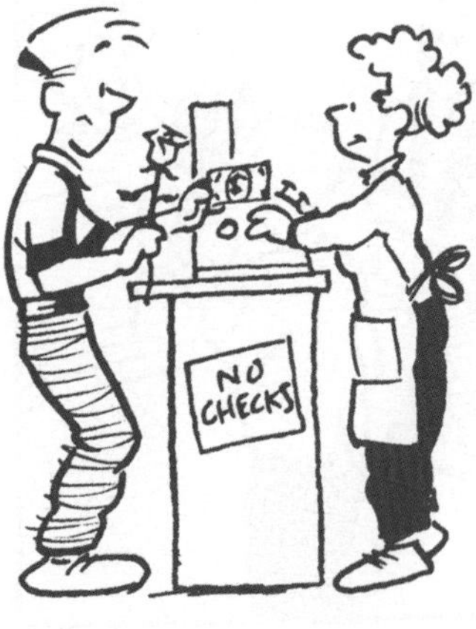
NO CHECKS

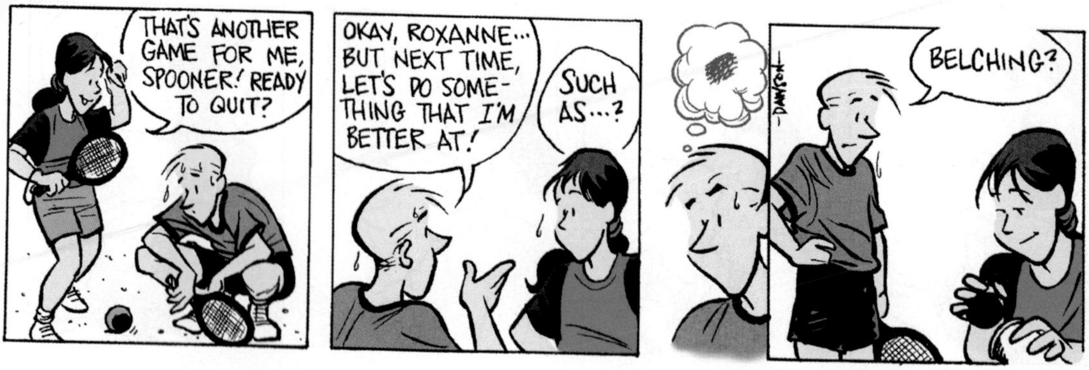
THAT'S ANOTHER GAME FOR ME, SPOONER! READY TO QUIT?
OKAY, ROXANNE... BUT NEXT TIME, LET'S DO SOME-THING THAT I'M BETTER AT!
SUCH AS...?
BELCHING?
-DAWSON-

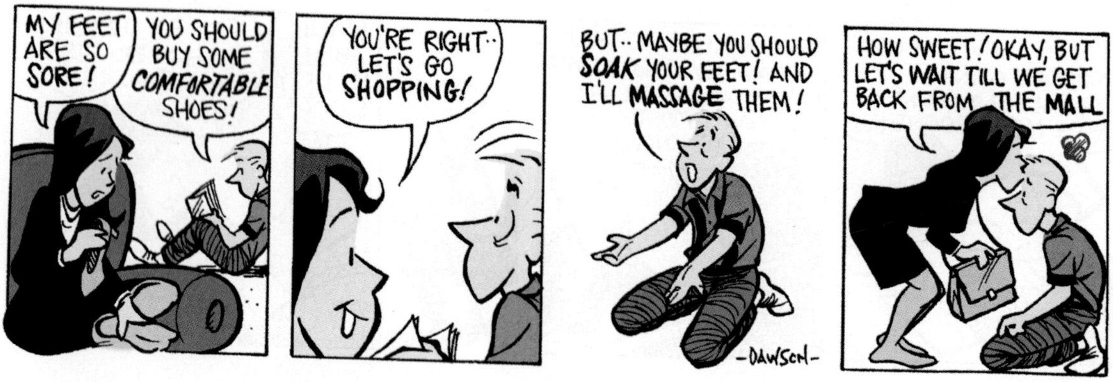
MY FEET ARE SO SORE!
YOU SHOULD BUY SOME COMFORTABLE SHOES!
YOU'RE RIGHT.. LET'S GO SHOPPING!
BUT.. MAYBE YOU SHOULD SOAK YOUR FEET! AND I'LL MASSAGE THEM!
-DAWSON-
HOW SWEET! OKAY, BUT LET'S WAIT TILL WE GET BACK FROM THE MALL

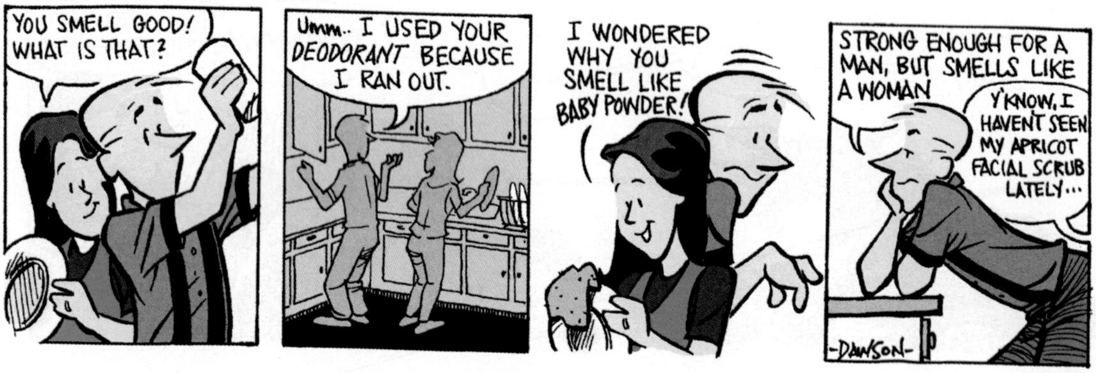
YOU SMELL GOOD! WHAT IS THAT?
Umm.. I USED YOUR DEODORANT BECAUSE I RAN OUT.
I WONDERED WHY YOU SMELL LIKE BABY POWDER!
STRONG ENOUGH FOR A MAN, BUT SMELLS LIKE A WOMAN
Y'KNOW, I HAVEN'T SEEN MY APRICOT FACIAL SCRUB LATELY...
-DAWSON-

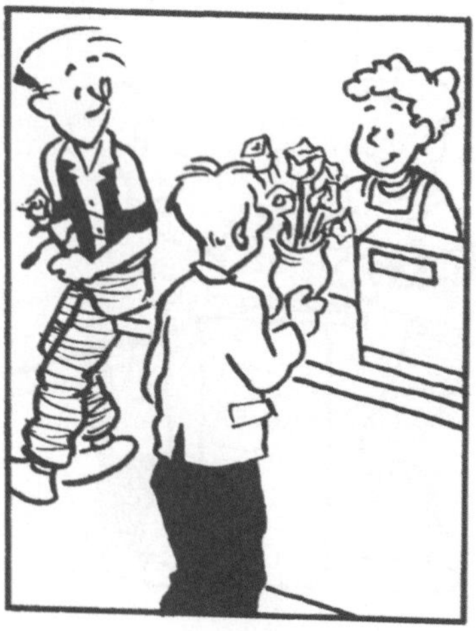

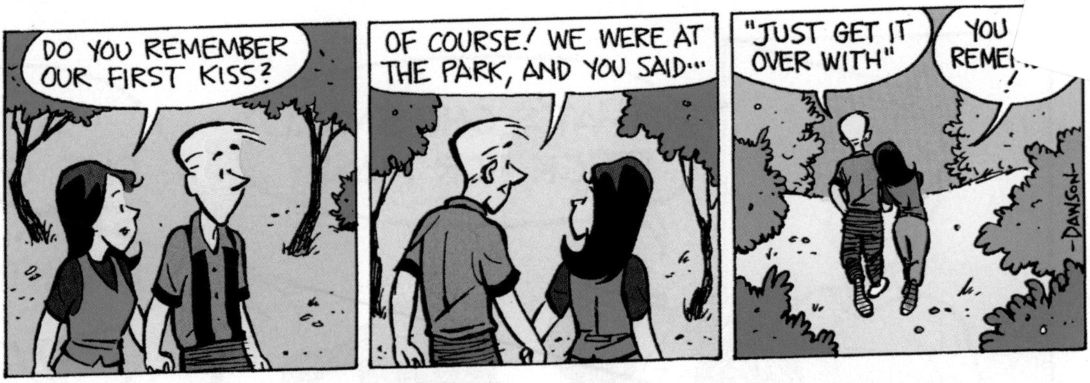
DO YOU REMEMBER OUR FIRST KISS?
OF COURSE! WE WERE AT THE PARK, AND YOU SAID...
"JUST GET IT OVER WITH"
-DAWSON-

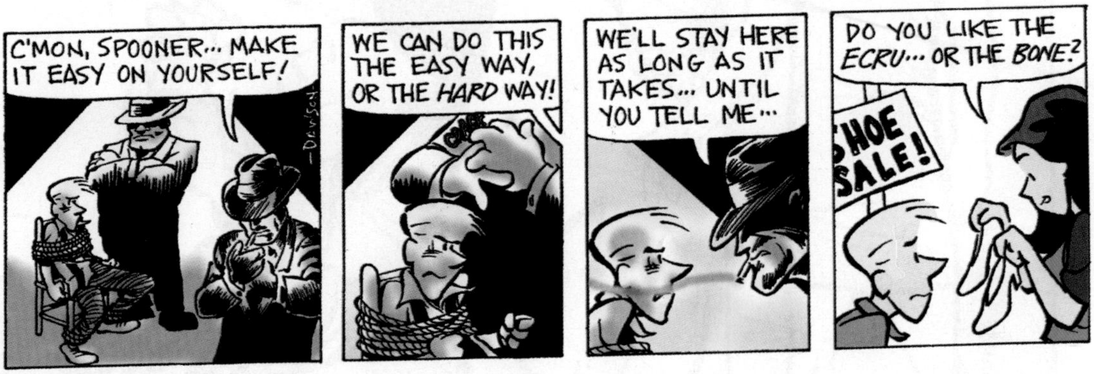
C'MON, SPOONER... MAKE IT EASY ON YOURSELF!
WE CAN DO THIS THE EASY WAY, OR THE *HARD* WAY!
WE'LL STAY HERE AS LONG AS IT TAKES... UNTIL YOU TELL ME...
DO YOU LIKE THE *ECRU*... OR THE *BONE*?
SHOE SALE!

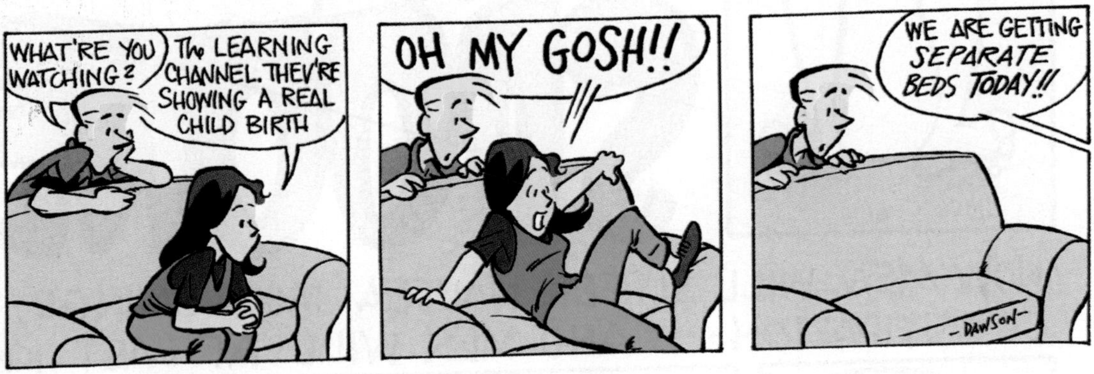
WHAT'RE YOU WATCHING?
The LEARNING CHANNEL. THEY'RE SHOWING A REAL CHILD BIRTH
OH MY GOSH!!
WE ARE GETTING *SEPARATE* BEDS *TODAY*!!
-DAWSON-

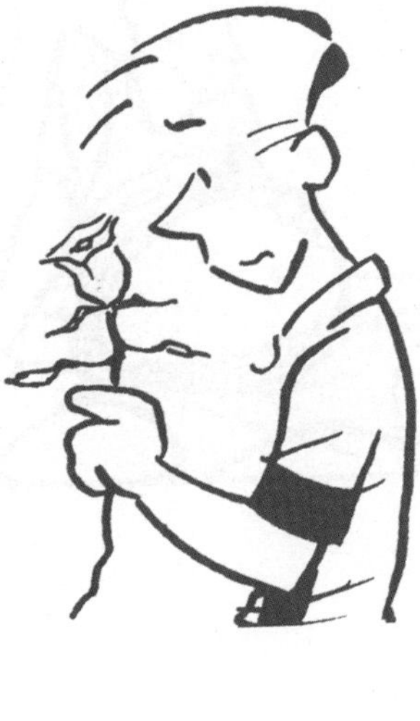

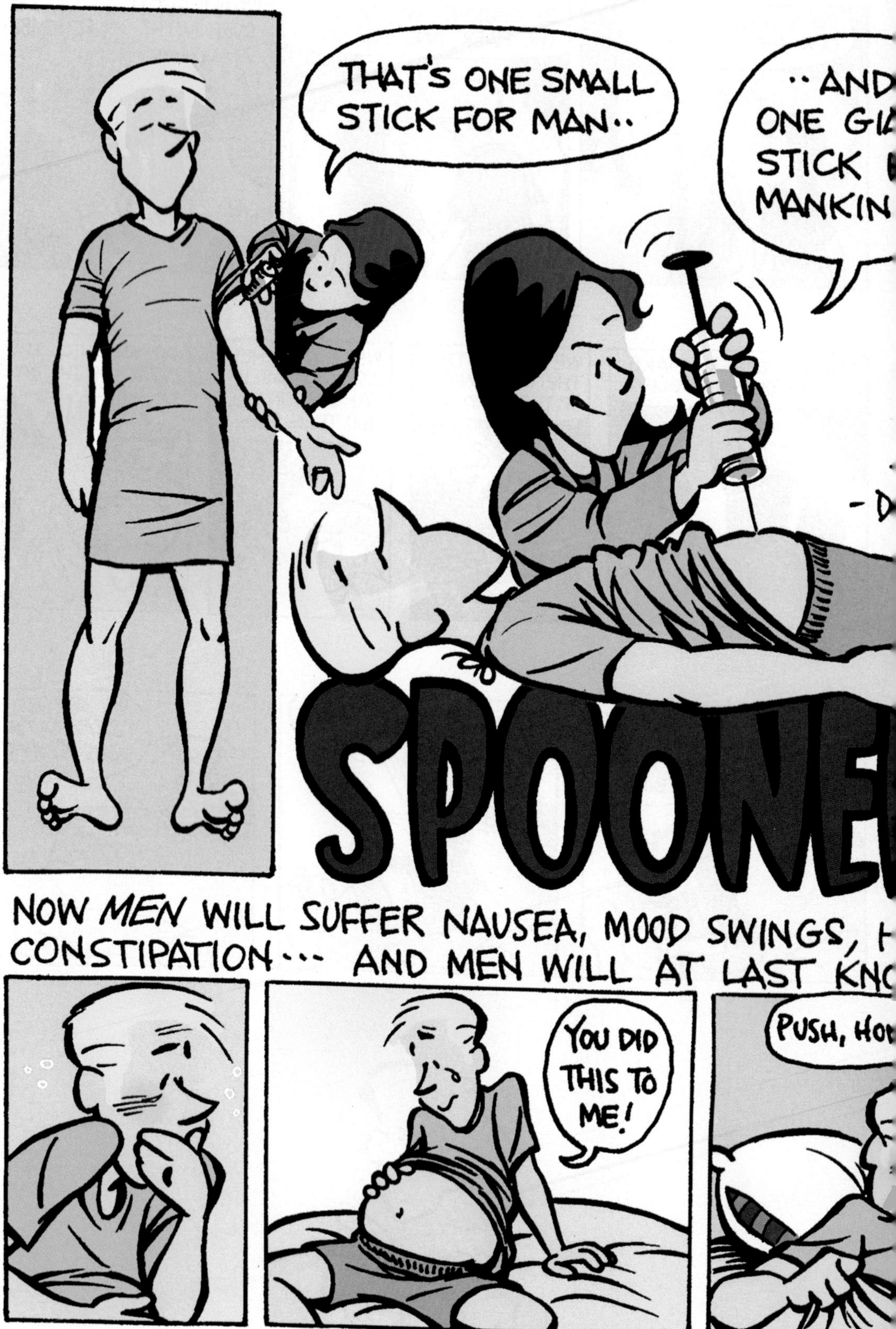
THAT'S ONE SMALL STICK FOR MAN..
..AND ONE GIA STICK MANKIN
SPOONE
NOW MEN WILL SUFFER NAUSEA, MOOD SWINGS, H
CONSTIPATION... AND MEN WILL AT LAST KNO
YOU DID THIS TO ME!
PUSH, HO

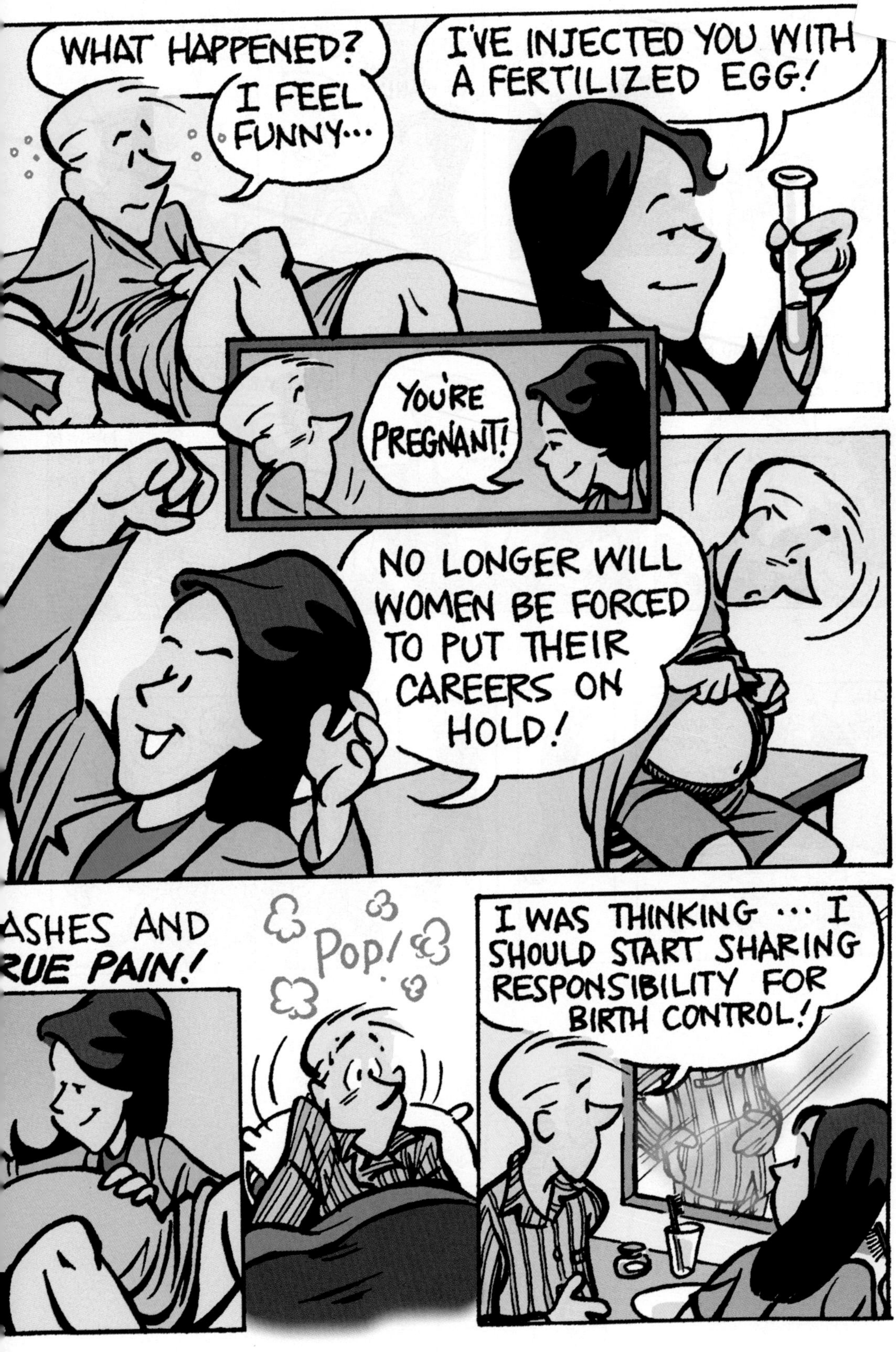
WHAT HAPPENED? I FEEL FUNNY...
I'VE INJECTED YOU WITH A FERTILIZED EGG!
YOU'RE PREGNANT!
NO LONGER WILL WOMEN BE FORCED TO PUT THEIR CAREERS ON HOLD!
ASHES AND
RUE PAIN!
Pop!
I WAS THINKING ... I SHOULD START SHARING RESPONSIBILITY FOR BIRTH CONTROL!

SPOONER, CAN YOU OPEN THIS JAR FOR ME, PLEASE?
SURE, SWEETIE
PSHHUPP
COULD YOU REALLY NOT OPEN IT, OR WERE YOU JUST LETTING ME BE MANLY?
DOES IT MATTER?
NOPE
-DAWSON-

WILL YOU STILL FIND ME ATTRACTIVE WHEN I'M OLD, GRAY & WRINKLED?
DID I MENTION YOU'LL BE OLD, GRAY, WRINKLED & BALD?
You'll always be my red hot mama
-DAWSON-

WHATCHA READING, ROXANNE?
"JANE EYRE"
THANK YOU
WELCOME
-DAWSON-

NO CHECKS

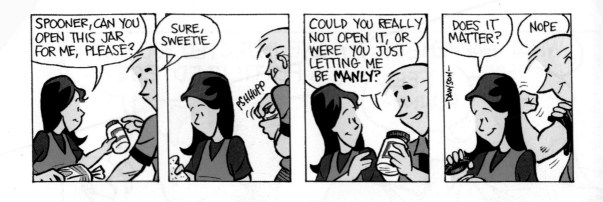

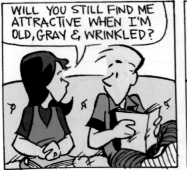

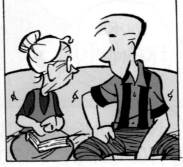

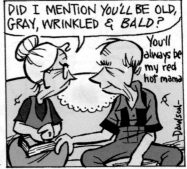

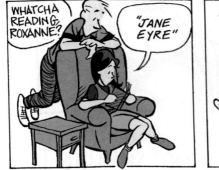

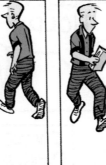

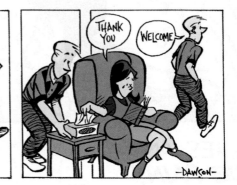

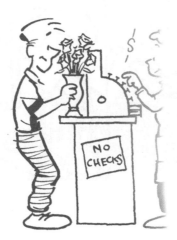

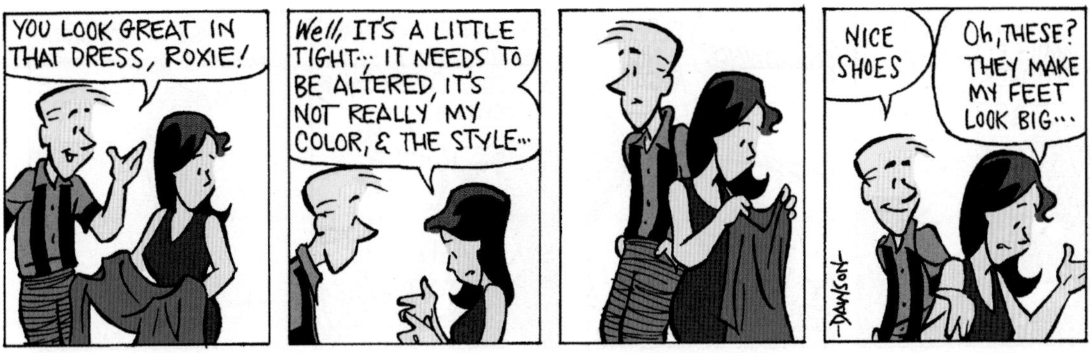
YOU LOOK GREAT IN THAT DRESS, ROXIE!
Well, IT'S A LITTLE TIGHT... IT NEEDS TO BE ALTERED, IT'S NOT REALLY MY COLOR, & THE STYLE...
NICE SHOES
Oh, THESE? THEY MAKE MY FEET LOOK BIG...
DAWSON

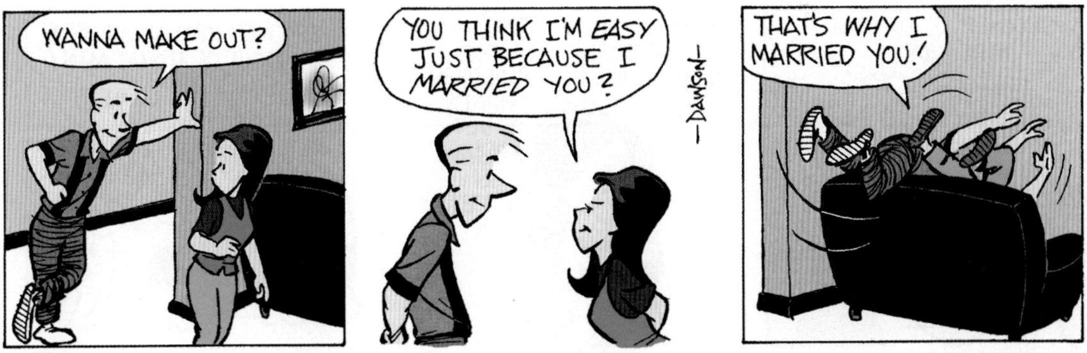
WANNA MAKE OUT?
YOU THINK I'M EASY JUST BECAUSE I MARRIED YOU?
DAWSON
THAT'S WHY I MARRIED YOU!

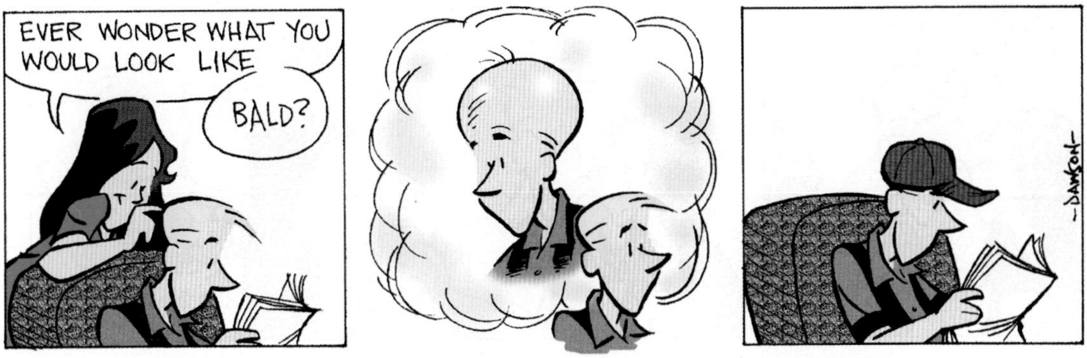
EVER WONDER WHAT YOU WOULD LOOK LIKE
BALD?
DAWSON

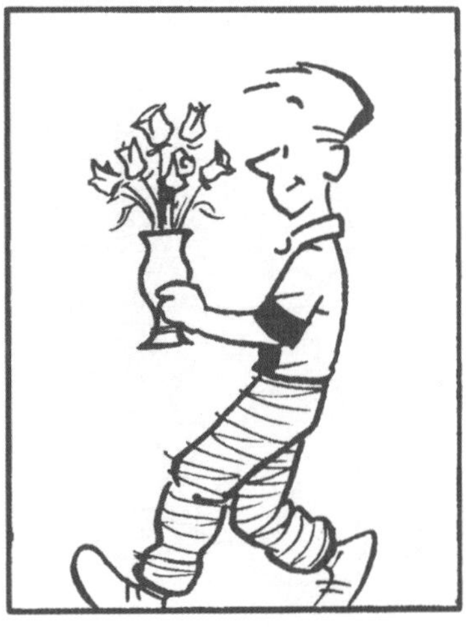

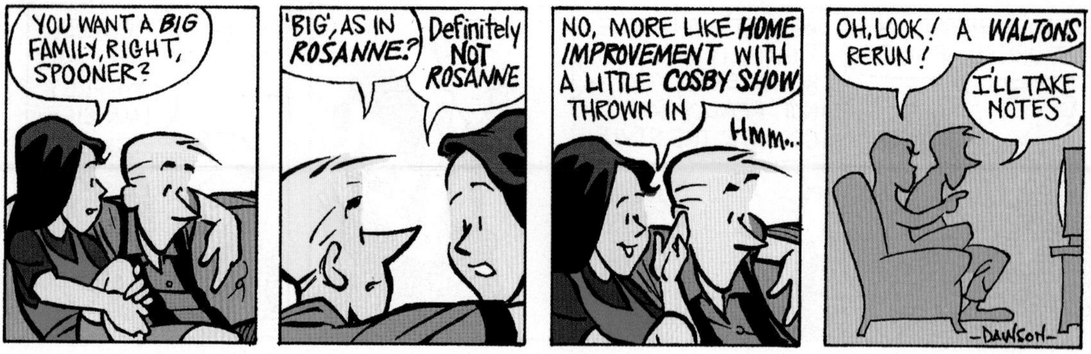
YOU WANT A BIG FAMILY, RIGHT, SPOONER?
'BIG', AS IN ROSANNE?
Definitely NOT ROSANNE
NO, MORE LIKE HOME IMPROVEMENT WITH A LITTLE COSBY SHOW THROWN IN
Hmm..
OH, LOOK! A WALTONS RERUN!
I'LL TAKE NOTES
-DAWSON-

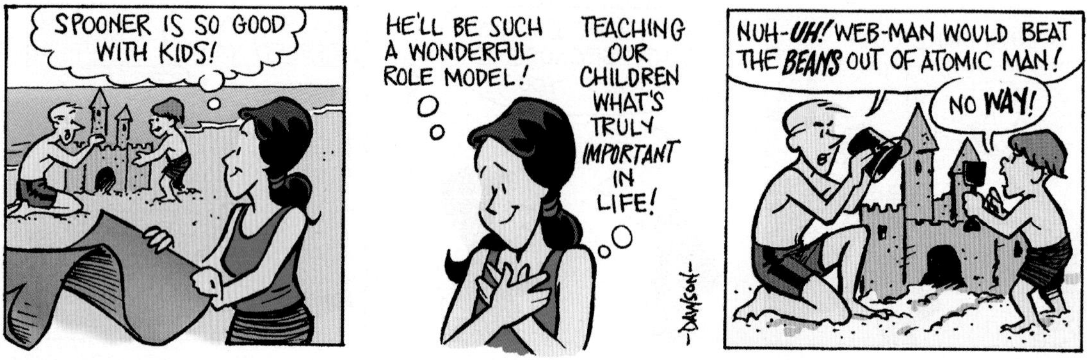
SPOONER IS SO GOOD WITH KIDS!
HE'LL BE SUCH A WONDERFUL ROLE MODEL!
TEACHING OUR CHILDREN WHAT'S TRULY IMPORTANT IN LIFE!
-DAWSON-
NUH-UH! WEB-MAN WOULD BEAT THE BEANS OUT OF ATOMIC MAN!
NO WAY!

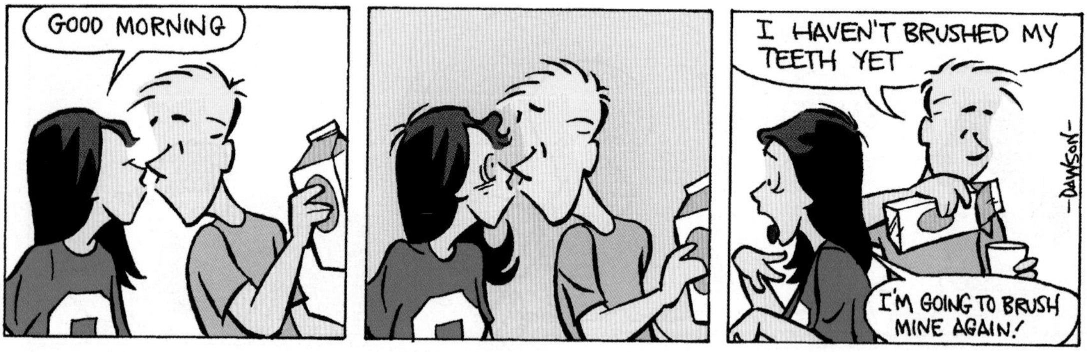
GOOD MORNING
I HAVEN'T BRUSHED MY TEETH YET
I'M GOING TO BRUSH MINE AGAIN!
-DAWSON-

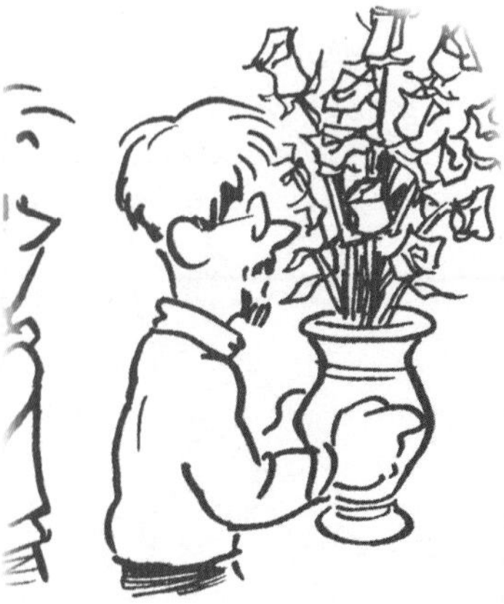

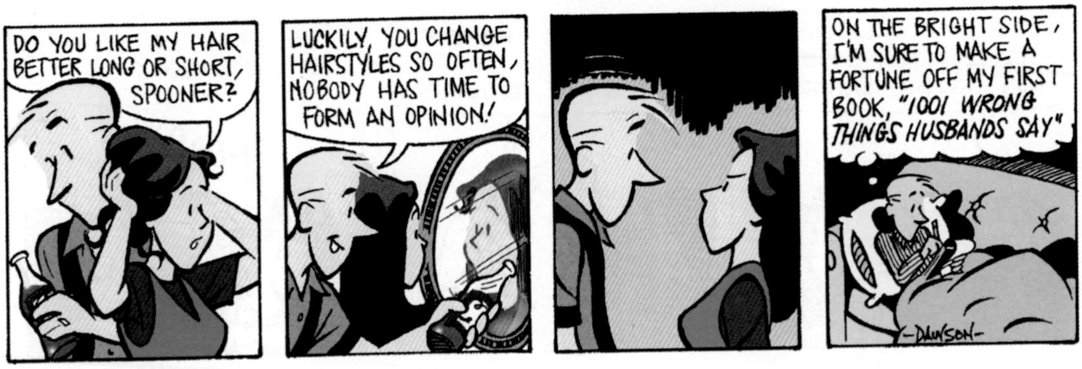
DO YOU LIKE MY HAIR BETTER LONG OR SHORT, SPOONER?
LUCKILY, YOU CHANGE HAIRSTYLES SO OFTEN, NOBODY HAS TIME TO FORM AN OPINION!
ON THE BRIGHT SIDE, I'M SURE TO MAKE A FORTUNE OFF MY FIRST BOOK, "1001 *WRONG THINGS HUSBANDS SAY*"
-DAWSON-

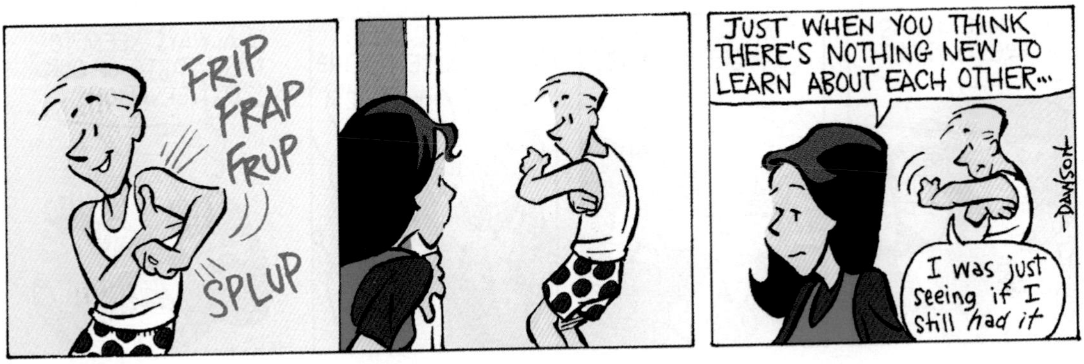
FRIP
FRAP
FRUP
SPLUP
JUST WHEN YOU THINK THERE'S NOTHING NEW TO LEARN ABOUT EACH OTHER...
I was just seeing if I still *had it*
-DAWSON-

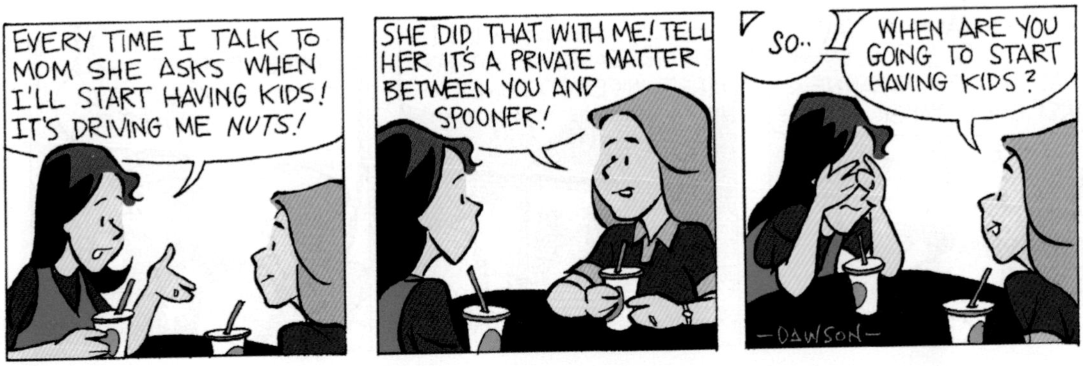
EVERY TIME I TALK TO MOM SHE ASKS WHEN I'LL START HAVING KIDS! IT'S DRIVING ME *NUTS*!
SHE DID THAT WITH ME! TELL HER IT'S A PRIVATE MATTER BETWEEN YOU AND SPOONER!
SO..
WHEN ARE YOU GOING TO START HAVING KIDS?
-DAWSON-

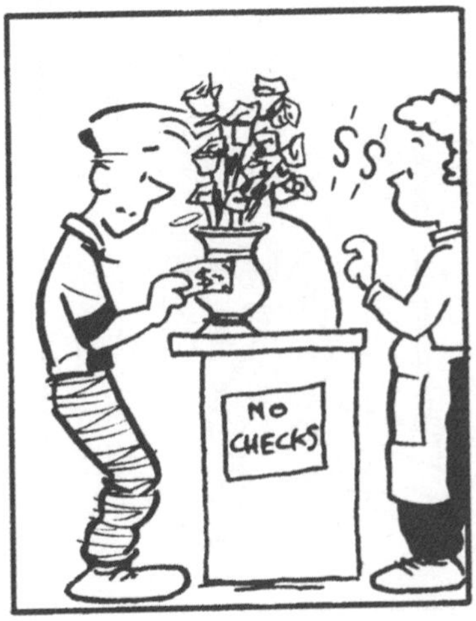
NO CHECKS

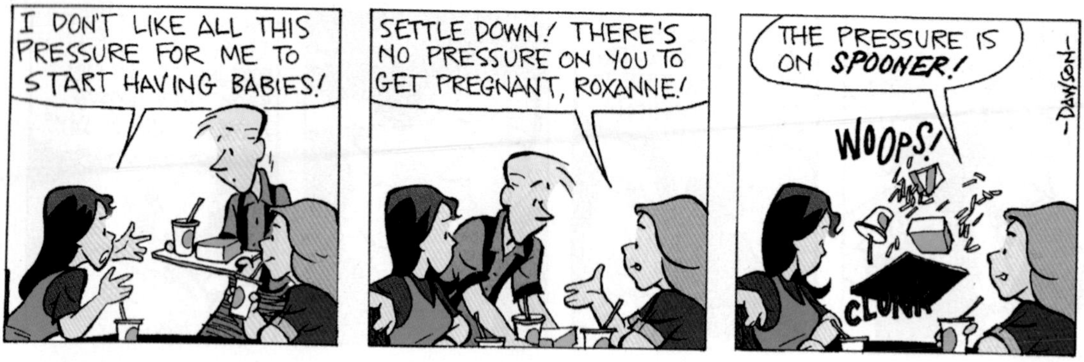
I DON'T LIKE ALL THIS PRESSURE FOR ME TO START HAVING BABIES!
SETTLE DOWN! THERE'S NO PRESSURE ON YOU TO GET PREGNANT, ROXANNE!
THE PRESSURE IS ON SPOONER!
WOOPS!
CLUNK
-DAWSON-

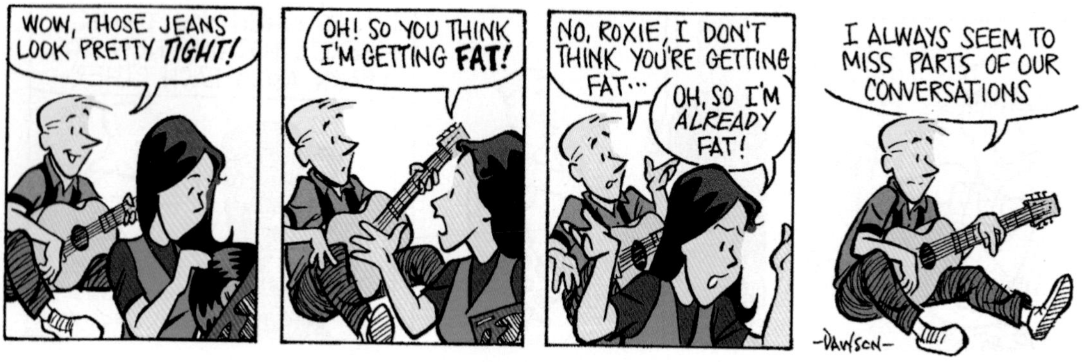
WOW, THOSE JEANS LOOK PRETTY TIGHT!
OH! SO YOU THINK I'M GETTING FAT!
NO, ROXIE, I DON'T THINK YOU'RE GETTING FAT...
OH, SO I'M ALREADY FAT!
I ALWAYS SEEM TO MISS PARTS OF OUR CONVERSATIONS
-DAWSON-

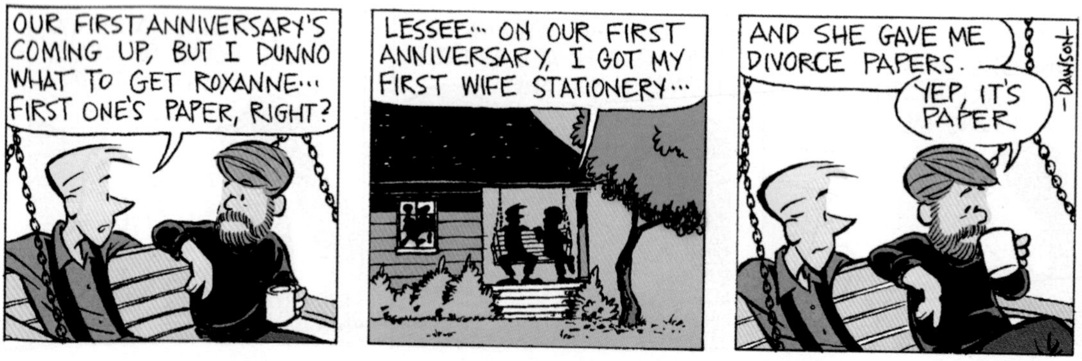
OUR FIRST ANNIVERSARY'S COMING UP, BUT I DUNNO WHAT TO GET ROXANNE... FIRST ONE'S PAPER, RIGHT?
LESSEE... ON OUR FIRST ANNIVERSARY, I GOT MY FIRST WIFE STATIONERY...
AND SHE GAVE ME DIVORCE PAPERS.
YEP, IT'S PAPER
-DAWSON-

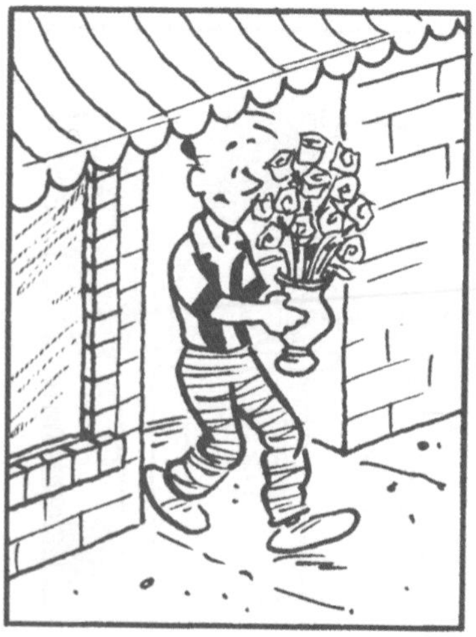

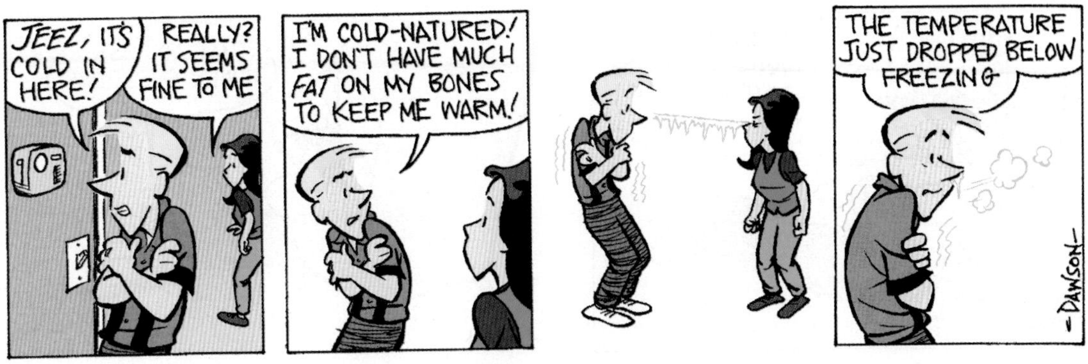
JEEZ, IT'S COLD IN HERE!
REALLY? IT SEEMS FINE TO ME
I'M COLD-NATURED! I DON'T HAVE MUCH FAT ON MY BONES TO KEEP ME WARM!
THE TEMPERATURE JUST DROPPED BELOW FREEZING
-DAWSON-

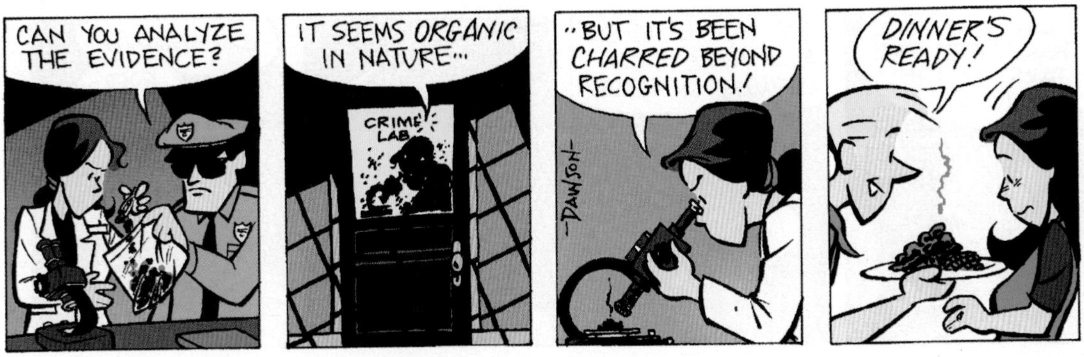
CAN YOU ANALYZE THE EVIDENCE?
IT SEEMS ORGANIC IN NATURE...
CRIME LAB
...BUT IT'S BEEN CHARRED BEYOND RECOGNITION!
-DAWSON-
DINNER'S READY!

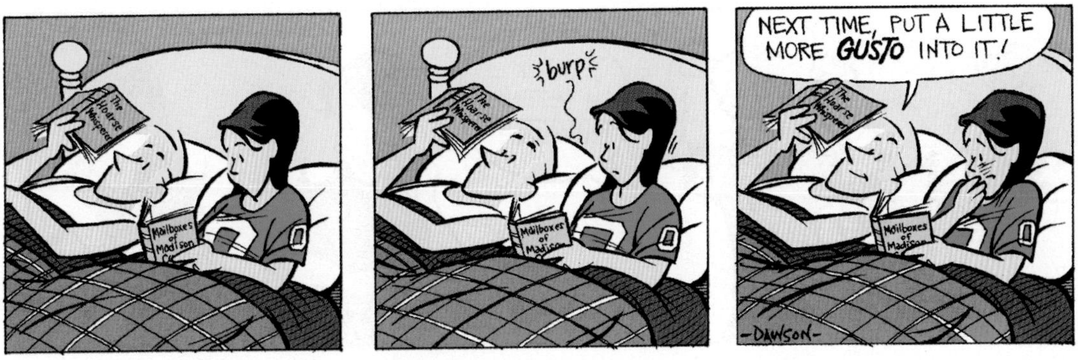
The Hoarse Whisperer
Mailboxes of Madison
burp
NEXT TIME, PUT A LITTLE MORE GUSTO INTO IT!
-DAWSON-

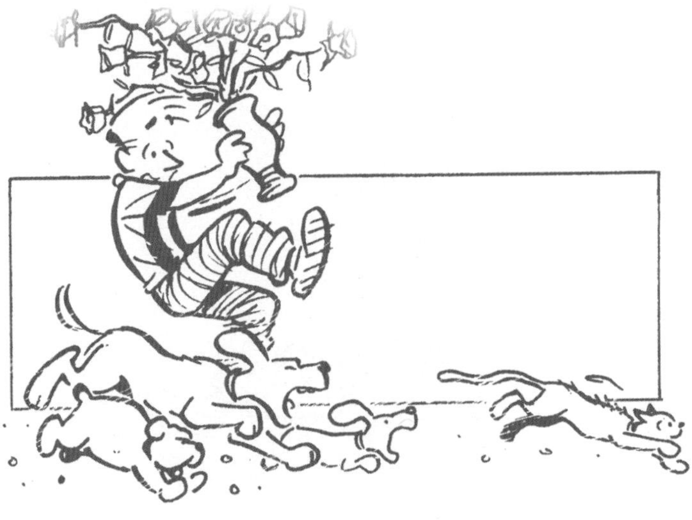

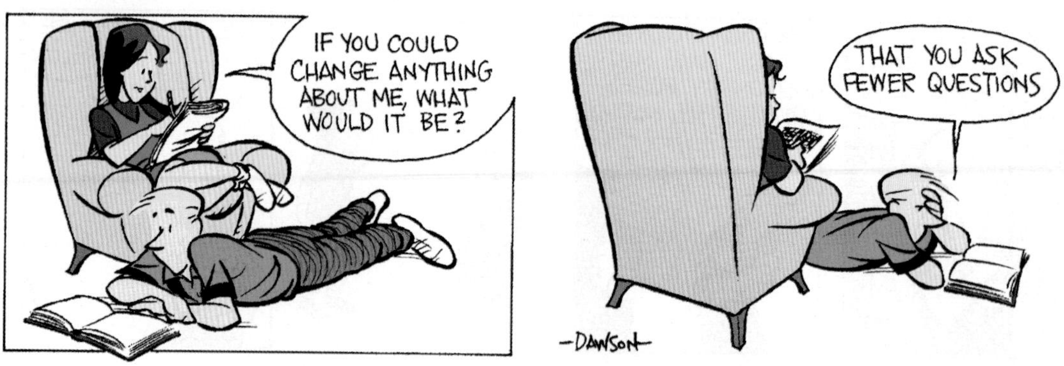
IF YOU COULD CHANGE ANYTHING ABOUT ME, WHAT WOULD IT BE?
THAT YOU ASK FEWER QUESTIONS
-DAWSON-

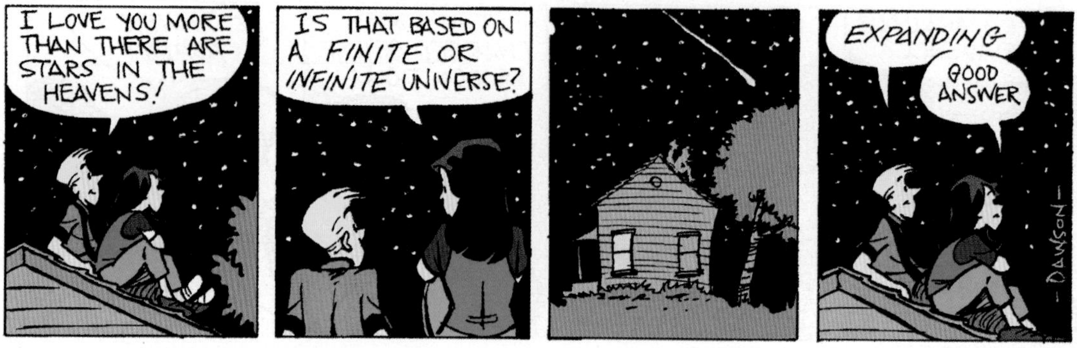
I LOVE YOU MORE THAN THERE ARE STARS IN THE HEAVENS!
IS THAT BASED ON A FINITE OR INFINITE UNIVERSE?
EXPANDING
GOOD ANSWER
-DAWSON-

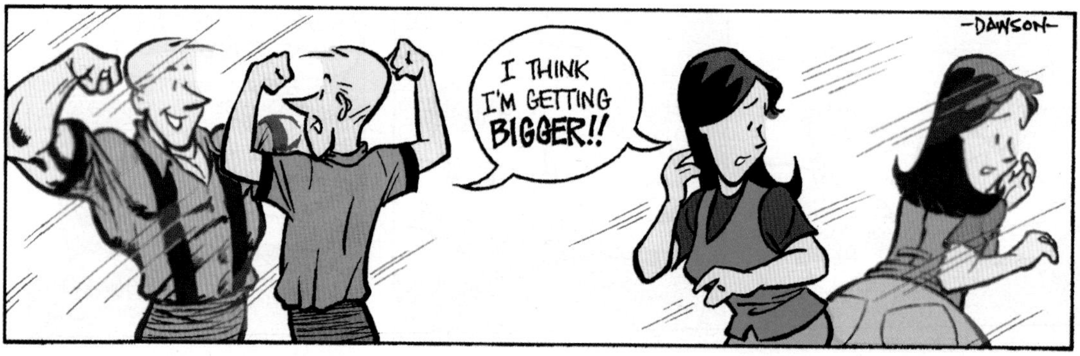
-DAWSON-
I THINK I'M GETTING BIGGER!!

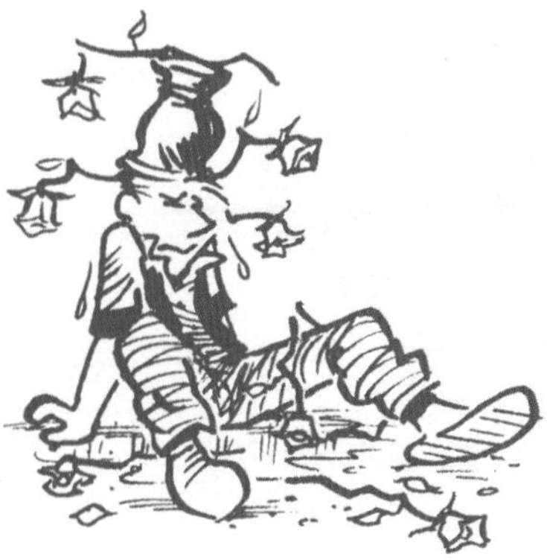

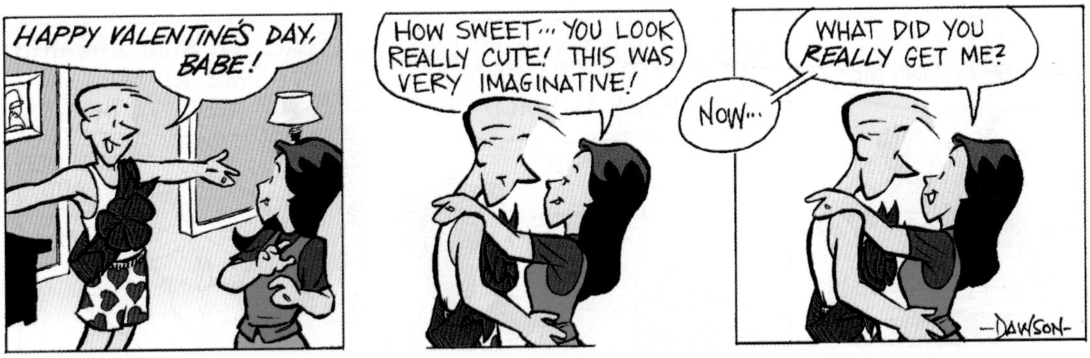
HAPPY VALENTINE'S DAY, BABE!
HOW SWEET... YOU LOOK REALLY CUTE! THIS WAS VERY IMAGINATIVE!
NOW...
WHAT DID YOU REALLY GET ME?
-DAWSON-

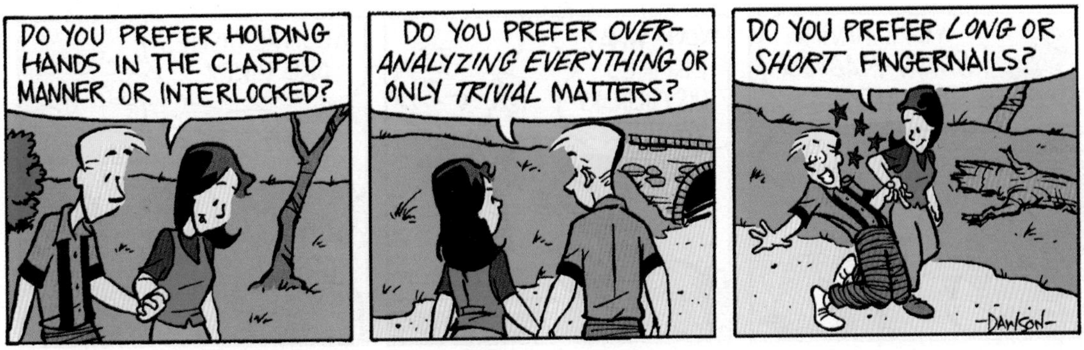
DO YOU PREFER HOLDING HANDS IN THE CLASPED MANNER OR INTERLOCKED?
DO YOU PREFER OVER-ANALYZING EVERYTHING OR ONLY TRIVIAL MATTERS?
DO YOU PREFER LONG OR SHORT FINGERNAILS?
-DAWSON-

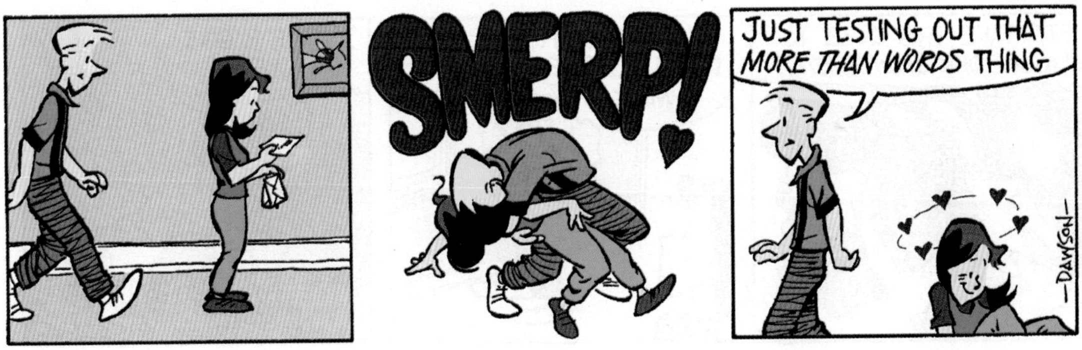
SMERP!
JUST TESTING OUT THAT MORE THAN WORDS THING
-DAWSON-

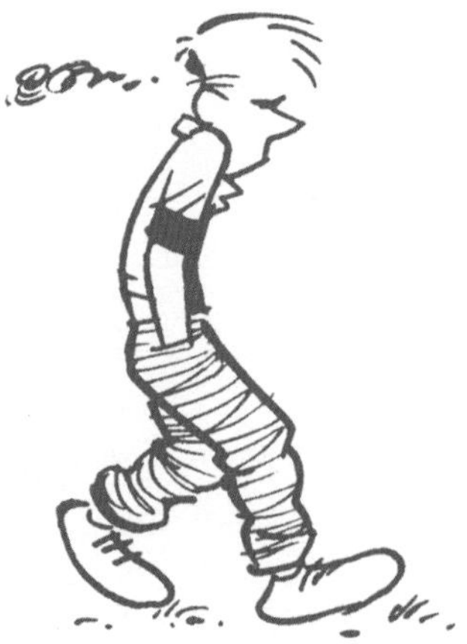

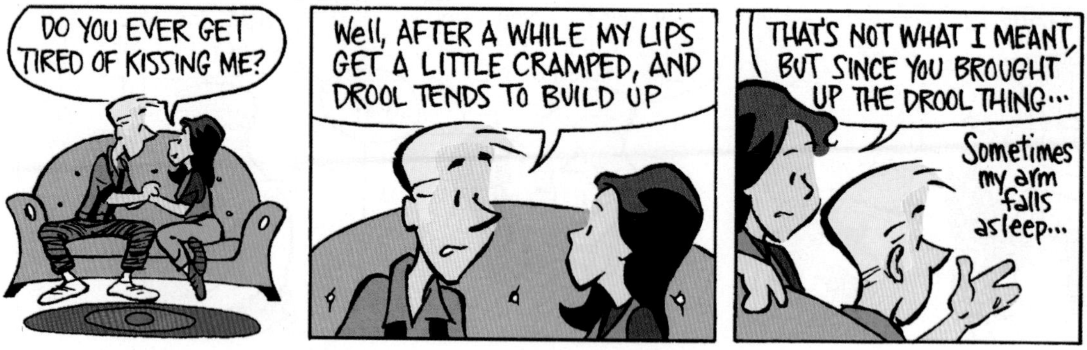
DO YOU EVER GET TIRED OF KISSING ME?
Well, AFTER A WHILE MY LIPS GET A LITTLE CRAMPED, AND DROOL TENDS TO BUILD UP
THAT'S NOT WHAT I MEANT, BUT SINCE YOU BROUGHT UP THE DROOL THING...
Sometimes my arm falls asleep...

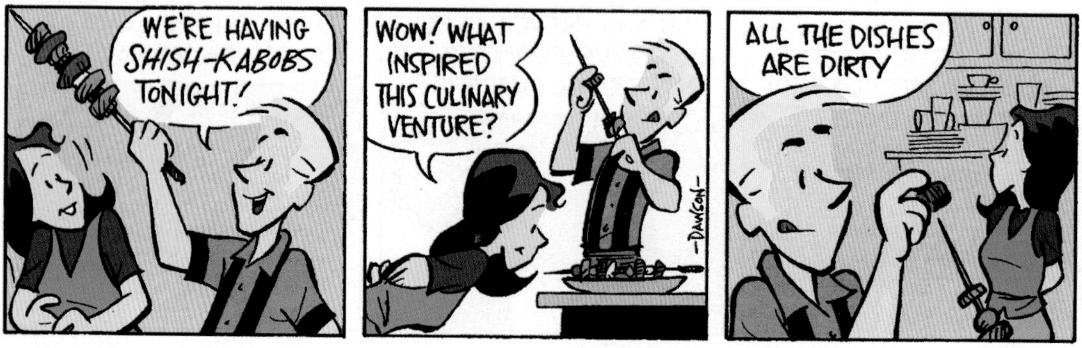
WE'RE HAVING SHISH-KABOBS TONIGHT!
WOW! WHAT INSPIRED THIS CULINARY VENTURE?
-DAWSON-
ALL THE DISHES ARE DIRTY

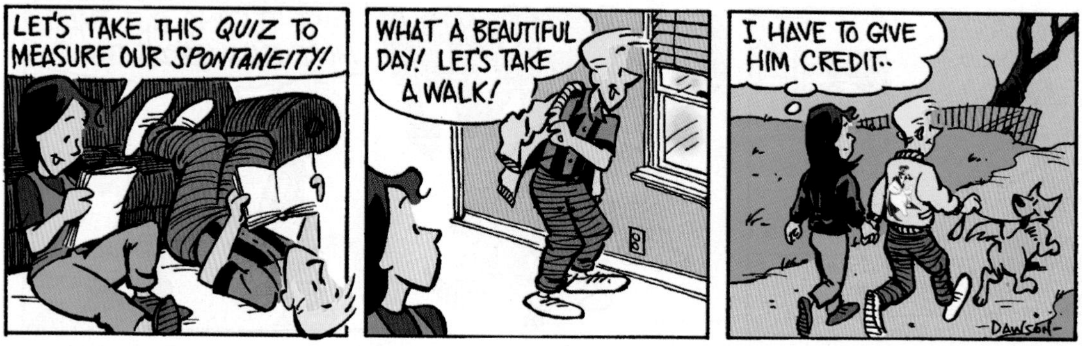
LET'S TAKE THIS QUIZ TO MEASURE OUR SPONTANEITY!
WHAT A BEAUTIFUL DAY! LET'S TAKE A WALK!
I HAVE TO GIVE HIM CREDIT..
-DAWSON-

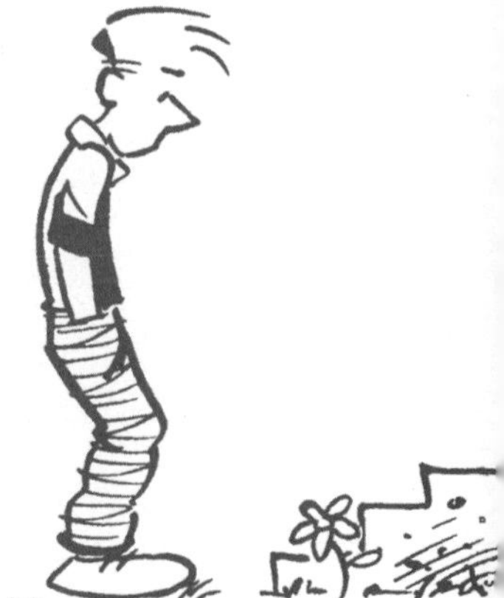

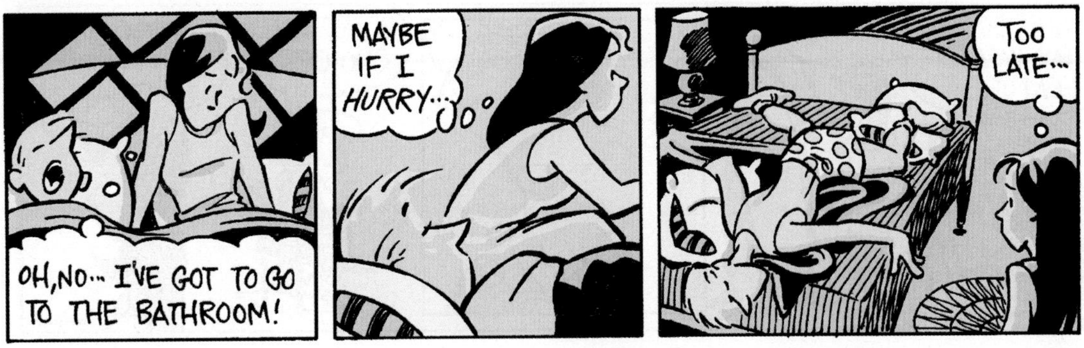
OH, NO... I'VE GOT TO GO TO THE BATHROOM!
MAYBE IF I HURRY...
TOO LATE...

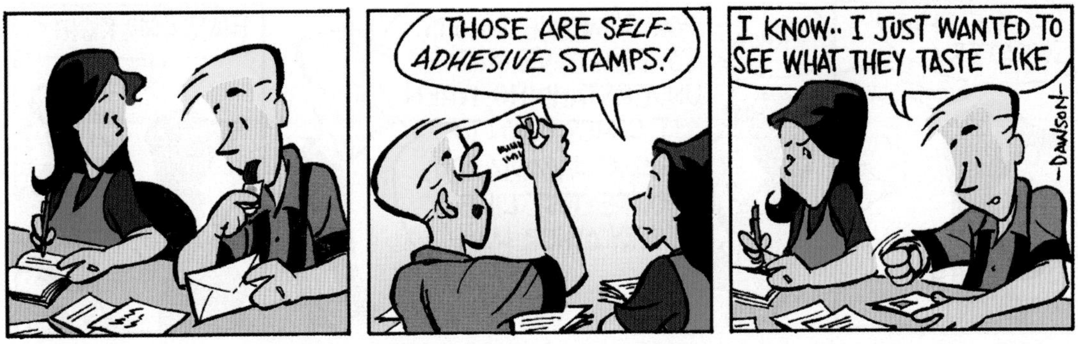
THOSE ARE SELF-ADHESIVE STAMPS!
I KNOW.. I JUST WANTED TO SEE WHAT THEY TASTE LIKE
-DAWSON-

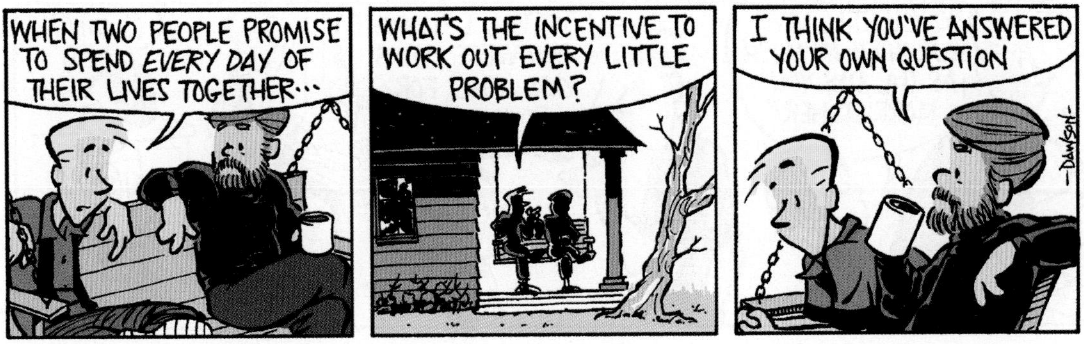
WHEN TWO PEOPLE PROMISE TO SPEND EVERY DAY OF THEIR LIVES TOGETHER...
WHAT'S THE INCENTIVE TO WORK OUT EVERY LITTLE PROBLEM?
I THINK YOU'VE ANSWERED YOUR OWN QUESTION
-DAWSON-

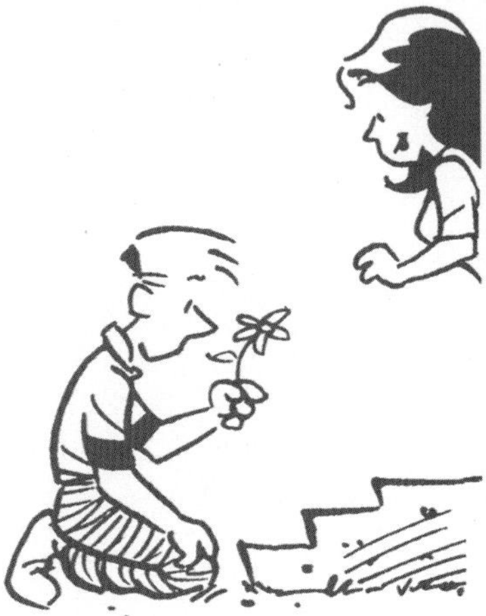

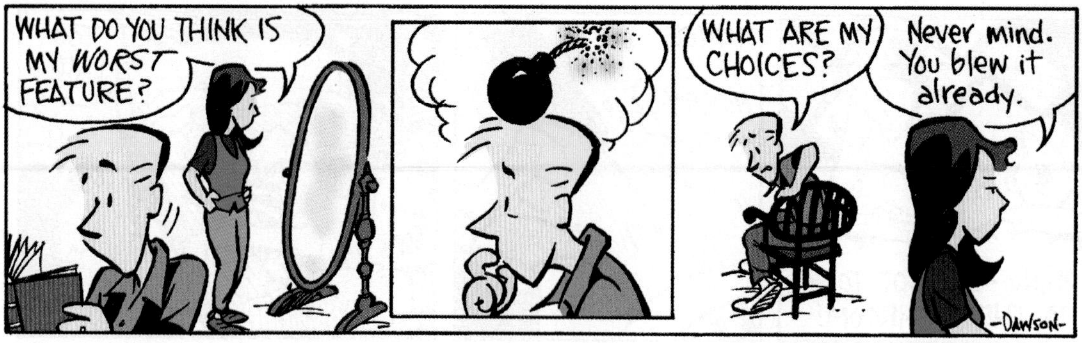
WHAT DO YOU THINK IS MY WORST FEATURE?
WHAT ARE MY CHOICES?
Never mind. You blew it already.
-DAWSON-

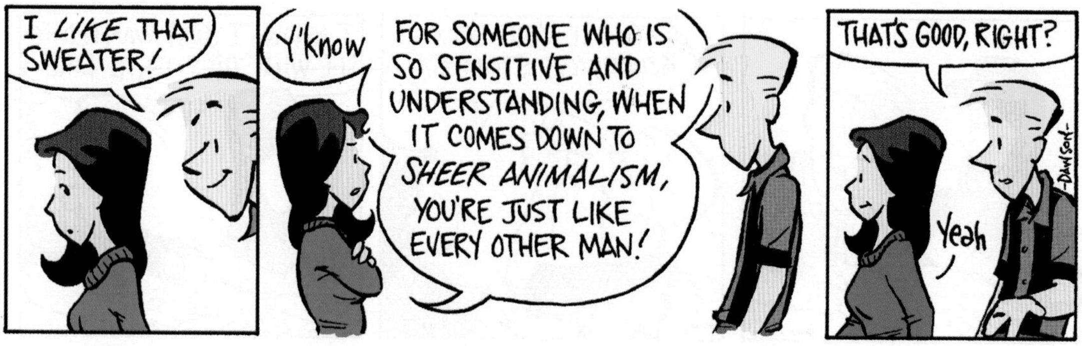
I LIKE THAT SWEATER!
Y'know
FOR SOMEONE WHO IS SO SENSITIVE AND UNDERSTANDING, WHEN IT COMES DOWN TO SHEER ANIMALISM, YOU'RE JUST LIKE EVERY OTHER MAN!
THAT'S GOOD, RIGHT?
Yeah
-DAWSON-

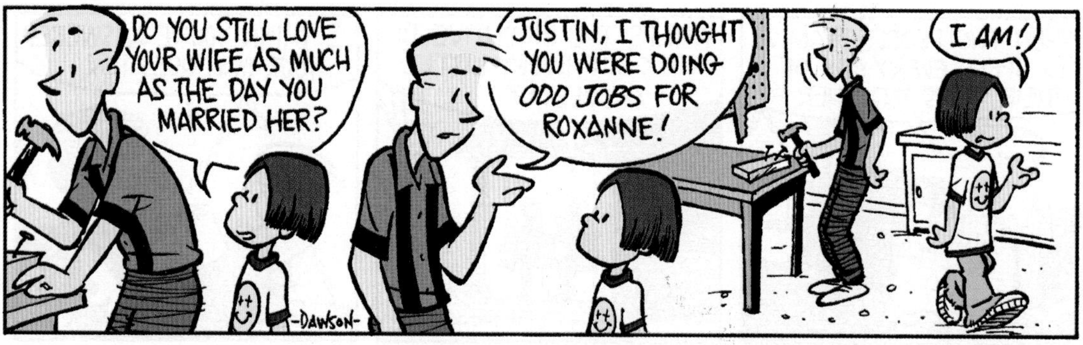
DO YOU STILL LOVE YOUR WIFE AS MUCH AS THE DAY YOU MARRIED HER?
-DAWSON-
JUSTIN, I THOUGHT YOU WERE DOING ODD JOBS FOR ROXANNE!
I AM!

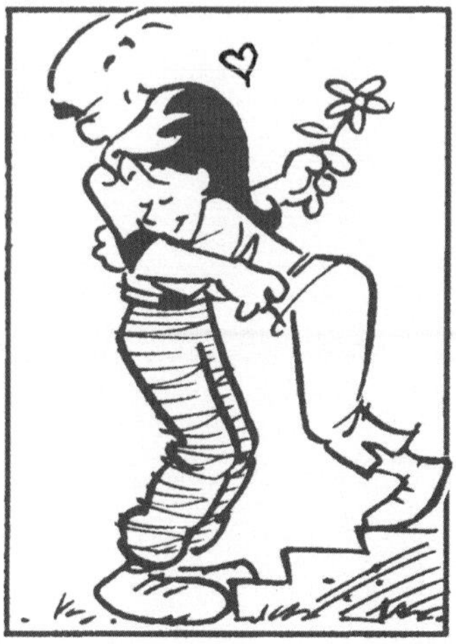

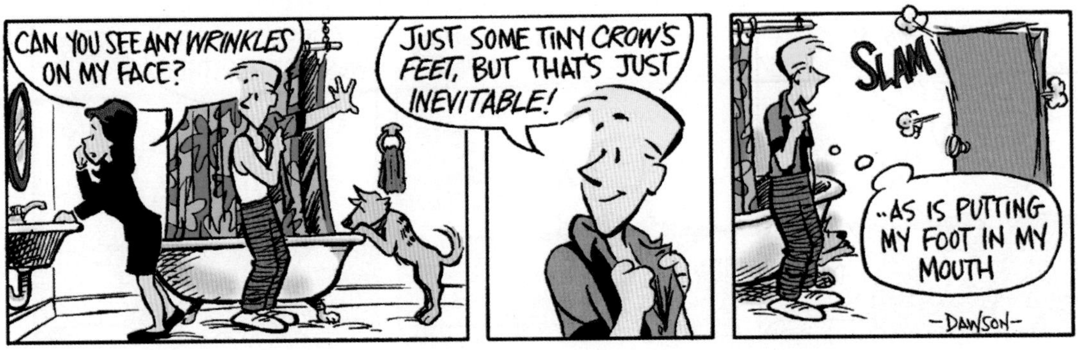
CAN YOU SEE ANY WRINKLES ON MY FACE?
JUST SOME TINY CROW'S FEET, BUT THAT'S JUST INEVITABLE!
SLAM
..AS IS PUTTING MY FOOT IN MY MOUTH
-DAWSON-

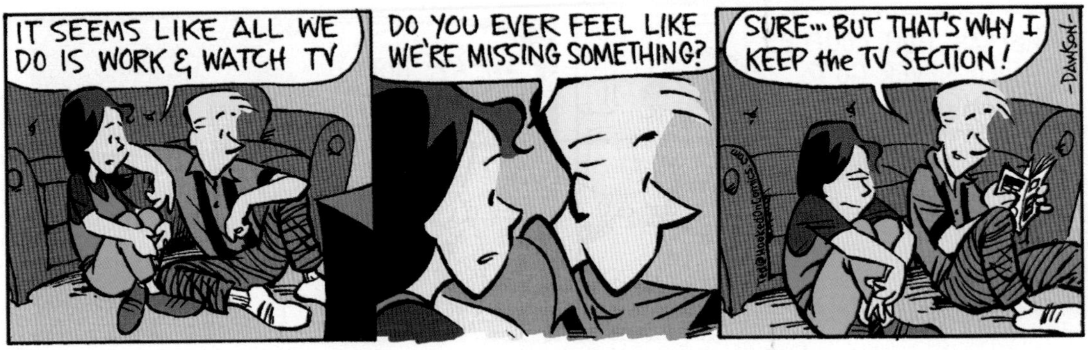
IT SEEMS LIKE ALL WE DO IS WORK & WATCH TV
DO YOU EVER FEEL LIKE WE'RE MISSING SOMETHING?
SURE... BUT THAT'S WHY I KEEP the TV SECTION!
-DAWSON-

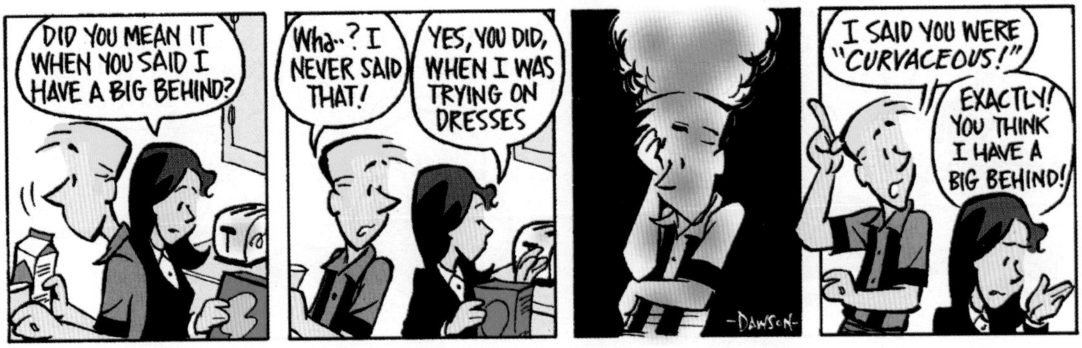
DID YOU MEAN IT WHEN YOU SAID I HAVE A BIG BEHIND?
Wha..? I NEVER SAID THAT!
YES, YOU DID, WHEN I WAS TRYING ON DRESSES
-DAWSON-
I SAID YOU WERE "CURVACEOUS!"
EXACTLY! YOU THINK I HAVE A BIG BEHIND!

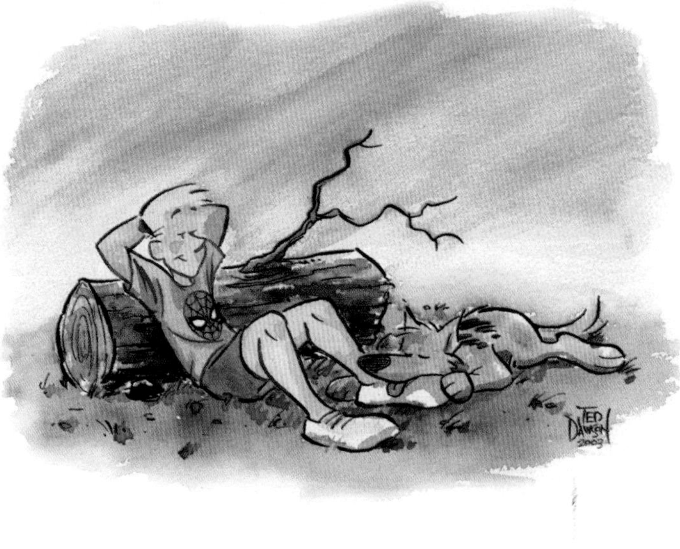
TED DAWSON

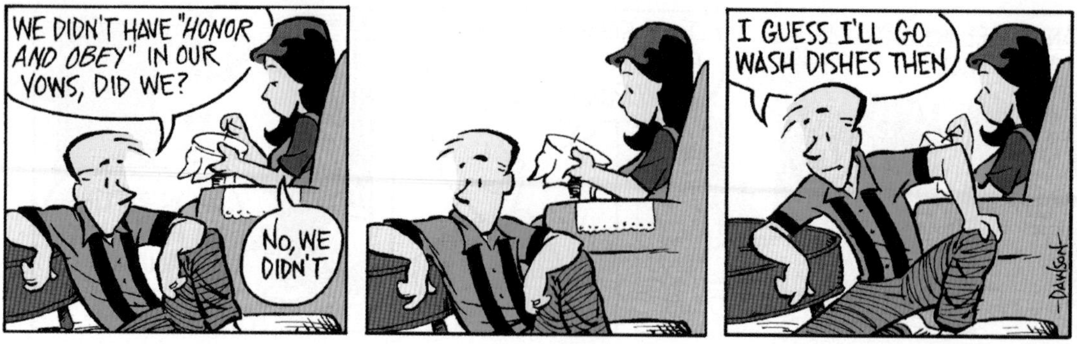
WE DIDN'T HAVE "HONOR AND OBEY" IN OUR VOWS, DID WE?
No, WE DIDN'T
I GUESS I'LL GO WASH DISHES THEN
-DAWSON-

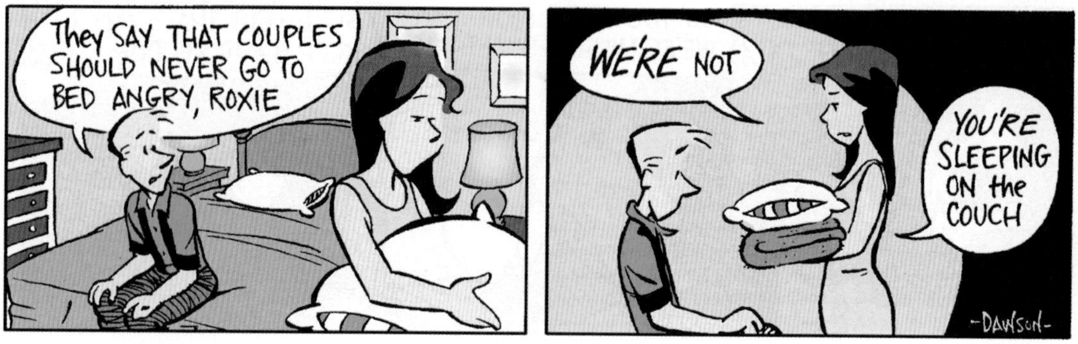
They SAY THAT COUPLES SHOULD NEVER GO TO BED ANGRY, ROXIE
WE'RE NOT
YOU'RE SLEEPING ON the COUCH
-DAWSON-

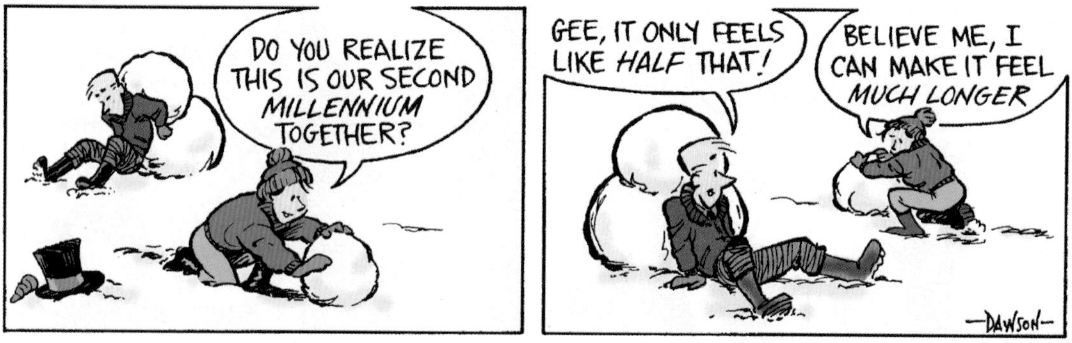
DO YOU REALIZE THIS IS OUR SECOND MILLENNIUM TOGETHER?
GEE, IT ONLY FEELS LIKE HALF THAT!
BELIEVE ME, I CAN MAKE IT FEEL MUCH LONGER
-DAWSON-

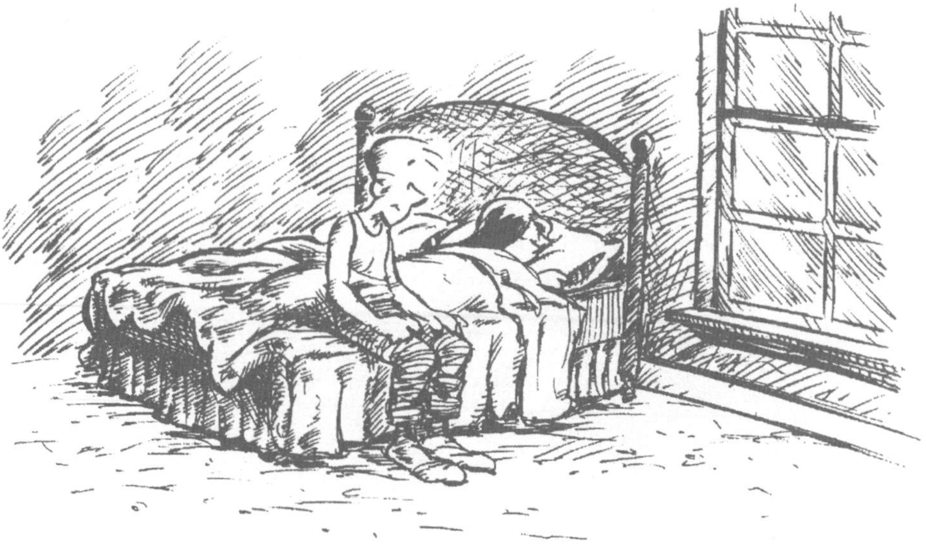

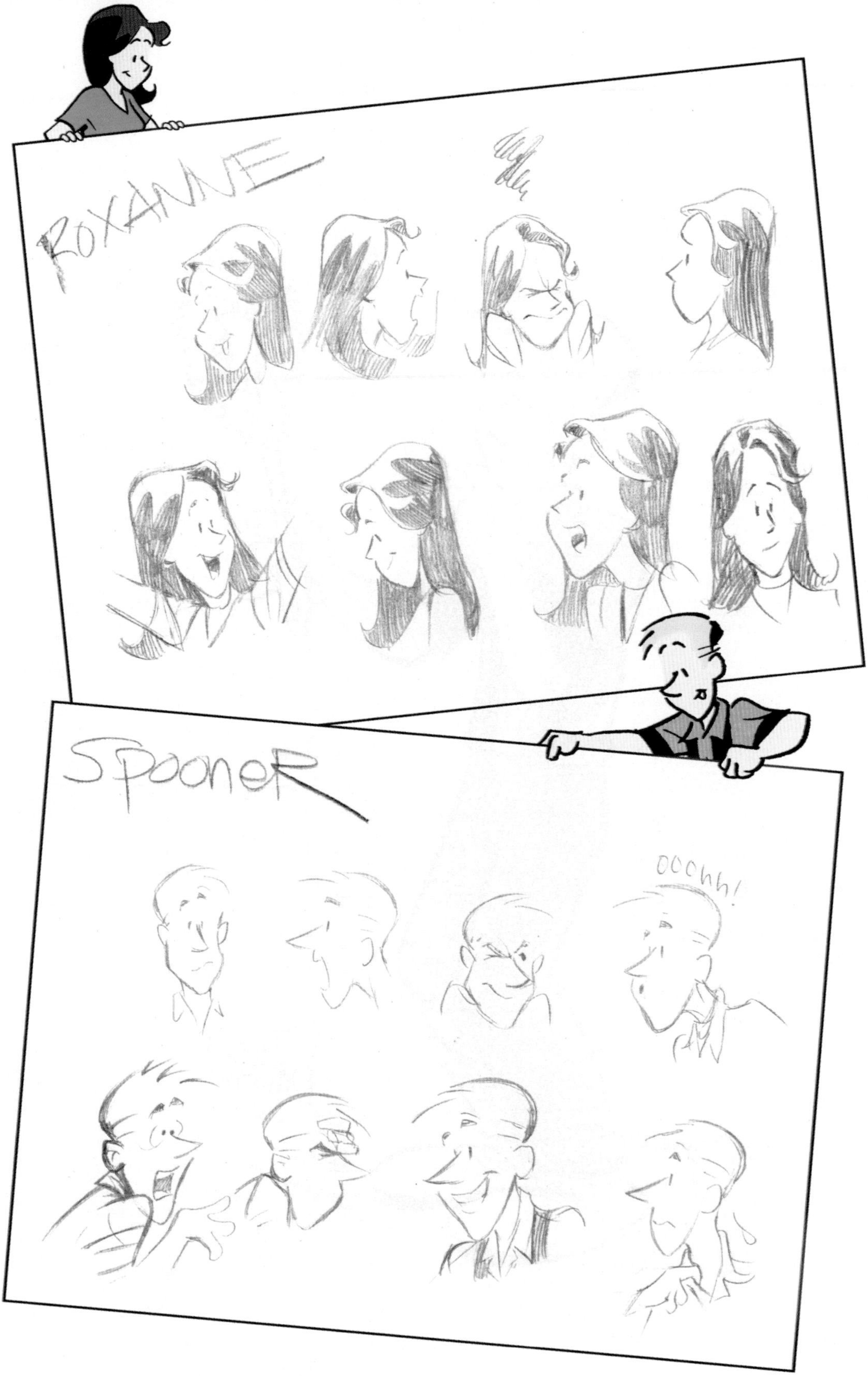
ROXANNE
SPOONER
OOOhh!

Early character sketches
of Spooner and Roxanne.

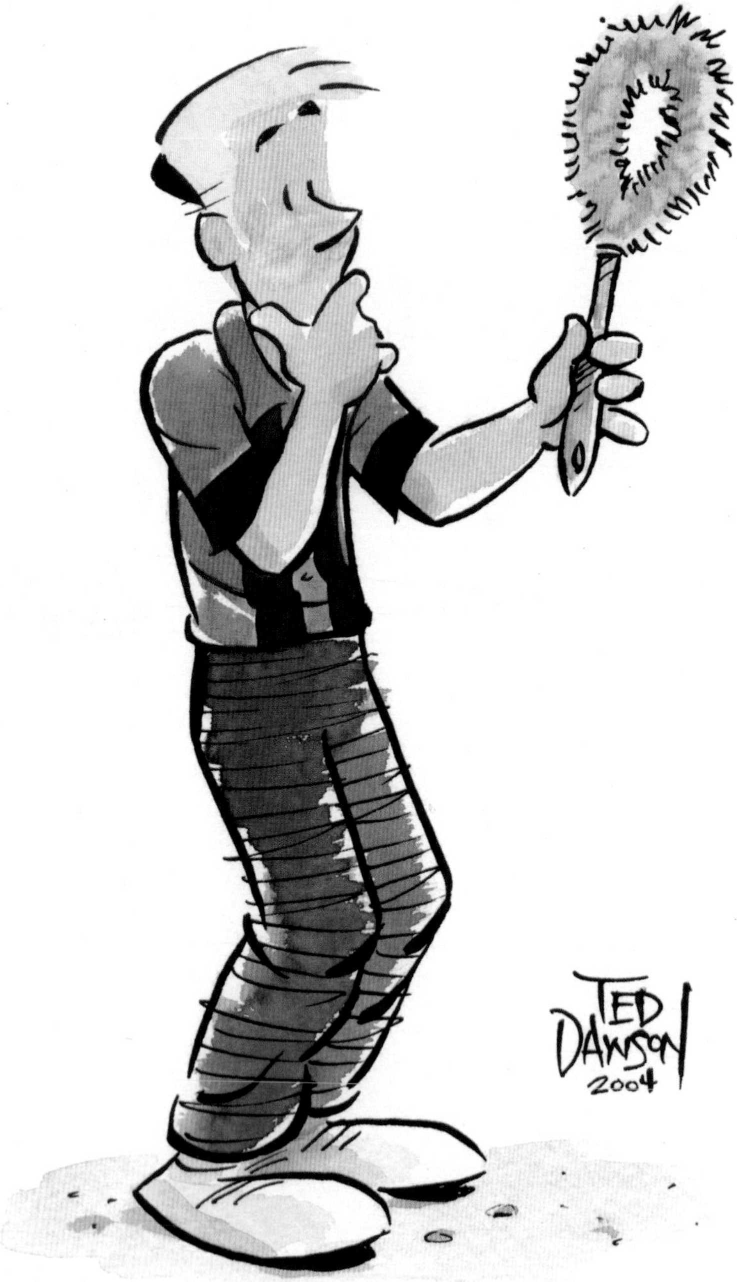
TED DAWSON
2004

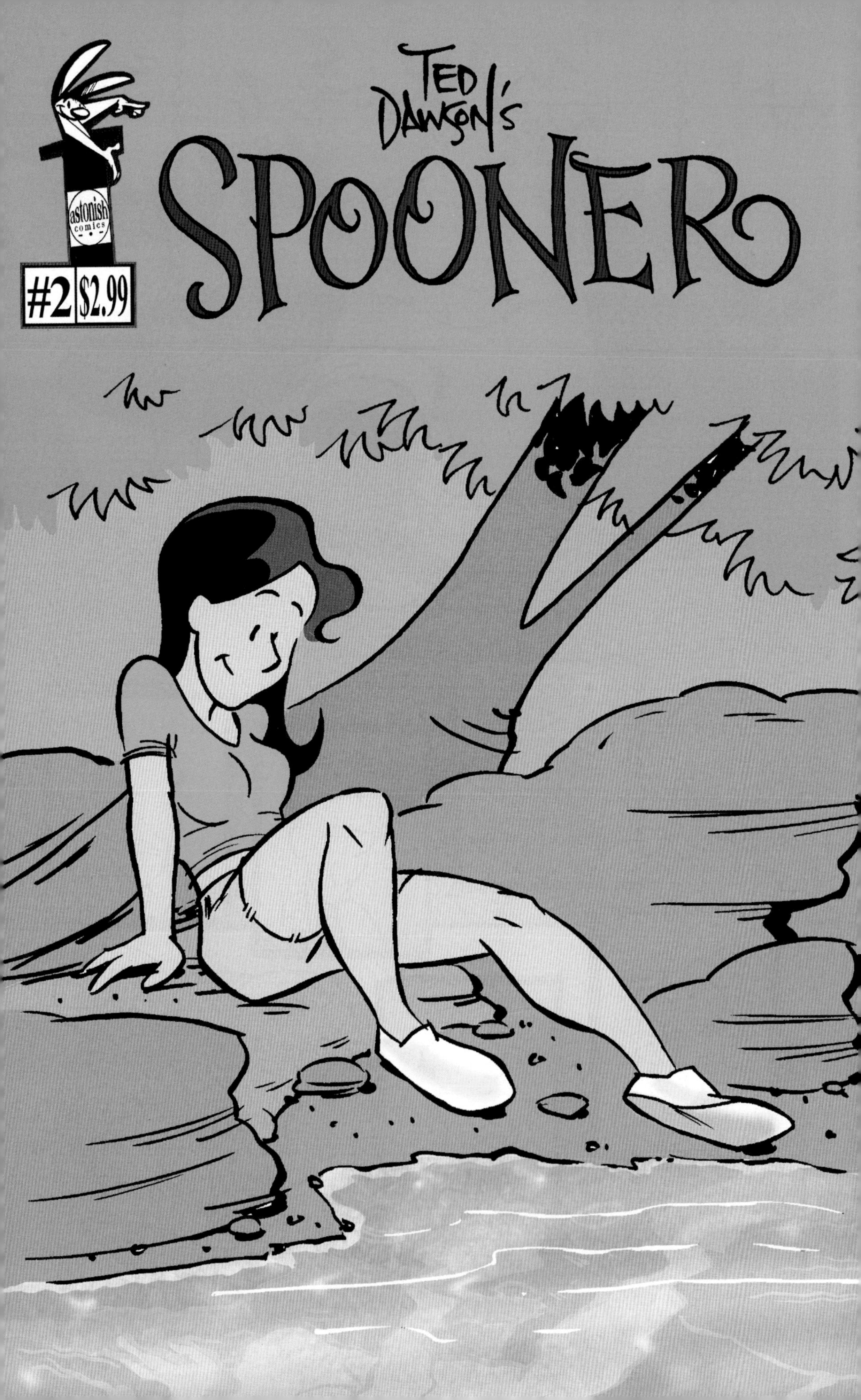
TED DAWSON'S
SPOONER
astonish comics
#2 $2.99

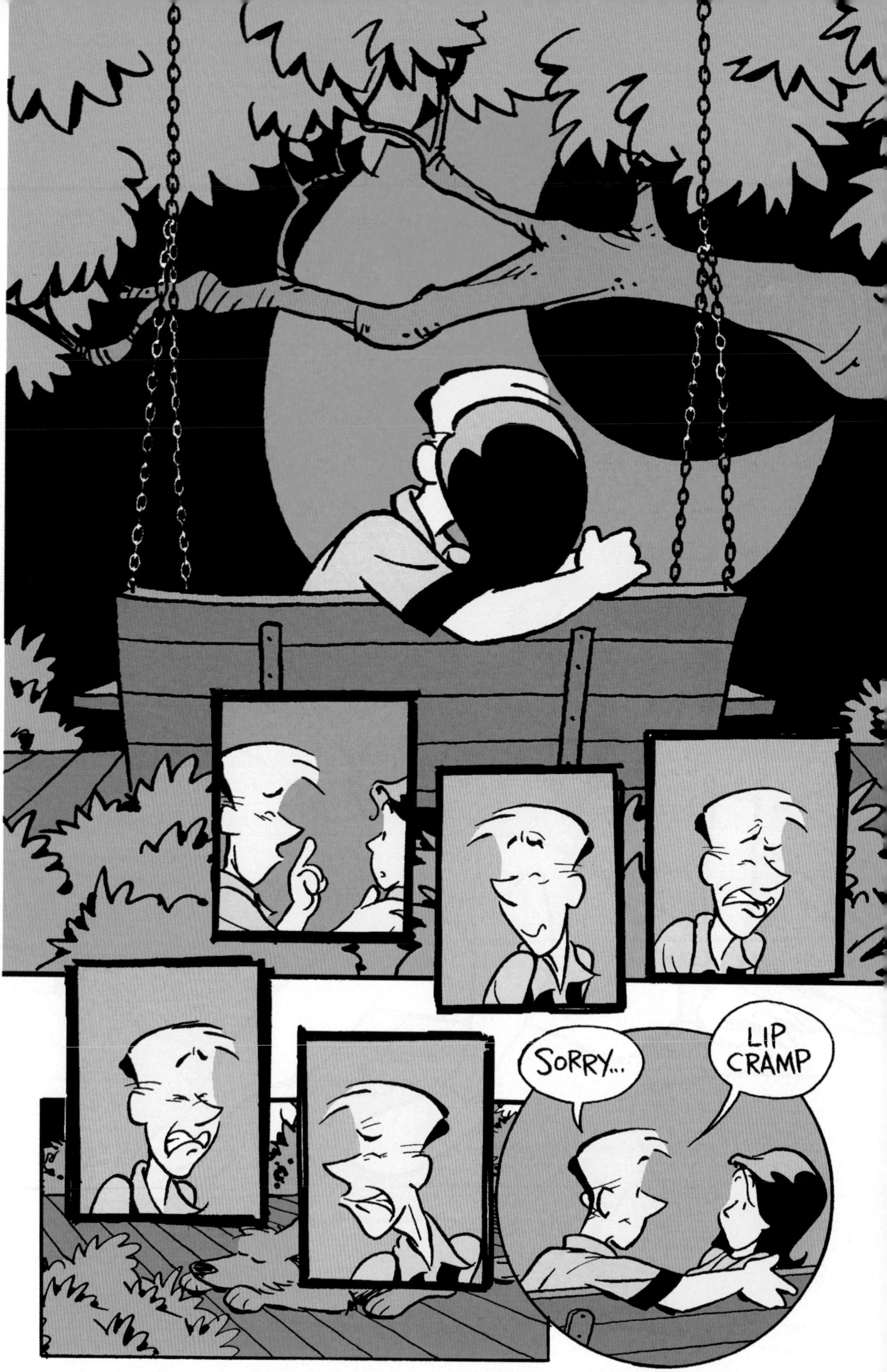
SORRY...
LIP CRAMP

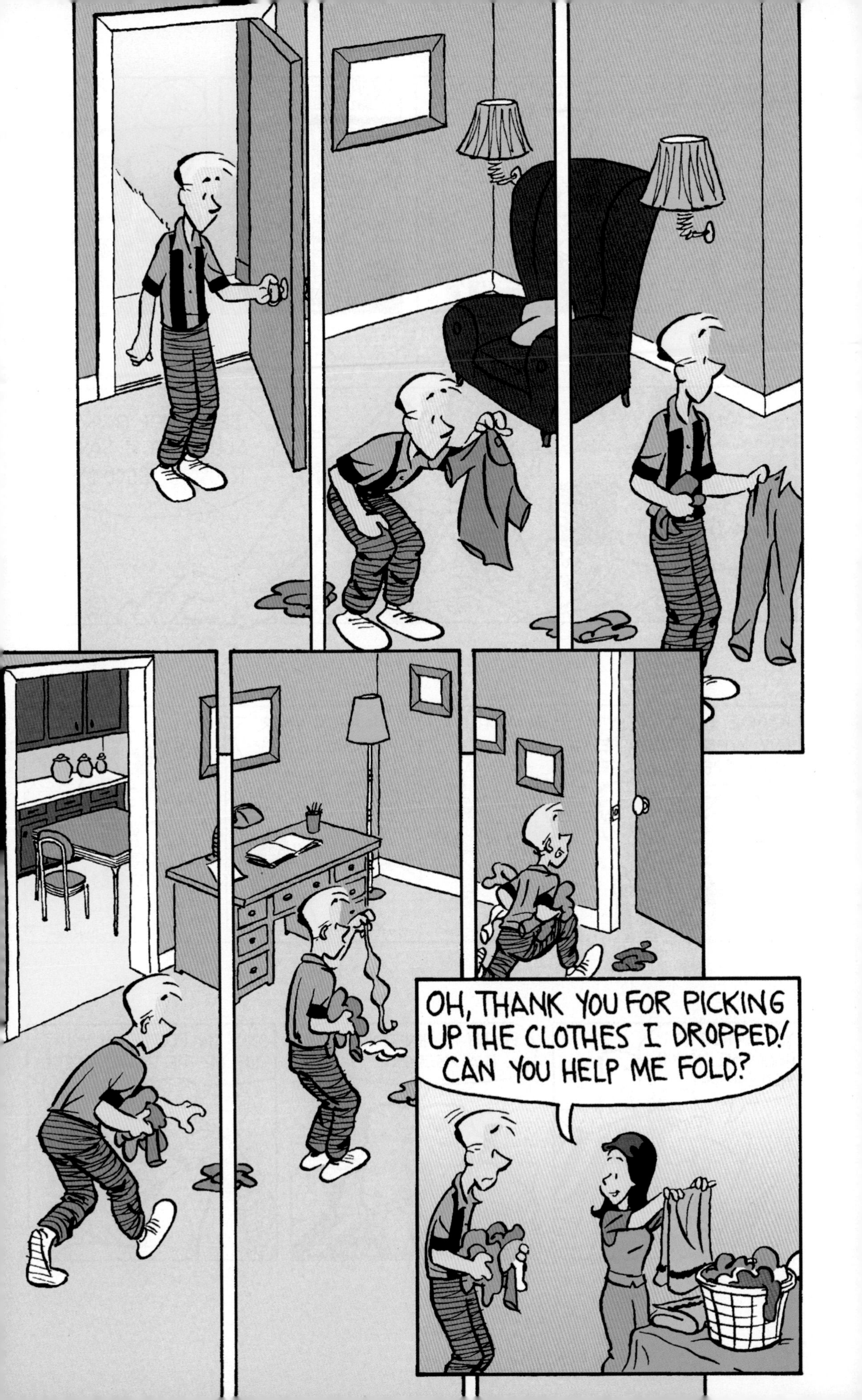
OH, THANK YOU FOR PICKING UP THE CLOTHES I DROPPED! CAN YOU HELP ME FOLD?

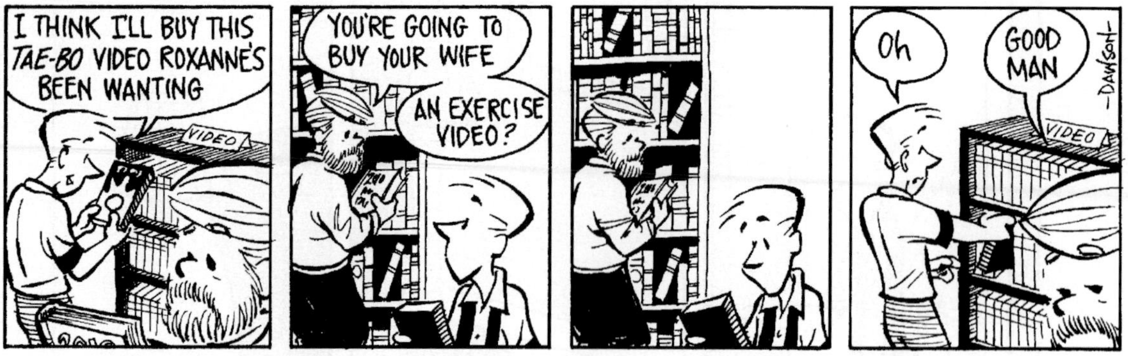
I THINK I'LL BUY THIS *TAE-BO* VIDEO ROXANNE'S BEEN WANTING
VIDEO
YOU'RE GOING TO BUY YOUR WIFE
AN EXERCISE VIDEO?
Oh
GOOD MAN
VIDEO
-DAWSON-

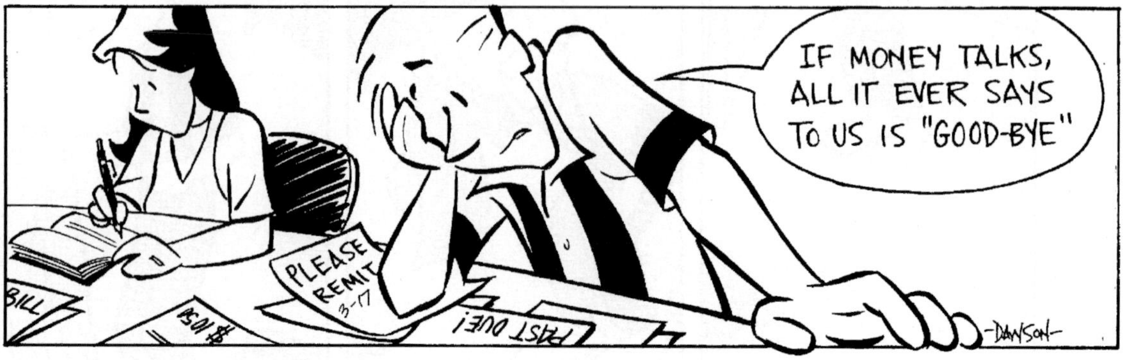
IF MONEY TALKS, ALL IT EVER SAYS TO US IS "GOOD-BYE"
PLEASE REMIT 3-17
BILL
PAST DUE!
-DAWSON-

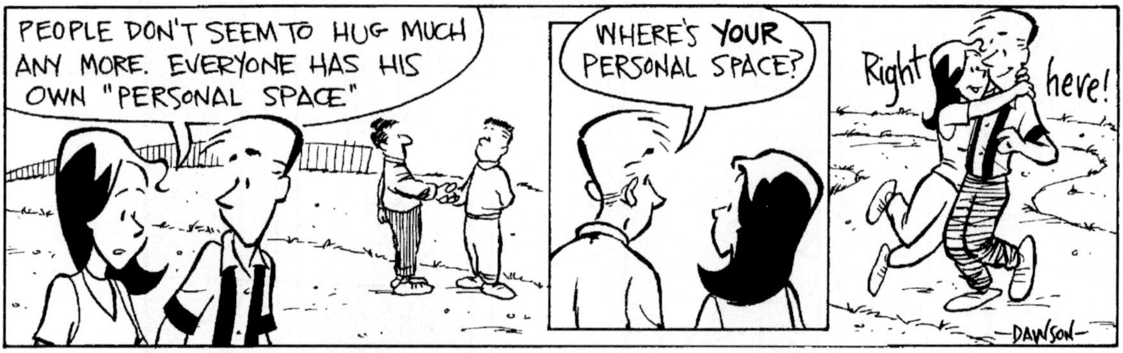
PEOPLE DON'T SEEM TO HUG MUCH ANY MORE. EVERYONE HAS HIS OWN "PERSONAL SPACE"
WHERE'S **YOUR** PERSONAL SPACE?
Right here!
-DAWSON-

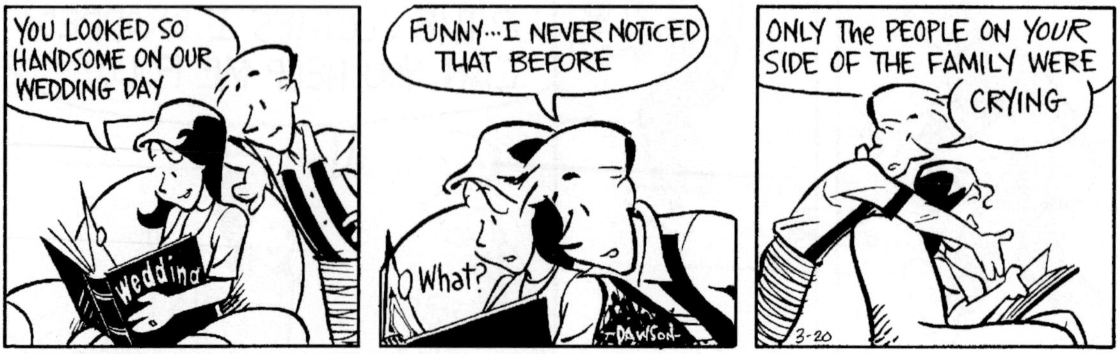
YOU LOOKED SO HANDSOME ON OUR WEDDING DAY
wedding
FUNNY...I NEVER NOTICED THAT BEFORE
What?
-DAWSON-
ONLY The PEOPLE ON *YOUR* SIDE OF THE FAMILY WERE
CRYING
3-20

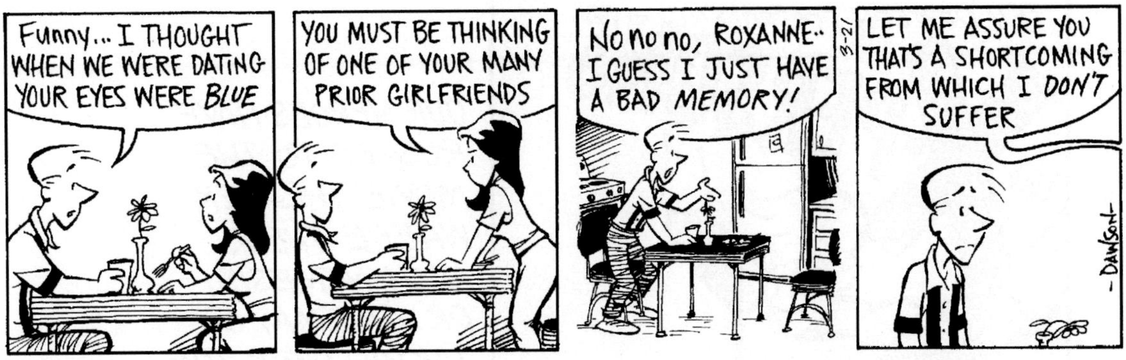
Funny... I THOUGHT WHEN WE WERE DATING YOUR EYES WERE *BLUE*
YOU MUST BE THINKING OF ONE OF YOUR MANY PRIOR GIRLFRIENDS
No no no, ROXANNE.. I GUESS I JUST HAVE A BAD *MEMORY!*
LET ME ASSURE YOU THAT'S A SHORTCOMING FROM WHICH I *DON'T* SUFFER

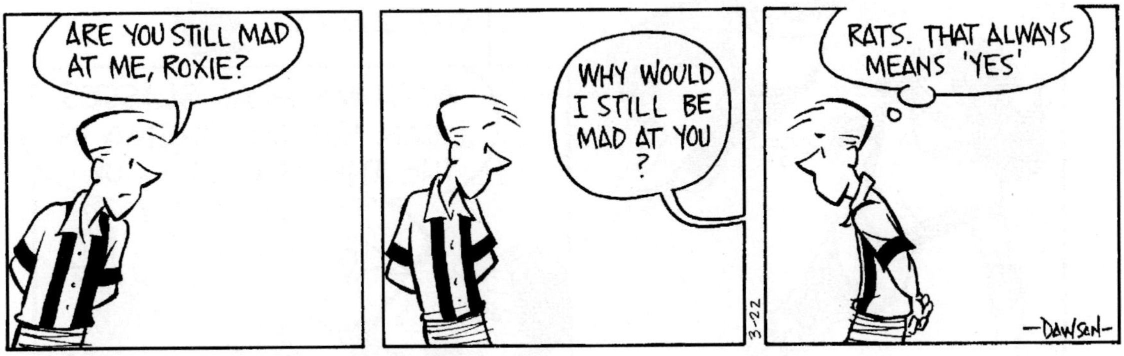
ARE YOU STILL MAD AT ME, ROXIE?
WHY WOULD I STILL BE MAD AT YOU ?
RATS. THAT ALWAYS MEANS 'YES'

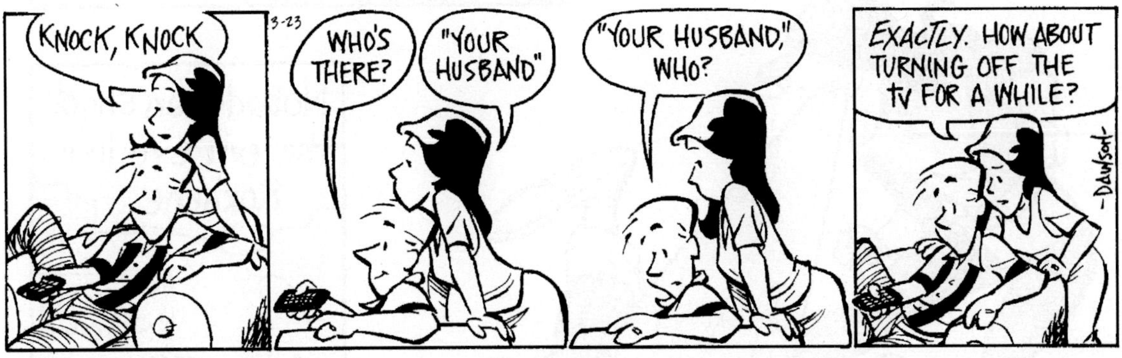
KNOCK, KNOCK
WHO'S THERE?
"YOUR HUSBAND"
"YOUR HUSBAND," WHO?
EXACTLY. HOW ABOUT TURNING OFF THE tv FOR A WHILE?

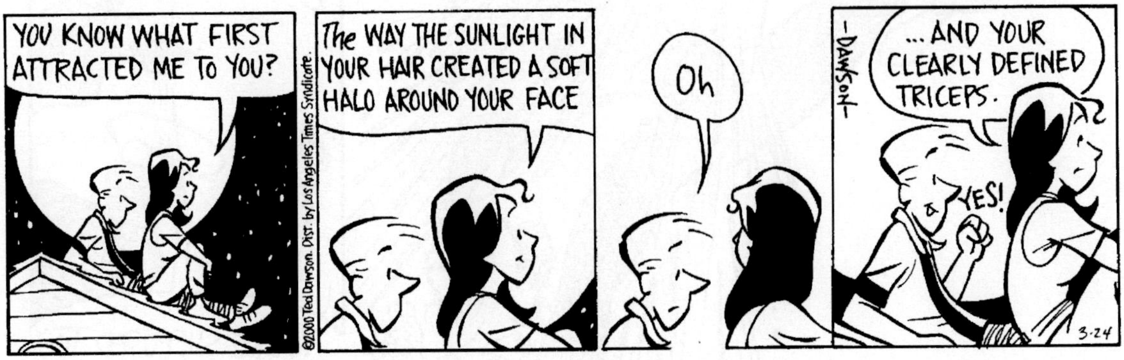
YOU KNOW WHAT FIRST ATTRACTED ME TO YOU?
The WAY THE SUNLIGHT IN YOUR HAIR CREATED A SOFT HALO AROUND YOUR FACE
Oh
...AND YOUR CLEARLY DEFINED TRICEPS.
YES!

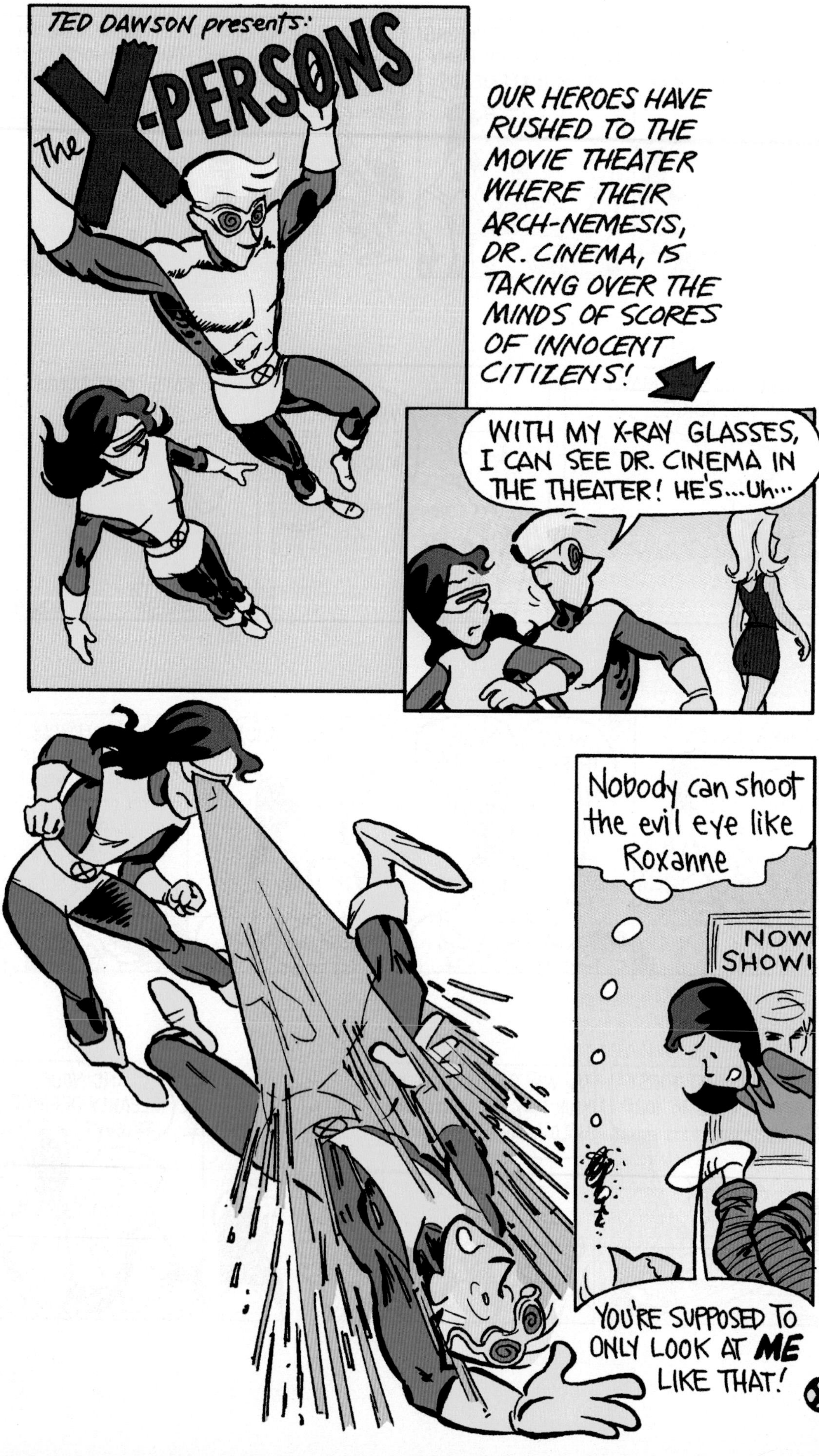
TED DAWSON presents:
The X-PERSONS
OUR HEROES HAVE RUSHED TO THE MOVIE THEATER WHERE THEIR ARCH-NEMESIS, DR. CINEMA, IS TAKING OVER THE MINDS OF SCORES OF INNOCENT CITIZENS!
WITH MY X-RAY GLASSES, I CAN SEE DR. CINEMA IN THE THEATER! HE'S...Uh...
Nobody can shoot the evil eye like Roxanne
NOW SHOWI
YOU'RE SUPPOSED TO ONLY LOOK AT ***ME*** LIKE THAT!

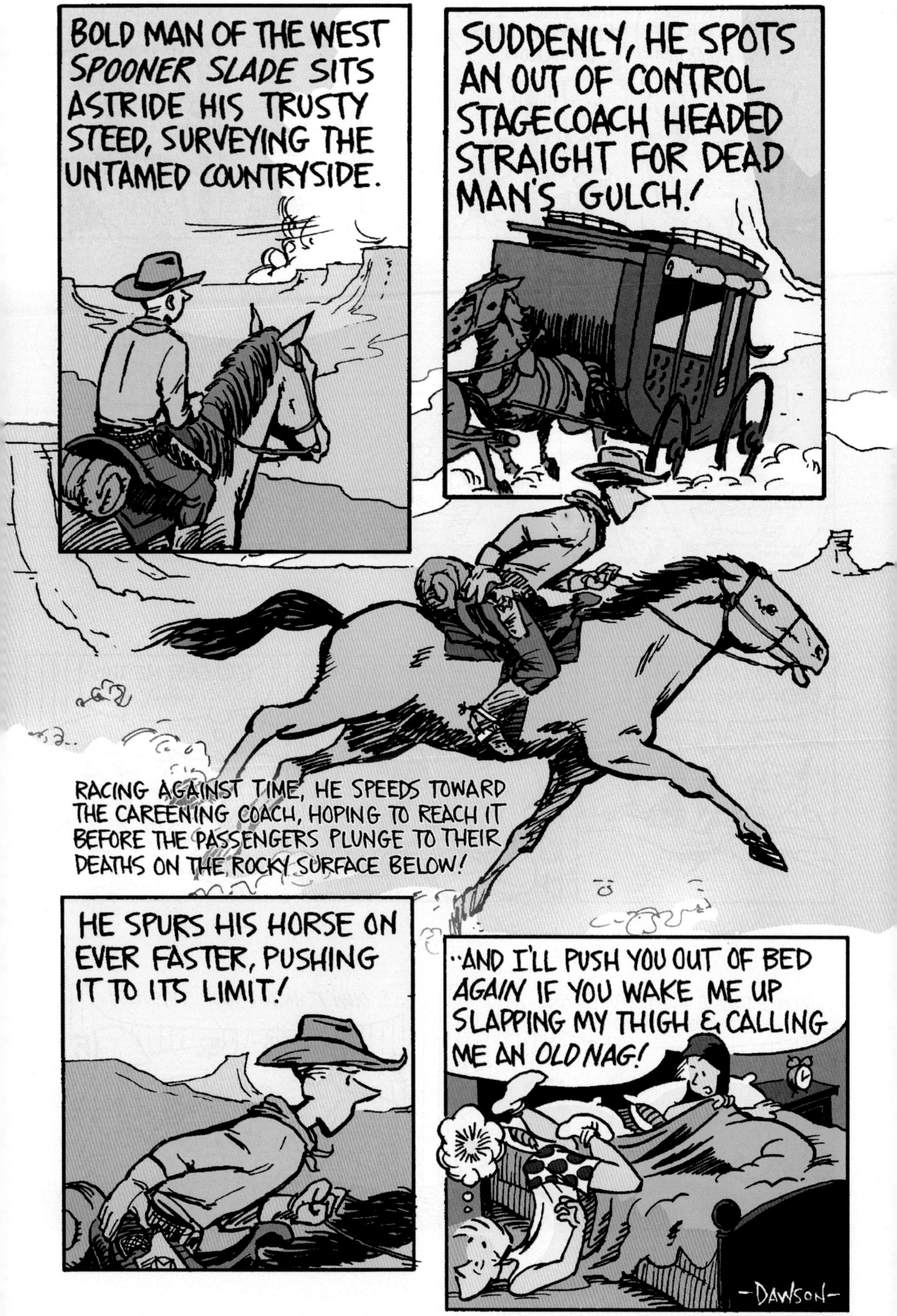
BOLD MAN OF THE WEST *SPOONER SLADE* SITS ASTRIDE HIS TRUSTY STEED, SURVEYING THE UNTAMED COUNTRYSIDE.
SUDDENLY, HE SPOTS AN OUT OF CONTROL STAGECOACH HEADED STRAIGHT FOR DEAD MAN'S GULCH!
RACING AGAINST TIME, HE SPEEDS TOWARD THE CAREENING COACH, HOPING TO REACH IT BEFORE THE PASSENGERS PLUNGE TO THEIR DEATHS ON THE ROCKY SURFACE BELOW!
HE SPURS HIS HORSE ON EVER FASTER, PUSHING IT TO ITS LIMIT!
..AND I'LL PUSH YOU OUT OF BED *AGAIN* IF YOU WAKE ME UP SLAPPING MY THIGH & CALLING ME AN *OLD NAG!*
-DAWSON-

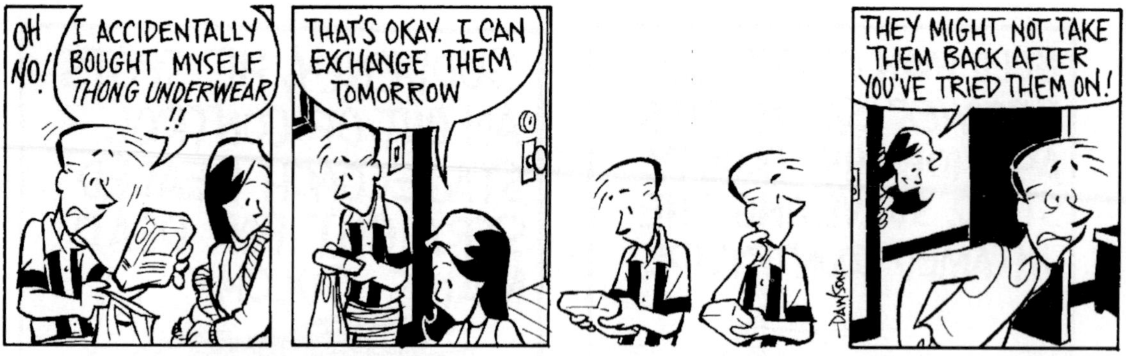
OH NO!
I ACCIDENTALLY BOUGHT MYSELF THONG UNDERWEAR!!
THAT'S OKAY. I CAN EXCHANGE THEM TOMORROW
THEY MIGHT NOT TAKE THEM BACK AFTER YOU'VE TRIED THEM ON!
DAWSON

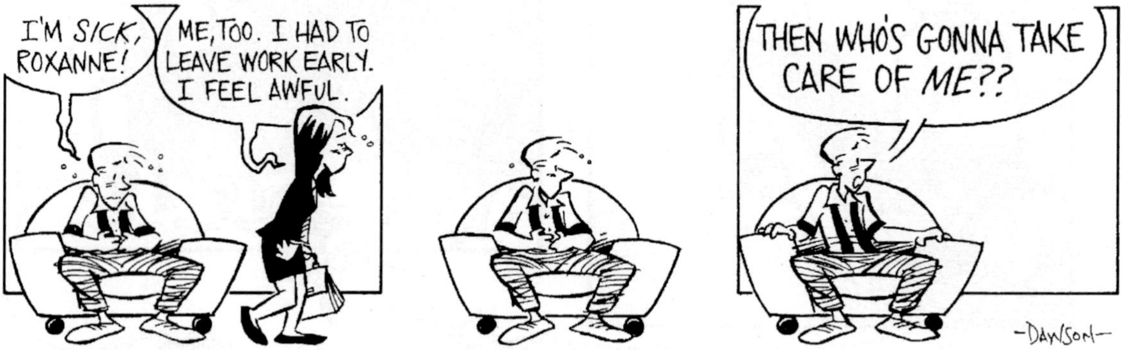
I'M SICK, ROXANNE!
ME, TOO. I HAD TO LEAVE WORK EARLY. I FEEL AWFUL.
THEN WHO'S GONNA TAKE CARE OF ME??
-DAWSON-

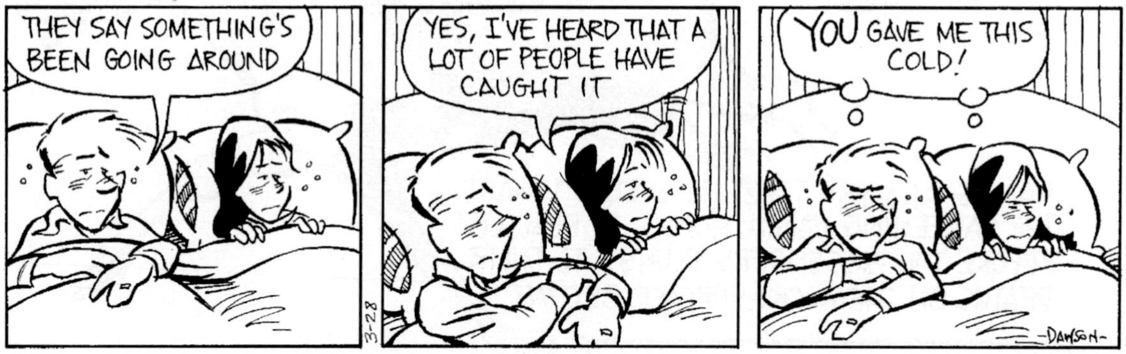
THEY SAY SOMETHING'S BEEN GOING AROUND
3-28
YES, I'VE HEARD THAT A LOT OF PEOPLE HAVE CAUGHT IT
YOU GAVE ME THIS COLD!
-DAWSON-

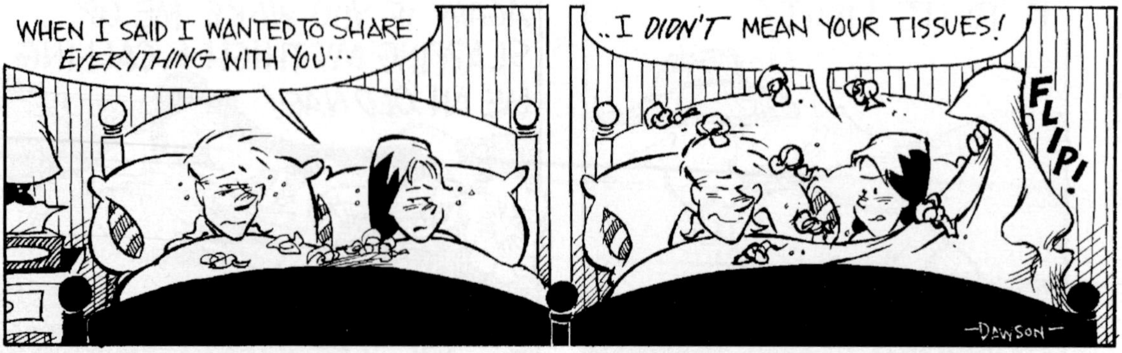
WHEN I SAID I WANTED TO SHARE EVERYTHING WITH YOU...
..I DIDN'T MEAN YOUR TISSUES!
FLIP!
-DAWSON-

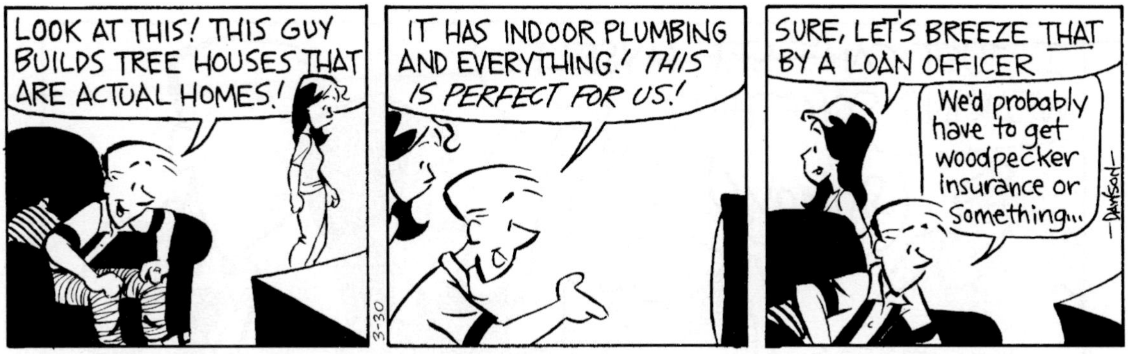
LOOK AT THIS! THIS GUY BUILDS TREE HOUSES THAT ARE ACTUAL HOMES!
3-30
IT HAS INDOOR PLUMBING AND EVERYTHING! *THIS IS PERFECT FOR US!*
SURE, LET'S BREEZE THAT BY A LOAN OFFICER
We'd probably have to get woodpecker insurance or something...
DAWSON

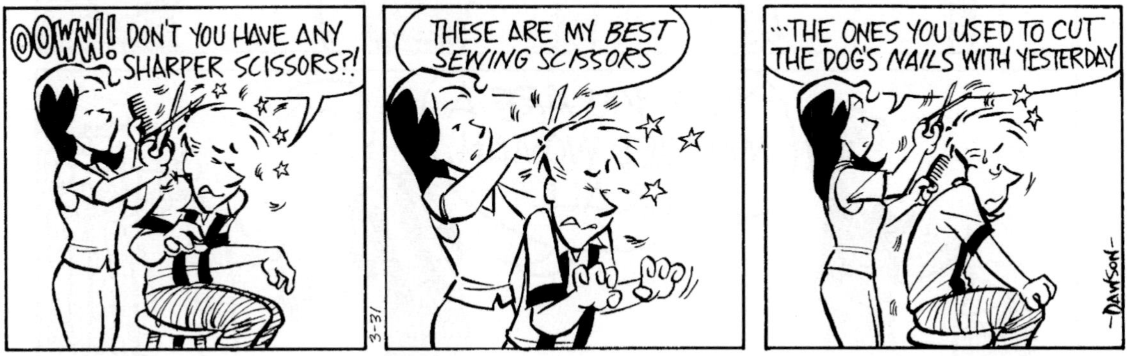
OOWW! DON'T YOU HAVE ANY SHARPER SCISSORS?!
3-31
THESE ARE MY *BEST SEWING SCISSORS*
...THE ONES YOU USED TO CUT THE DOG'S *NAILS* WITH YESTERDAY
DAWSON

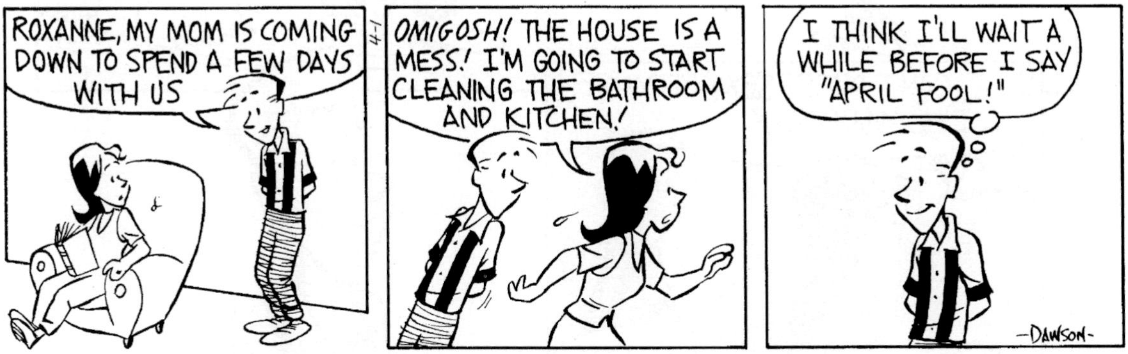
ROXANNE, MY MOM IS COMING DOWN TO SPEND A FEW DAYS WITH US
4-1
OMIGOSH! THE HOUSE IS A MESS! I'M GOING TO START CLEANING THE BATHROOM AND KITCHEN!
I THINK I'LL WAIT A WHILE BEFORE I SAY "APRIL FOOL!"
DAWSON

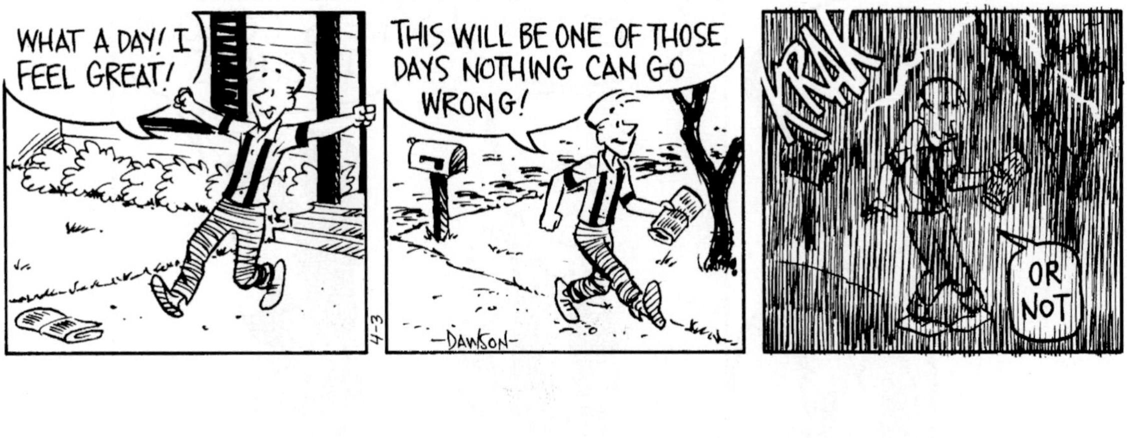
WHAT A DAY! I FEEL GREAT!
4-3
THIS WILL BE ONE OF THOSE DAYS NOTHING CAN GO WRONG!
DAWSON
KRAK
OR NOT

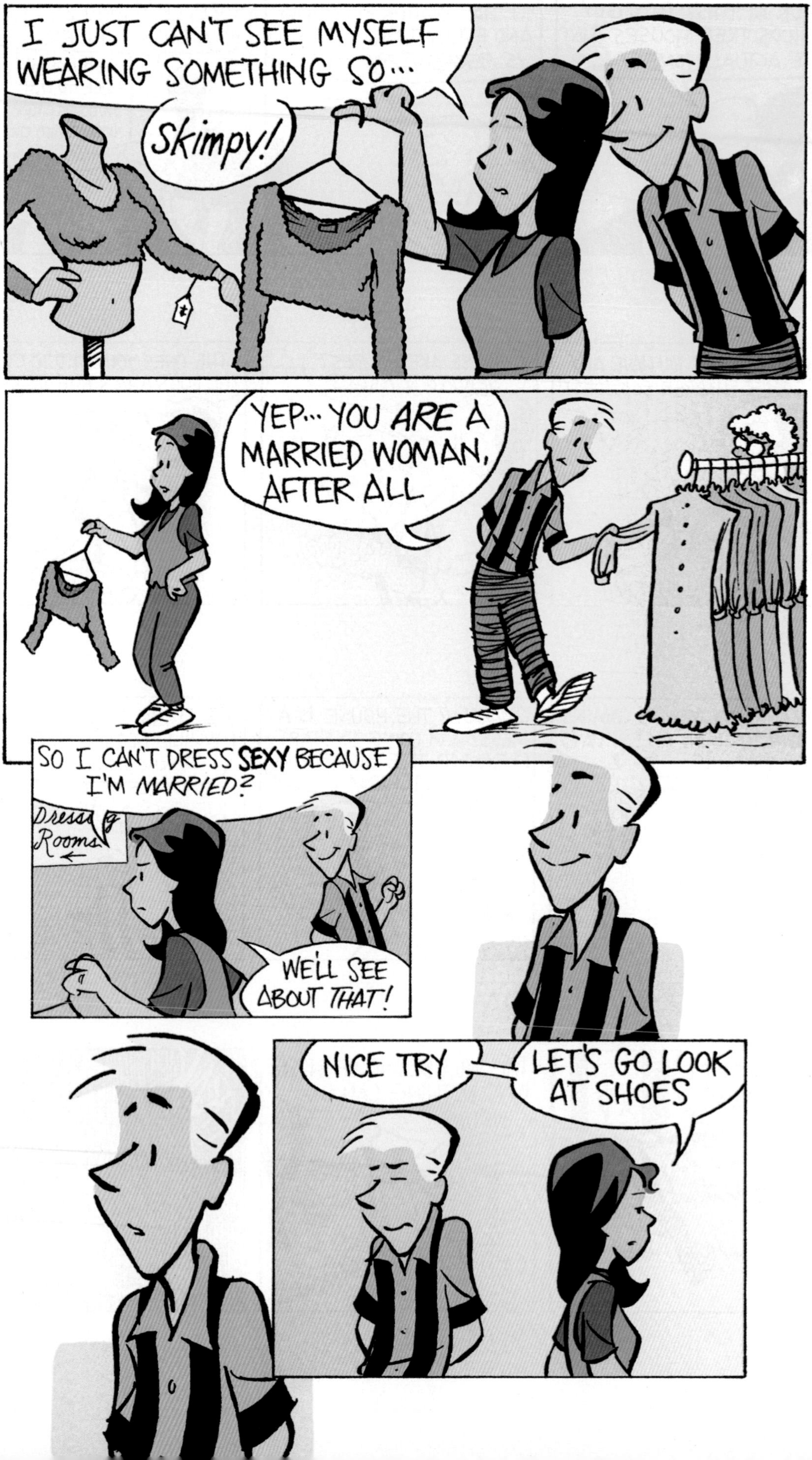
I JUST CAN'T SEE MYSELF WEARING SOMETHING SO...
Skimpy!
YEP... YOU ARE A MARRIED WOMAN, AFTER ALL
SO I CAN'T DRESS SEXY BECAUSE I'M MARRIED?
Dressing Rooms
WE'LL SEE ABOUT THAT!
NICE TRY
LET'S GO LOOK AT SHOES

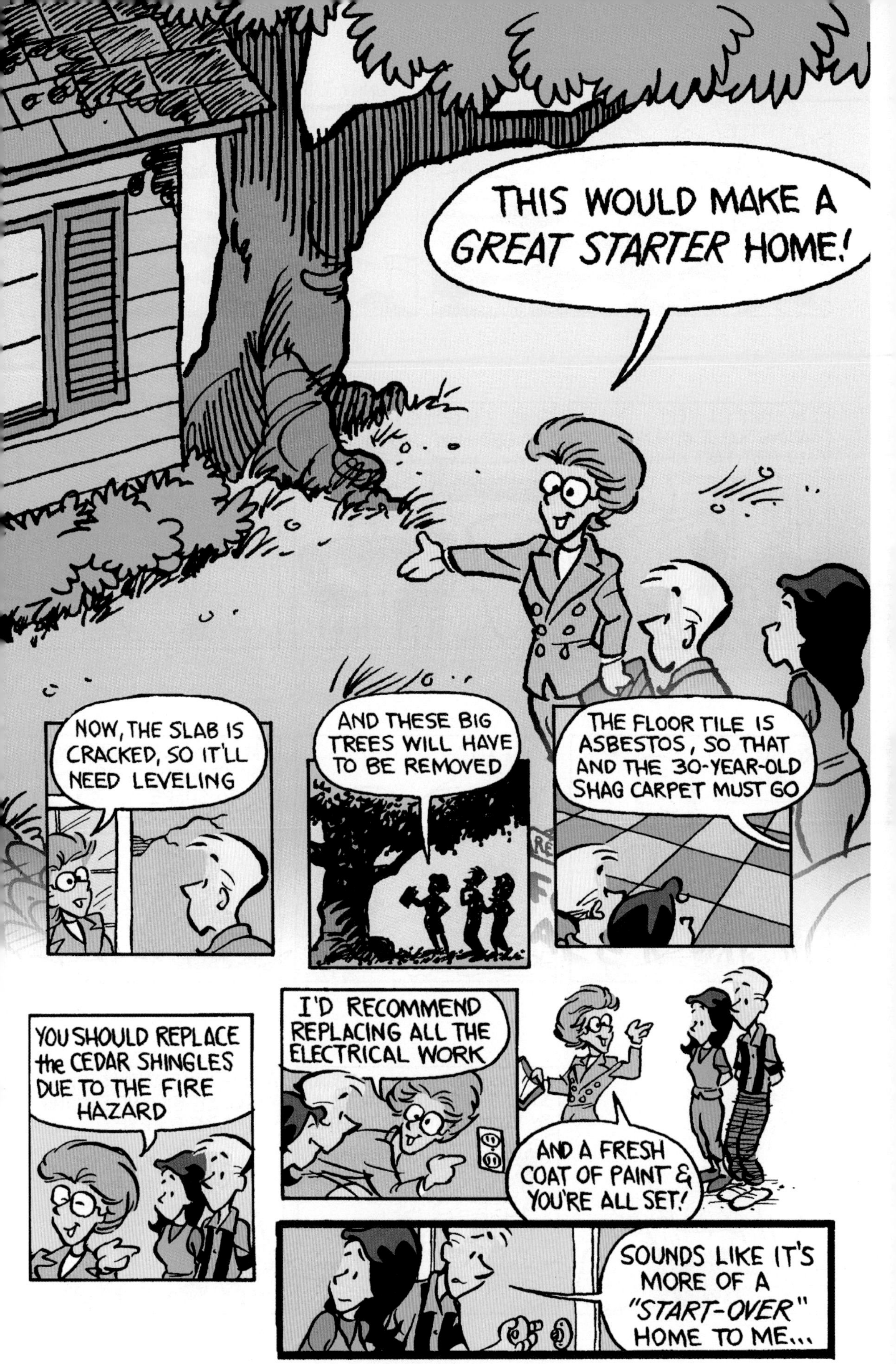
THIS WOULD MAKE A GREAT STARTER HOME!
NOW, THE SLAB IS CRACKED, SO IT'LL NEED LEVELING
AND THESE BIG TREES WILL HAVE TO BE REMOVED
THE FLOOR TILE IS ASBESTOS, SO THAT AND THE 30-YEAR-OLD SHAG CARPET MUST GO
YOU SHOULD REPLACE the CEDAR SHINGLES DUE TO THE FIRE HAZARD
I'D RECOMMEND REPLACING ALL THE ELECTRICAL WORK
AND A FRESH COAT OF PAINT & YOU'RE ALL SET!
SOUNDS LIKE IT'S MORE OF A "START-OVER" HOME TO ME...

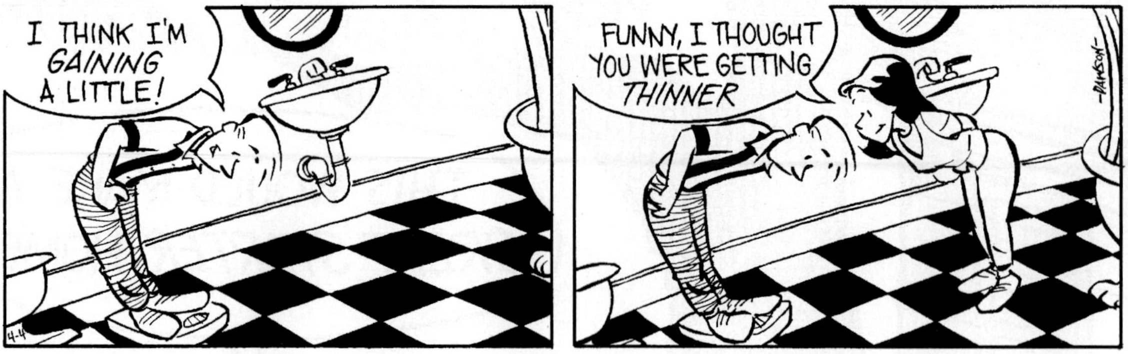
I THINK I'M GAINING A LITTLE!
FUNNY, I THOUGHT YOU WERE GETTING THINNER

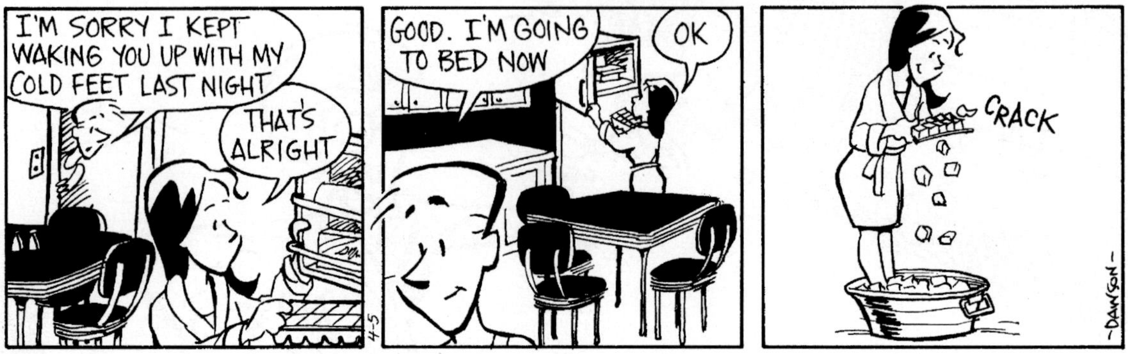
I'M SORRY I KEPT WAKING YOU UP WITH MY COLD FEET LAST NIGHT
THAT'S ALRIGHT
GOOD. I'M GOING TO BED NOW
OK
CRACK

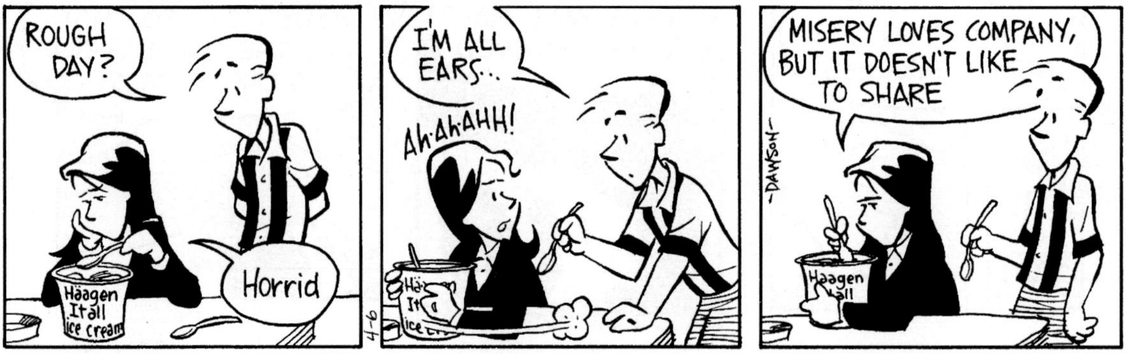
ROUGH DAY?
Horrid
I'M ALL EARS..
Ah·Ah·AHH!
MISERY LOVES COMPANY, BUT IT DOESN'T LIKE TO SHARE

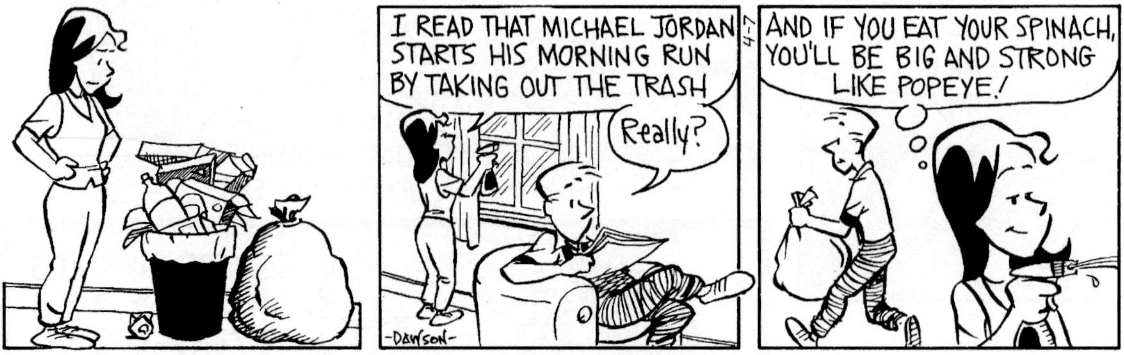
I READ THAT MICHAEL JORDAN STARTS HIS MORNING RUN BY TAKING OUT THE TRASH
Really?
AND IF YOU EAT YOUR SPINACH, YOU'LL BE BIG AND STRONG LIKE POPEYE!

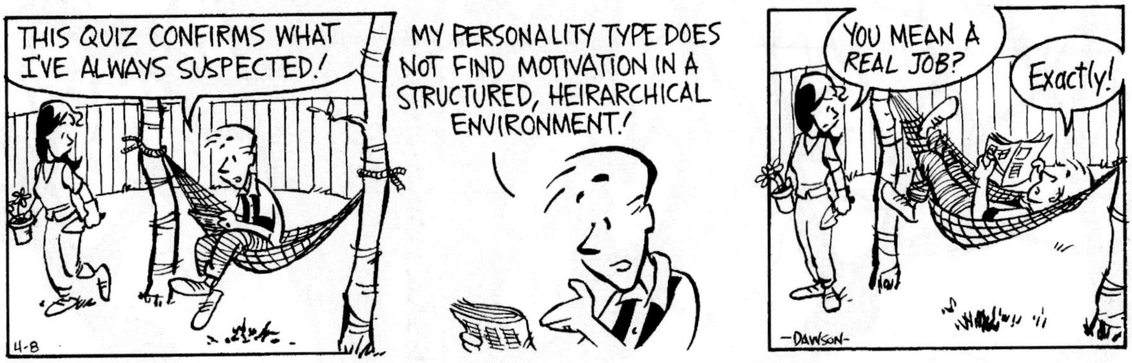
THIS QUIZ CONFIRMS WHAT I'VE ALWAYS SUSPECTED!
4-8
MY PERSONALITY TYPE DOES NOT FIND MOTIVATION IN A STRUCTURED, HEIRARCHICAL ENVIRONMENT!
YOU MEAN A REAL JOB?
Exactly!
-DAWSON-

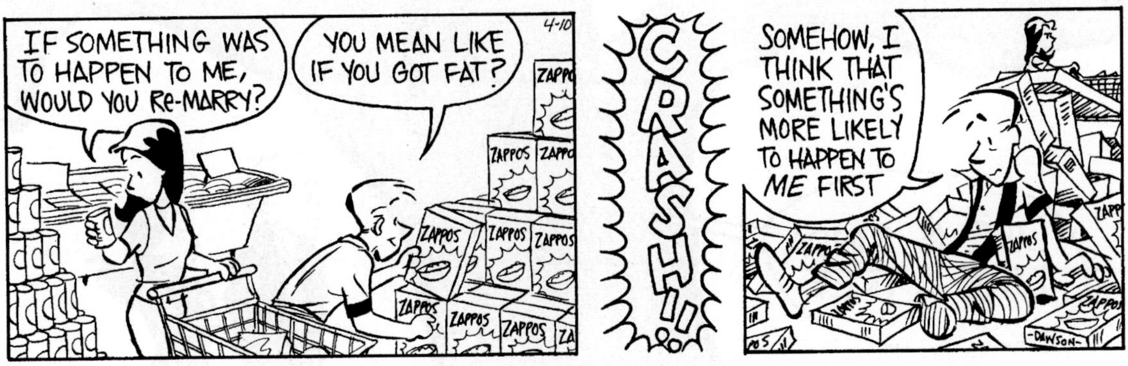
IF SOMETHING WAS TO HAPPEN TO ME, WOULD YOU Re-MARRY?
YOU MEAN LIKE IF YOU GOT FAT?
4-10
ZAPPOS
CRASH!!
SOMEHOW, I THINK THAT SOMETHING'S MORE LIKELY TO HAPPEN TO ME FIRST
-DAWSON-

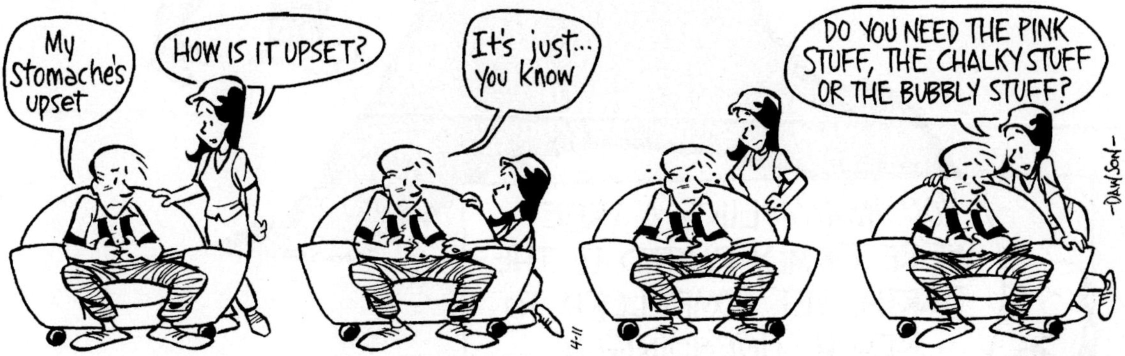
My Stomache's upset
HOW IS IT UPSET?
It's just... you know
4-11
DO YOU NEED THE PINK STUFF, THE CHALKY STUFF OR THE BUBBLY STUFF?
-DAWSON-

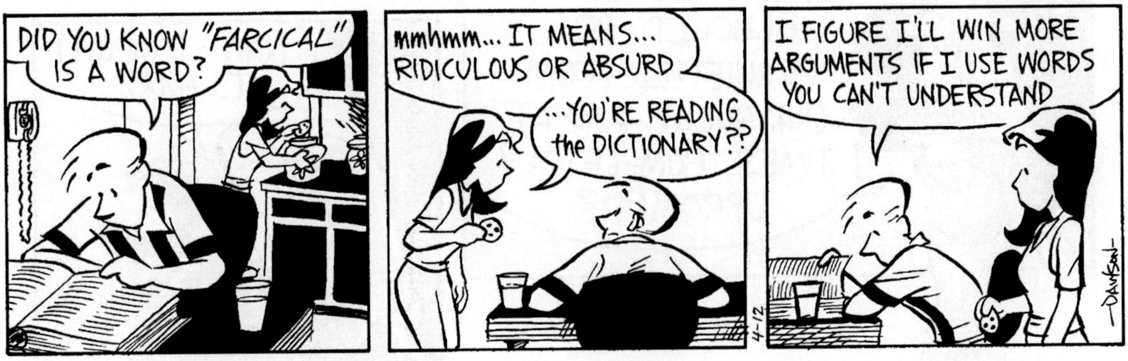
DID YOU KNOW "FARCICAL" IS A WORD?
mmhmm... IT MEANS... RIDICULOUS OR ABSURD
...YOU'RE READING the DICTIONARY??
4-12
I FIGURE I'LL WIN MORE ARGUMENTS IF I USE WORDS YOU CAN'T UNDERSTAND
-DAWSON-

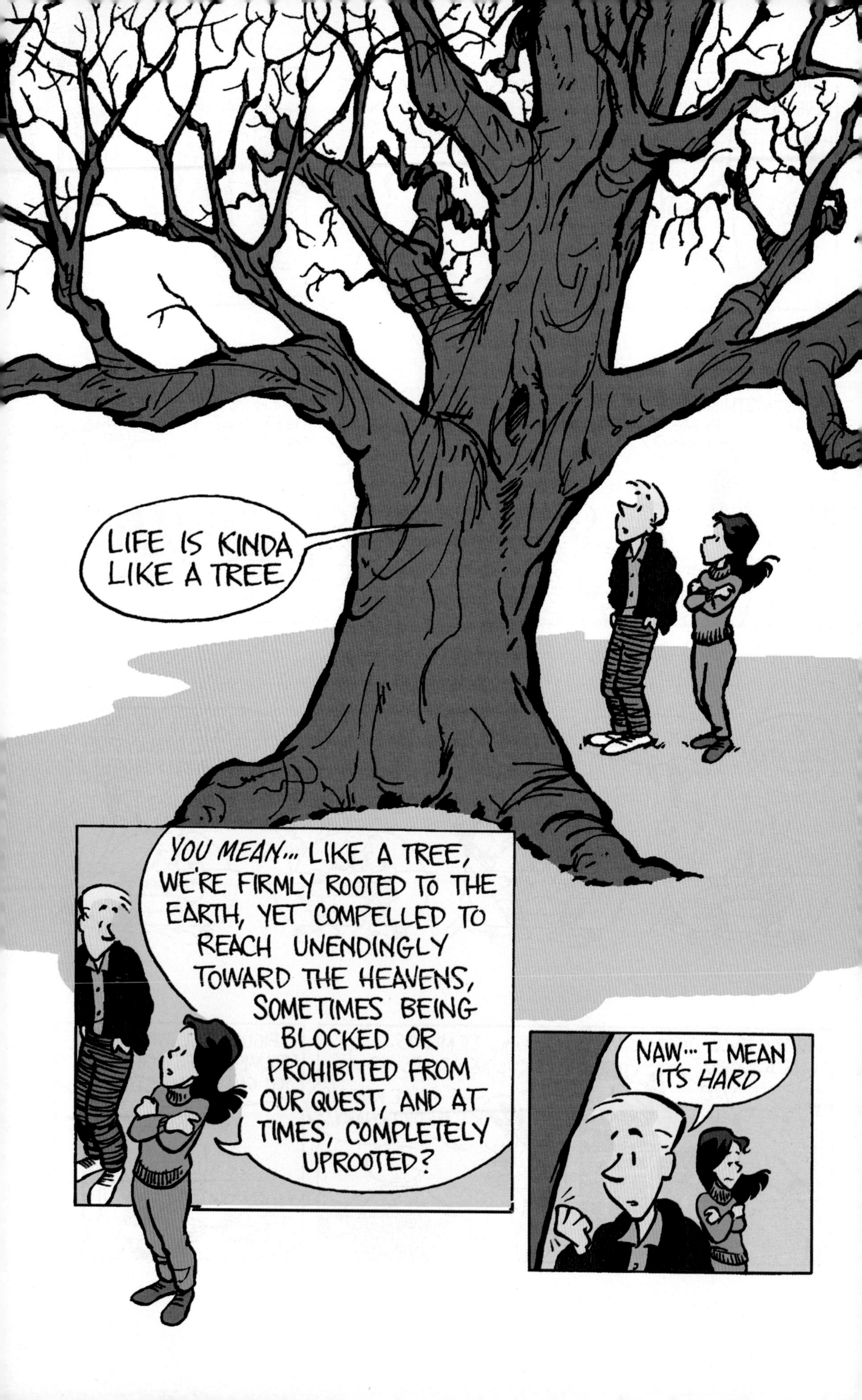
LIFE IS KINDA LIKE A TREE
YOU MEAN... LIKE A TREE, WE'RE FIRMLY ROOTED TO THE EARTH, YET COMPELLED TO REACH UNENDINGLY TOWARD THE HEAVENS, SOMETIMES BEING BLOCKED OR PROHIBITED FROM OUR QUEST, AND AT TIMES, COMPLETELY UPROOTED?
NAW... I MEAN IT'S *HARD*

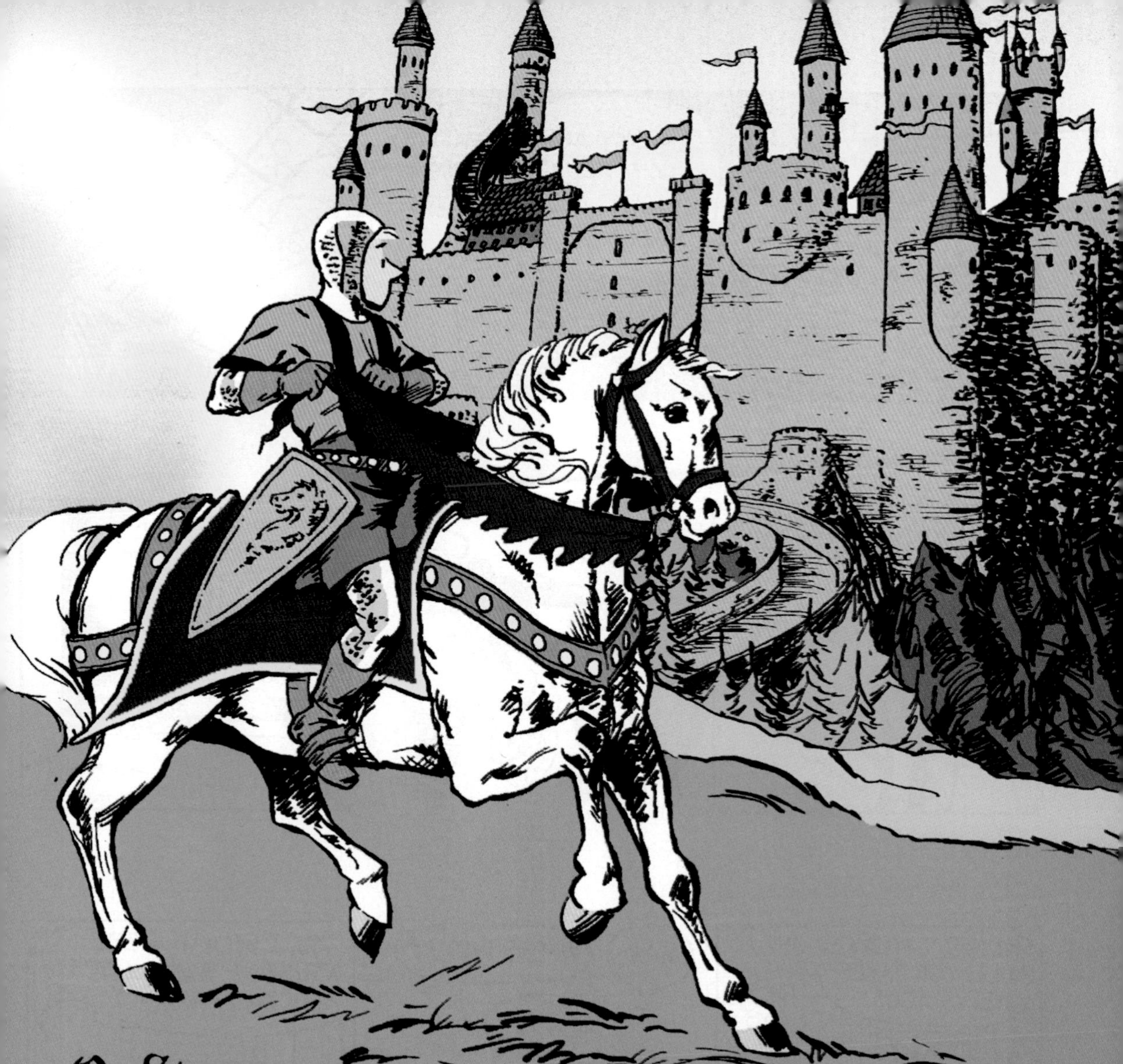

Our Story:

WHILE IN THE MIDST OF BATTLE AND ADVENTURE TO SAVE THE NEIGHBORING KINGDOM OF THE ROYALS FROM THE PIRATES OF THE NORTHLANDS, FIRST KNIGHT SIR SPOONER RECEIVED AN URGENT PLEA FROM LADY ROXANNE'S PERSONAL MESSENGER. *"RETURN ANON, AND MAKE HASTE!"* FEARFUL OF WHAT DANGER MIGHT BE THREATENING HIS LOVE, HE RODE NIGHT AND DAY ACROSS THE COUNTRYSIDE. *WOULD HE BE TOO LATE?*

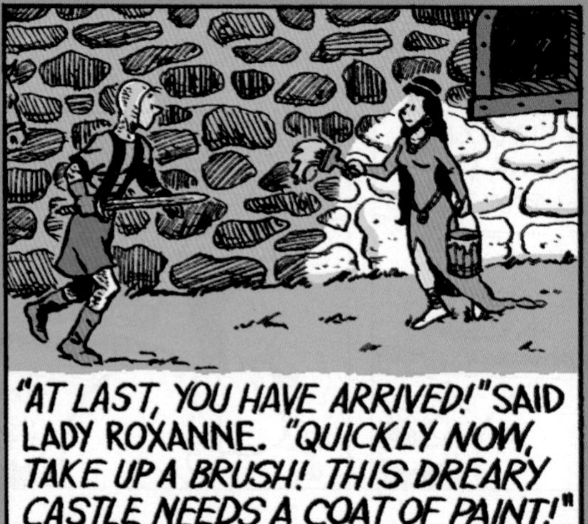
"AT LAST, YOU HAVE ARRIVED!" SAID LADY ROXANNE. "QUICKLY NOW, TAKE UP A BRUSH! THIS DREARY CASTLE NEEDS A COAT OF PAINT!"

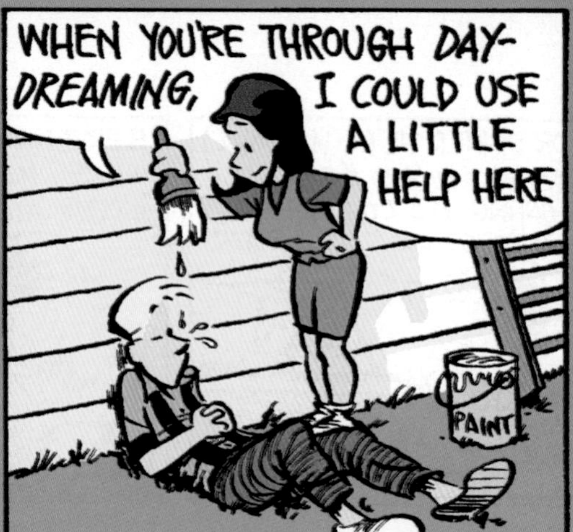
WHEN YOU'RE THROUGH DAY-DREAMING, I COULD USE A LITTLE HELP HERE
PAINT

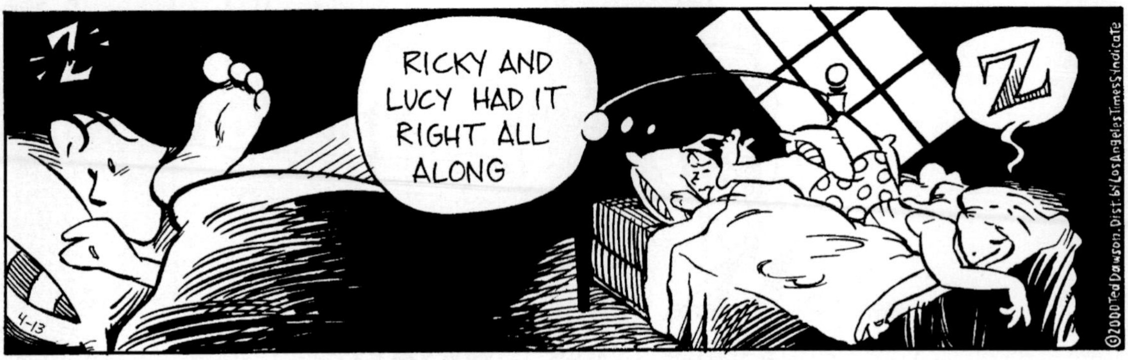
Z
RICKY AND LUCY HAD IT RIGHT ALL ALONG
Z
4-13
©2000 Ted Dawson. Dist. by Los Angeles Times Syndicate

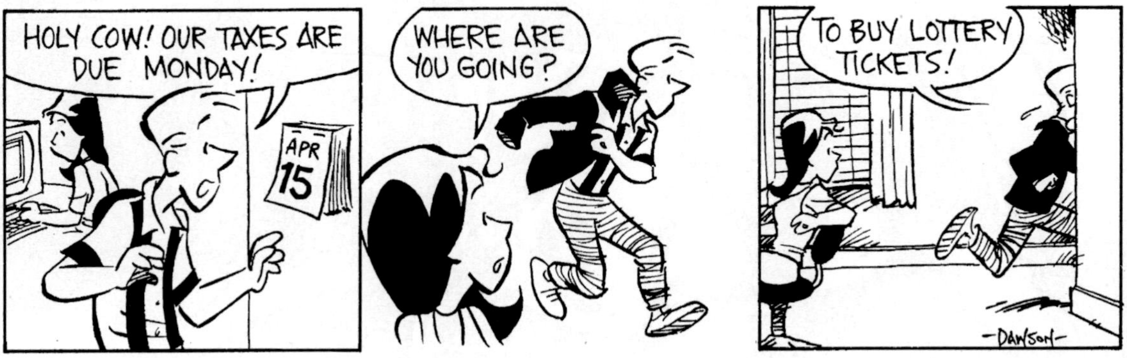
HOLY COW! OUR TAXES ARE DUE MONDAY!
APR 15
WHERE ARE YOU GOING?
TO BUY LOTTERY TICKETS!
-DAWSON-

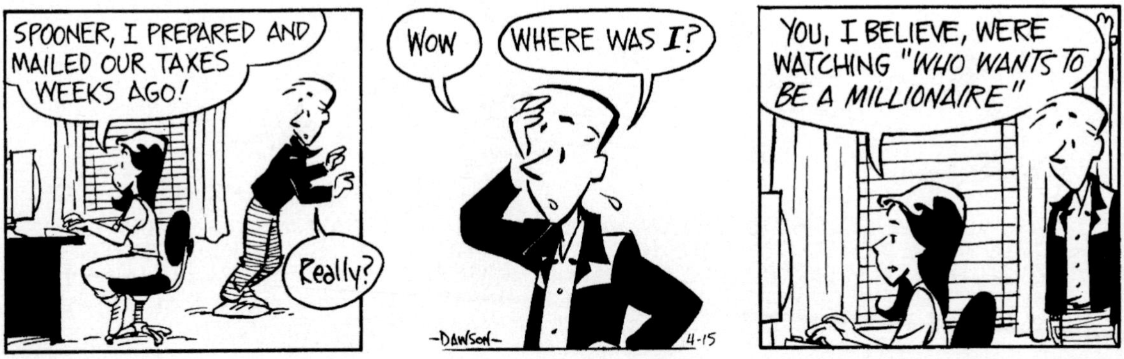
SPOONER, I PREPARED AND MAILED OUR TAXES WEEKS AGO!
Really?
WOW
WHERE WAS *I*?
-DAWSON-
4-15
YOU, I BELIEVE, WERE WATCHING "*WHO WANTS TO BE A MILLIONAIRE*"

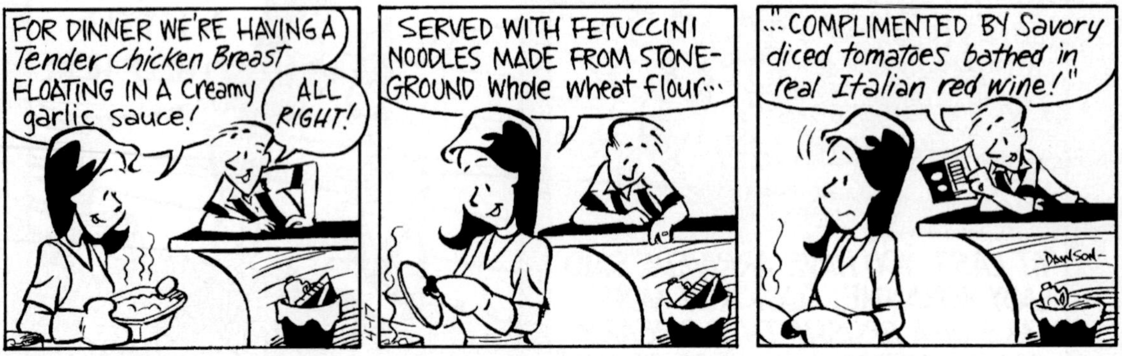
FOR DINNER WE'RE HAVING A *Tender Chicken Breast* FLOATING IN A Creamy garlic sauce!
ALL *RIGHT!*
4-17
SERVED WITH FETUCCINI NOODLES MADE FROM STONE-GROUND Whole wheat flour...
"...COMPLIMENTED BY *Savory diced tomatoes bathed in real Italian red wine!*"
-DAWSON-

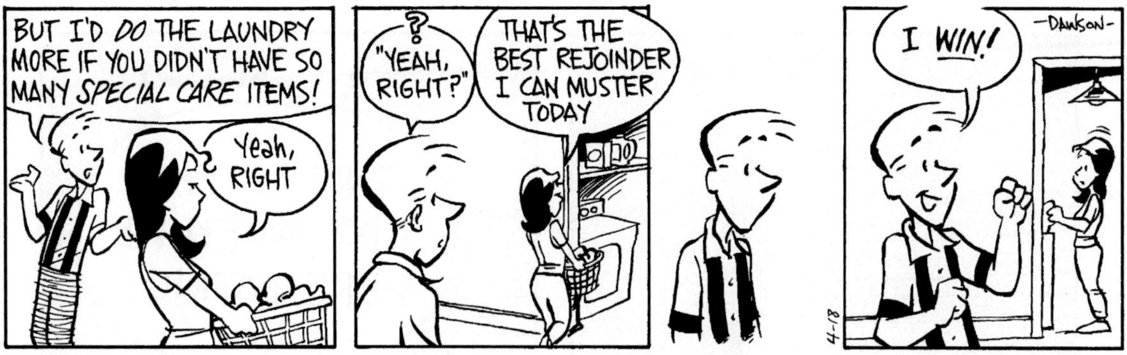
BUT I'D *DO* THE LAUNDRY MORE IF YOU DIDN'T HAVE SO MANY *SPECIAL CARE* ITEMS!
Yeah, RIGHT
?
"YEAH, RIGHT?"
THAT'S THE BEST REJOINDER I CAN MUSTER TODAY
I *WIN!*
-DAWSON-
4-18

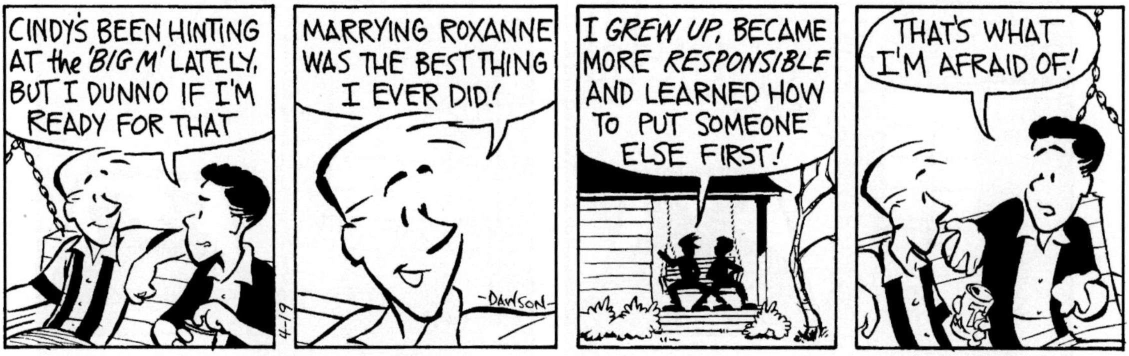
CINDY'S BEEN HINTING AT the '*BIG M*' LATELY, BUT I DUNNO IF I'M READY FOR THAT
4-19
MARRYING ROXANNE WAS THE BEST THING I EVER DID!
-DAWSON-
I *GREW UP*, BECAME MORE *RESPONSIBLE* AND LEARNED HOW TO PUT SOMEONE ELSE FIRST!
THAT'S WHAT I'M AFRAID OF!

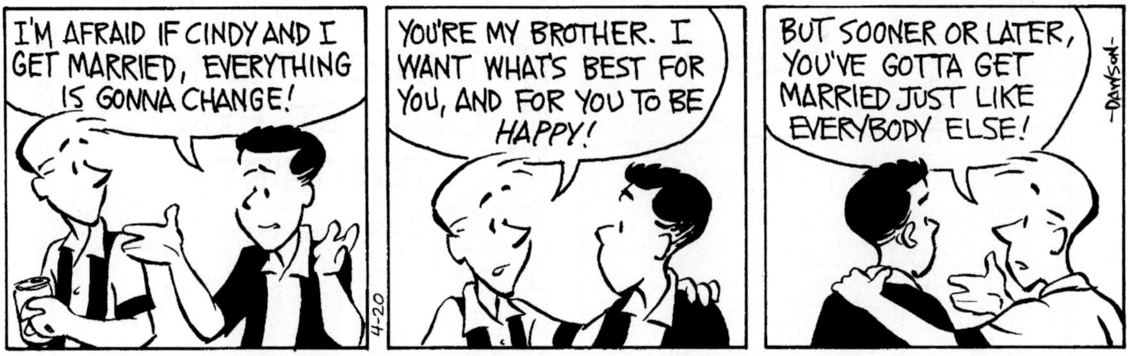
I'M AFRAID IF CINDY AND I GET MARRIED, EVERYTHING IS GONNA CHANGE!
4-20
YOU'RE MY BROTHER. I WANT WHAT'S BEST FOR YOU, AND FOR YOU TO BE *HAPPY!*
BUT SOONER OR LATER, YOU'VE GOTTA GET MARRIED JUST LIKE EVERYBODY ELSE!
-DAWSON-

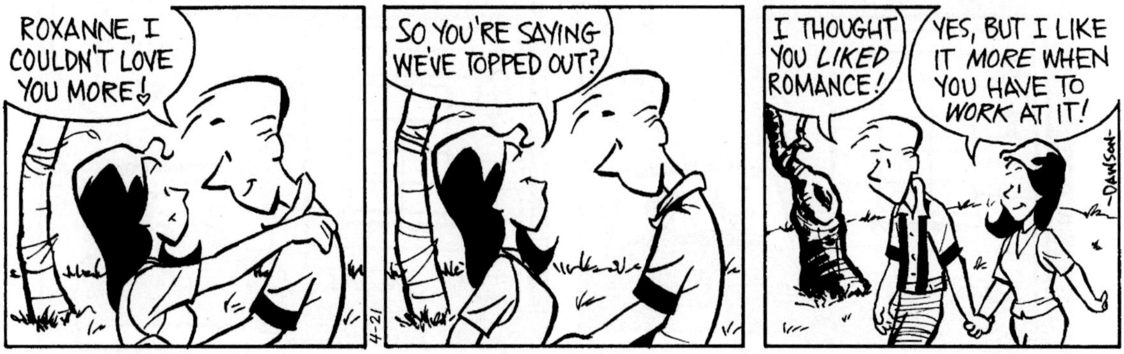
ROXANNE, I COULDN'T LOVE YOU MORE!
4-21
SO YOU'RE SAYING WE'VE TOPPED OUT?
I THOUGHT YOU *LIKED* ROMANCE!
YES, BUT I LIKE IT *MORE* WHEN YOU HAVE TO *WORK* AT IT!
-DAWSON-

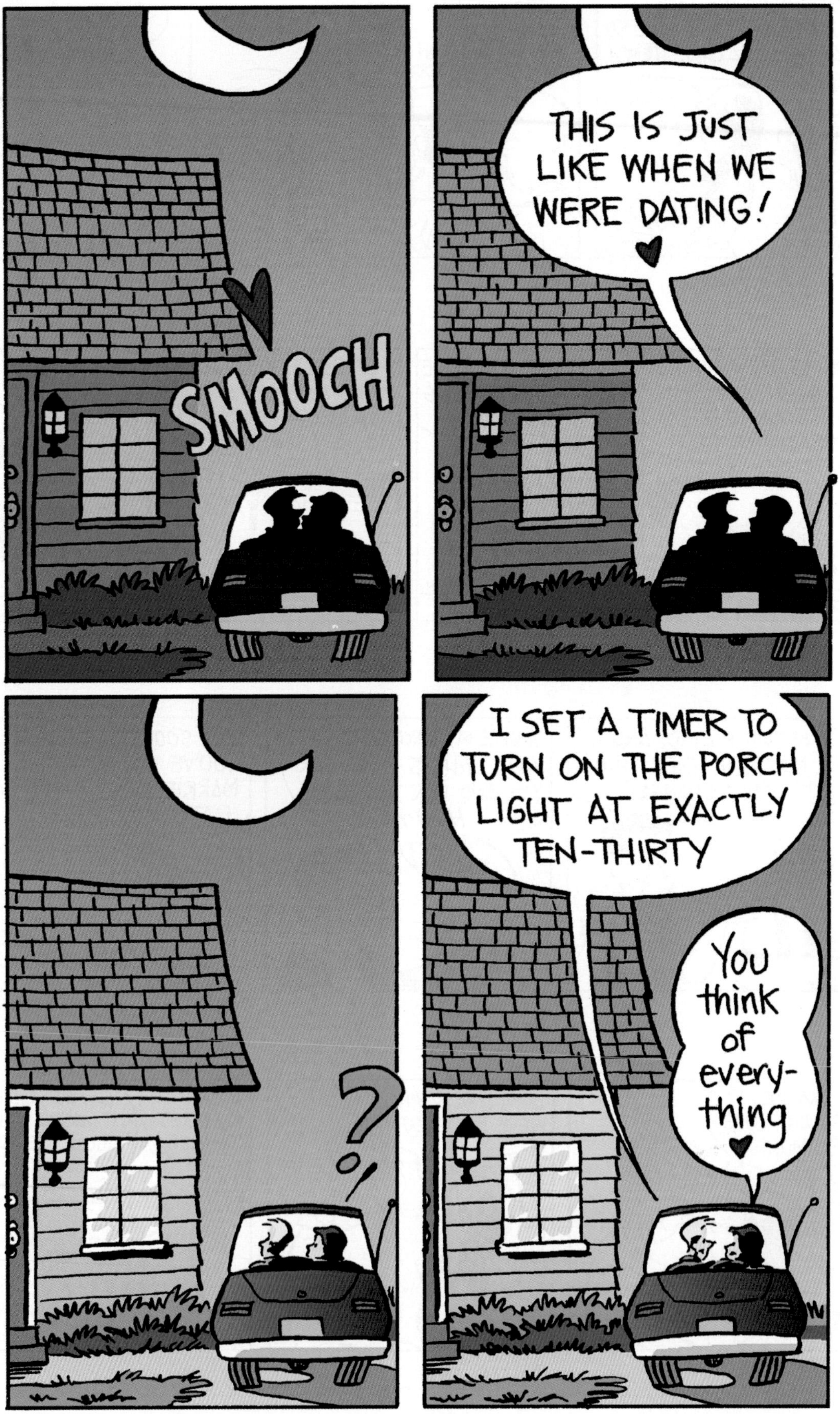
SMOOCH
THIS IS JUST LIKE WHEN WE WERE DATING!
I SET A TIMER TO TURN ON THE PORCH LIGHT AT EXACTLY TEN-THIRTY
You think of every-thing

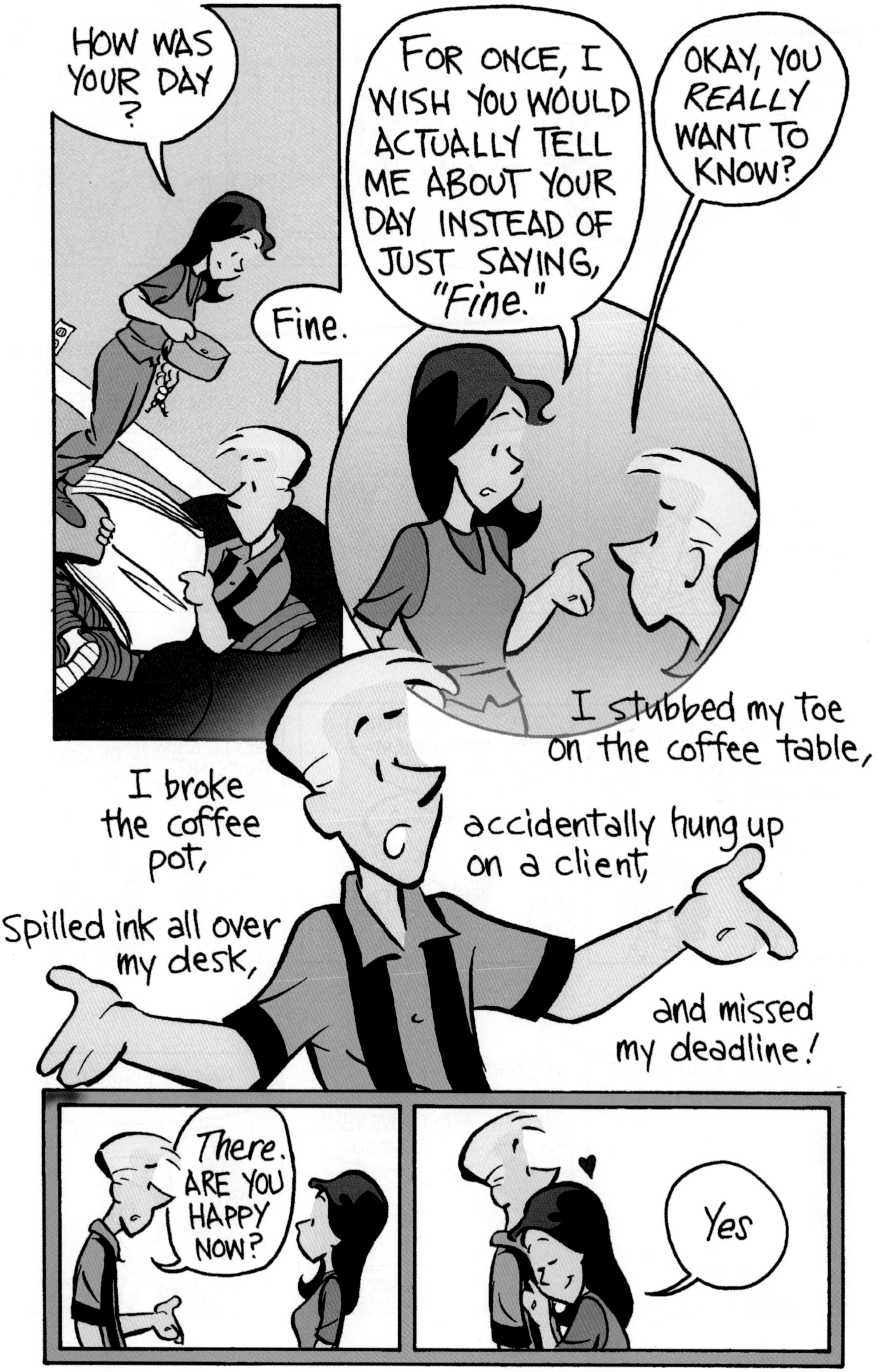
HOW WAS YOUR DAY ?
Fine.
FOR ONCE, I WISH YOU WOULD ACTUALLY TELL ME ABOUT YOUR DAY INSTEAD OF JUST SAYING, "Fine."
OKAY, YOU REALLY WANT TO KNOW?
I stubbed my toe on the coffee table,
I broke the coffee pot,
accidentally hung up on a client,
Spilled ink all over my desk,
and missed my deadline!
There. ARE YOU HAPPY NOW?
Yes

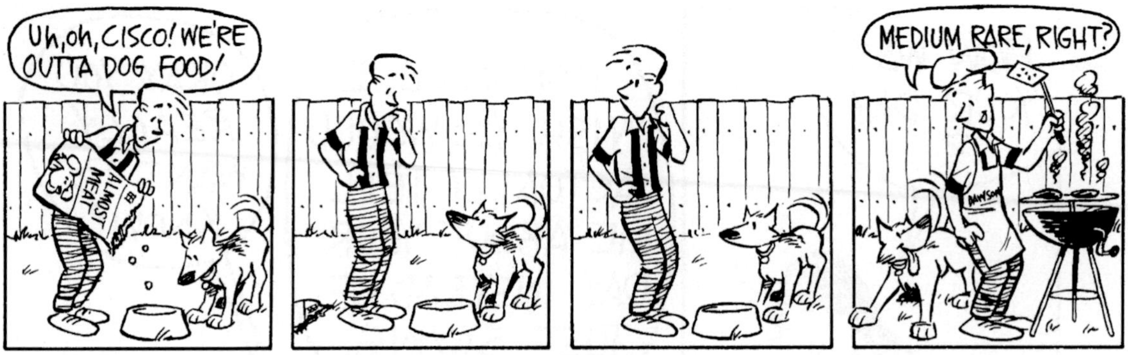
Uh, oh, CISCO! WE'RE OUTTA DOG FOOD!
ALMOST MEAT
MEDIUM RARE, RIGHT?
DAWSON

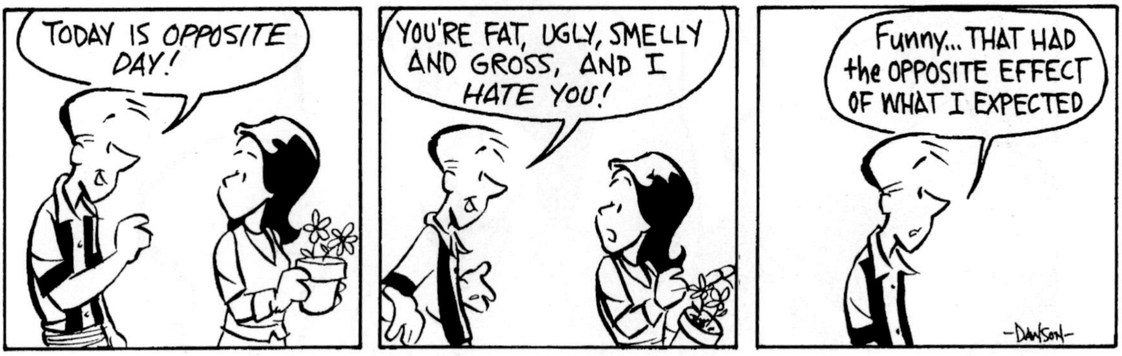
TODAY IS OPPOSITE DAY!
YOU'RE FAT, UGLY, SMELLY AND GROSS, AND I HATE YOU!
Funny... THAT HAD the OPPOSITE EFFECT OF WHAT I EXPECTED
-DAWSON-

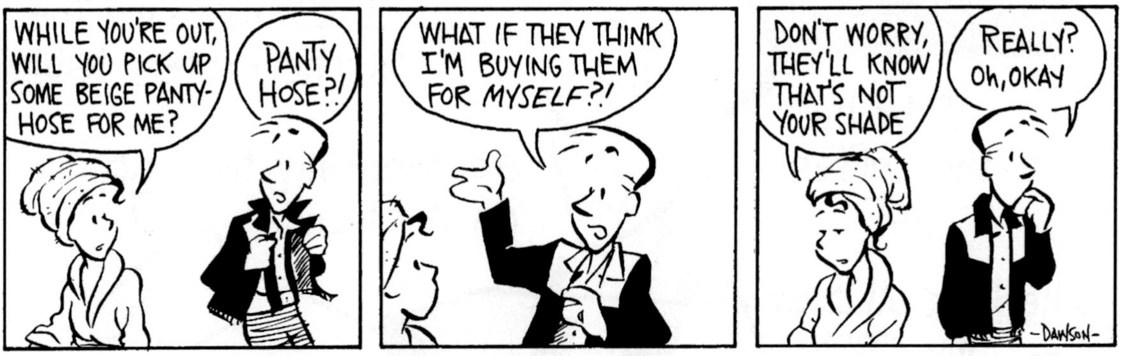
WHILE YOU'RE OUT, WILL YOU PICK UP SOME BEIGE PANTY-HOSE FOR ME?
PANTY HOSE?!
WHAT IF THEY THINK I'M BUYING THEM FOR MYSELF?!
DON'T WORRY, THEY'LL KNOW THAT'S NOT YOUR SHADE
REALLY? Oh, OKAY
-DAWSON-

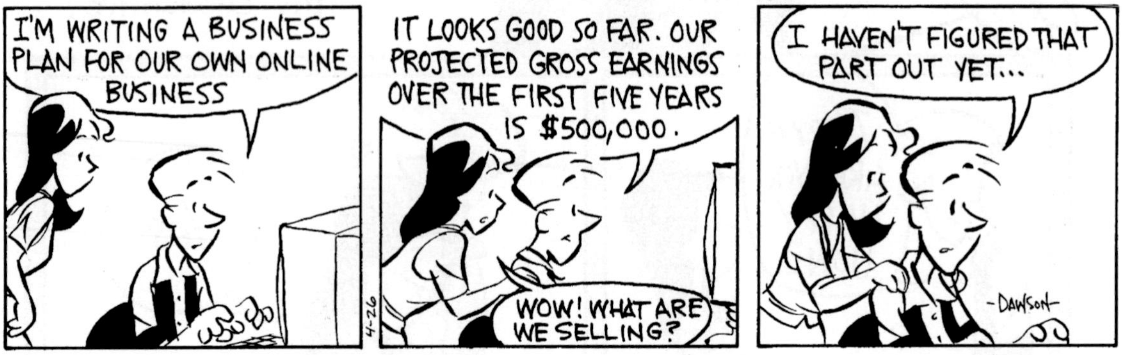
I'M WRITING A BUSINESS PLAN FOR OUR OWN ONLINE BUSINESS
4-26
IT LOOKS GOOD SO FAR. OUR PROJECTED GROSS EARNINGS OVER THE FIRST FIVE YEARS IS $500,000.
WOW! WHAT ARE WE SELLING?
I HAVEN'T FIGURED THAT PART OUT YET...
-DAWSON-

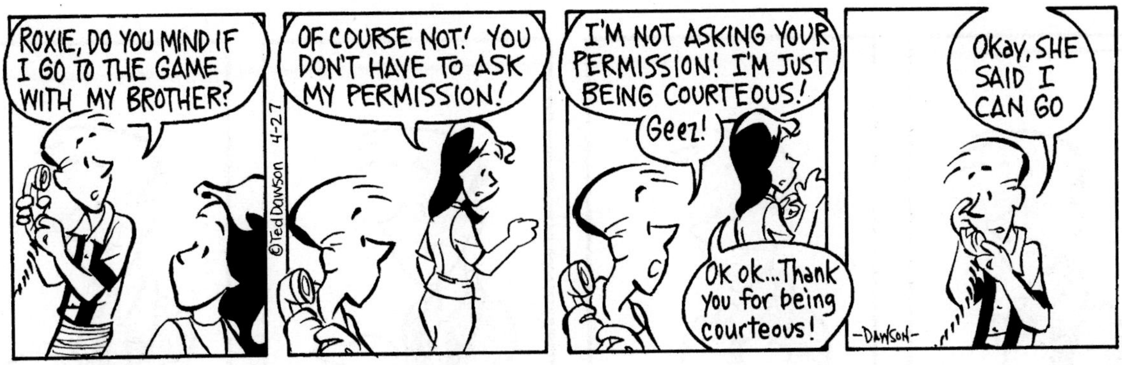
ROXIE, DO YOU MIND IF I GO TO THE GAME WITH MY BROTHER?
©Ted Dawson 4-27
OF COURSE NOT! YOU DON'T HAVE TO ASK MY PERMISSION!
I'M NOT ASKING YOUR PERMISSION! I'M JUST BEING COURTEOUS!
Geez!
Ok ok...Thank you for being courteous!
Okay, SHE SAID I CAN GO
-DAWSON-

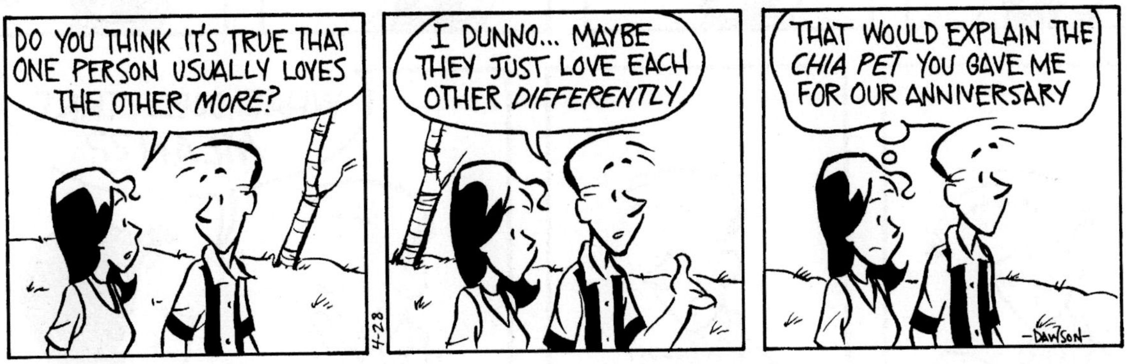
DO YOU THINK IT'S TRUE THAT ONE PERSON USUALLY LOVES THE OTHER *MORE?*
4-28
I DUNNO... MAYBE THEY JUST LOVE EACH OTHER *DIFFERENTLY*
THAT WOULD EXPLAIN THE *CHIA PET* YOU GAVE ME FOR OUR ANNIVERSARY
-DAWSON-

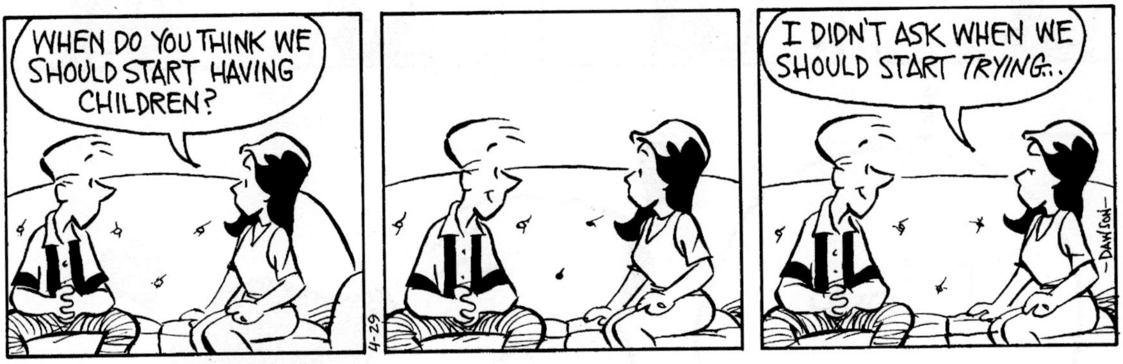
WHEN DO YOU THINK WE SHOULD START HAVING CHILDREN?
4-29
I DIDN'T ASK WHEN WE SHOULD START *TRYING*...
-DAWSON-

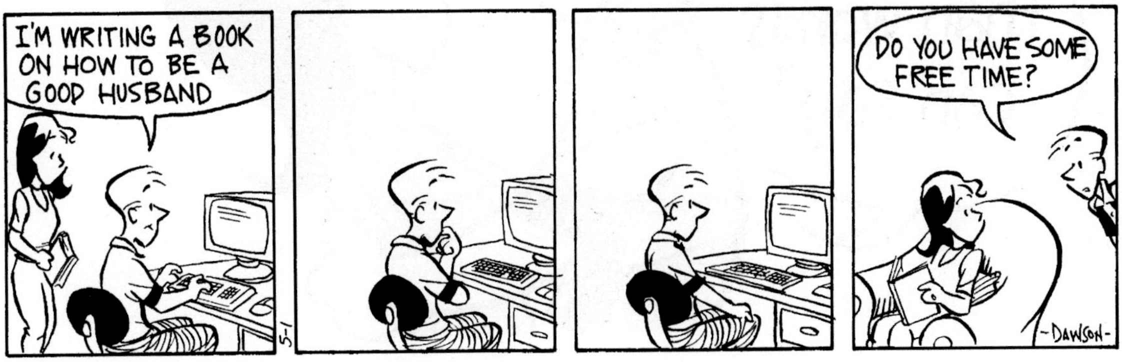
I'M WRITING A BOOK ON HOW TO BE A GOOD HUSBAND
5-1
DO YOU HAVE SOME FREE TIME?
-DAWSON-

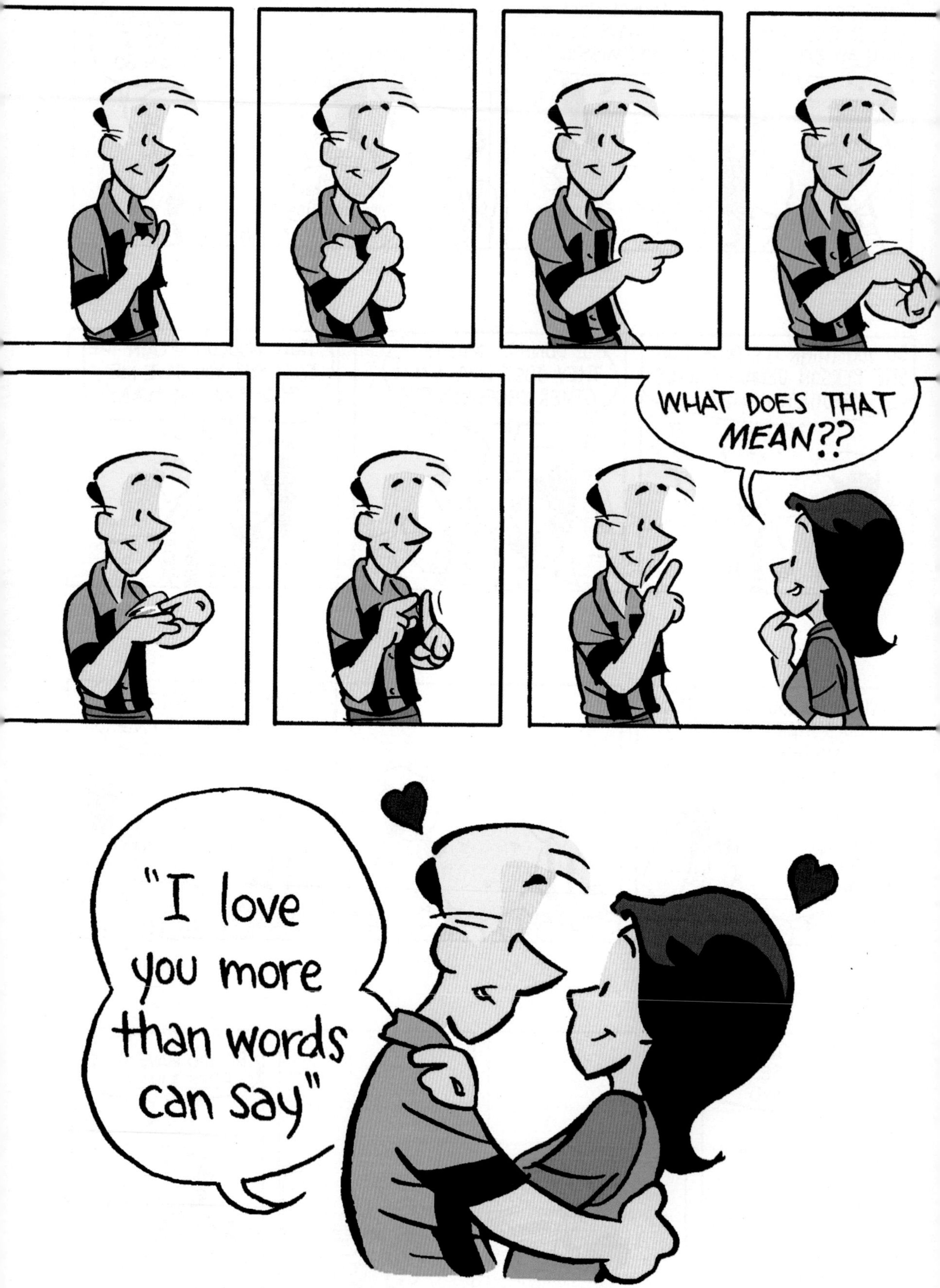
WHAT DOES THAT MEAN??
"I love you more than words can say"

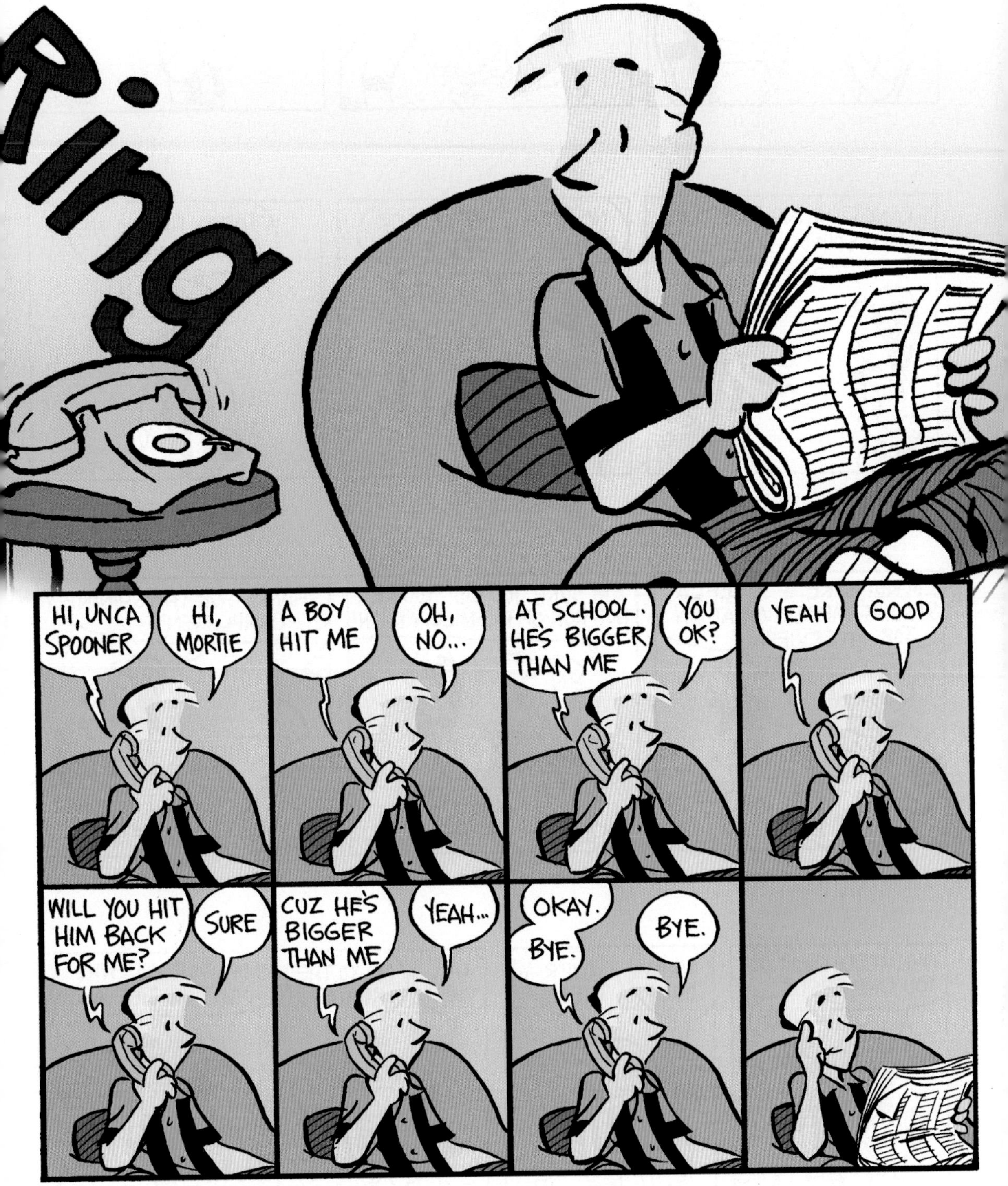
Ring
HI, UNCA SPOONER
HI, MORTIE
A BOY HIT ME
OH, NO...
AT SCHOOL. HE'S BIGGER THAN ME
YOU OK?
YEAH
GOOD
WILL YOU HIT HIM BACK FOR ME?
SURE
CUZ HE'S BIGGER THAN ME
YEAH...
OKAY. BYE.
BYE.

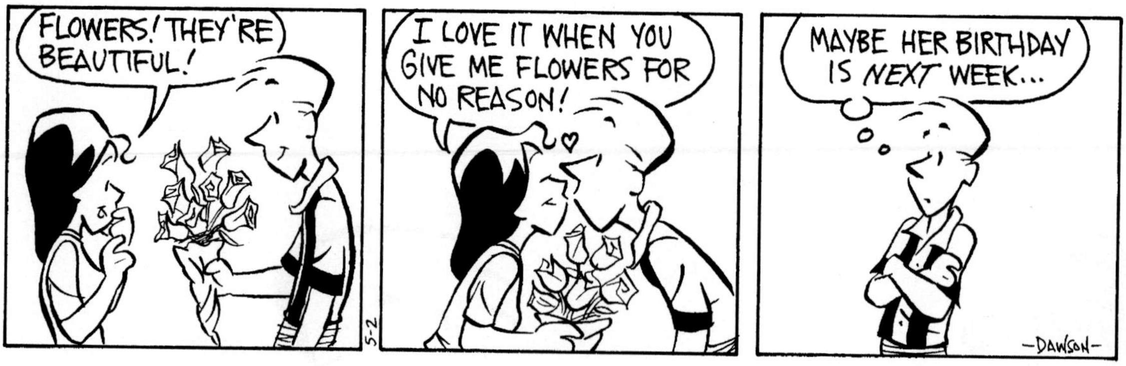
FLOWERS! THEY'RE BEAUTIFUL!
I LOVE IT WHEN YOU GIVE ME FLOWERS FOR NO REASON!
MAYBE HER BIRTHDAY IS *NEXT* WEEK...
5-2
-DAWSON-

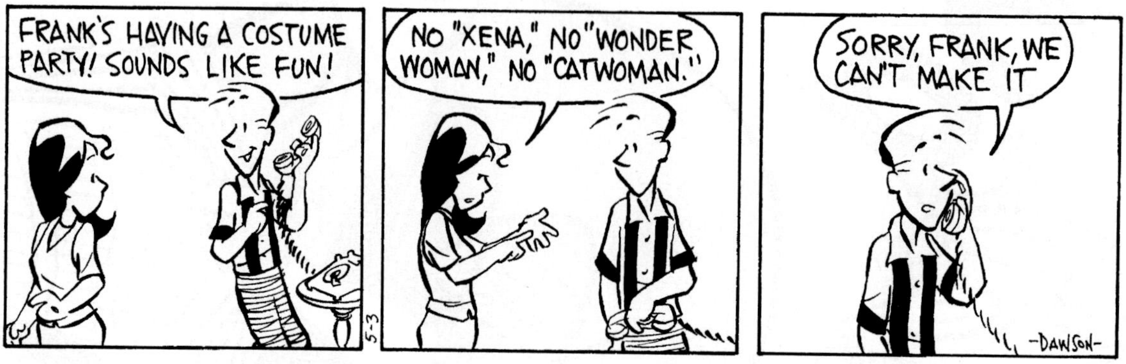
FRANK'S HAVING A COSTUME PARTY! SOUNDS LIKE FUN!
NO "XENA," NO "WONDER WOMAN," NO "CATWOMAN."
SORRY, FRANK, WE CAN'T MAKE IT
5-3
-DAWSON-

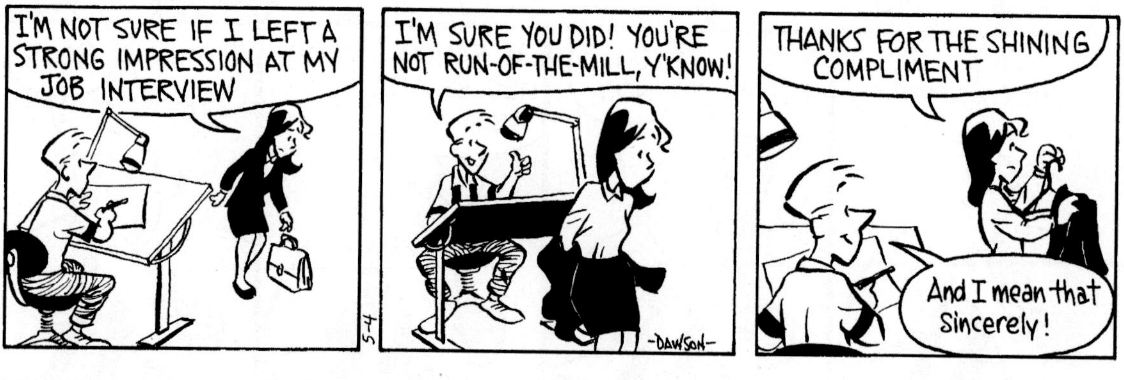
I'M NOT SURE IF I LEFT A STRONG IMPRESSION AT MY JOB INTERVIEW
I'M SURE YOU DID! YOU'RE NOT RUN-OF-THE-MILL, Y'KNOW!
THANKS FOR THE SHINING COMPLIMENT
And I mean that sincerely!
5-4
-DAWSON-

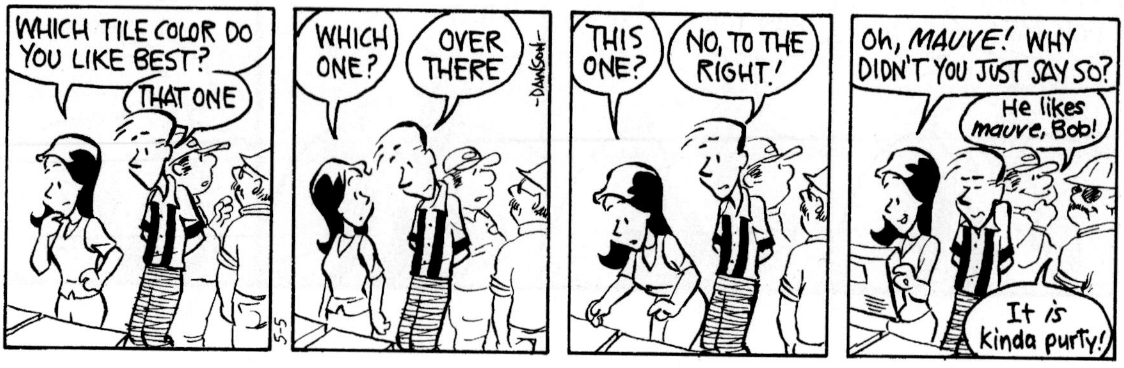
WHICH TILE COLOR DO YOU LIKE BEST?
THAT ONE
WHICH ONE?
OVER THERE
THIS ONE?
NO, TO THE RIGHT!
Oh, *MAUVE!* WHY DIDN'T YOU JUST SAY SO?
He likes *mauve*, Bob!
It *is* kinda purty!
5-5
-DAWSON-

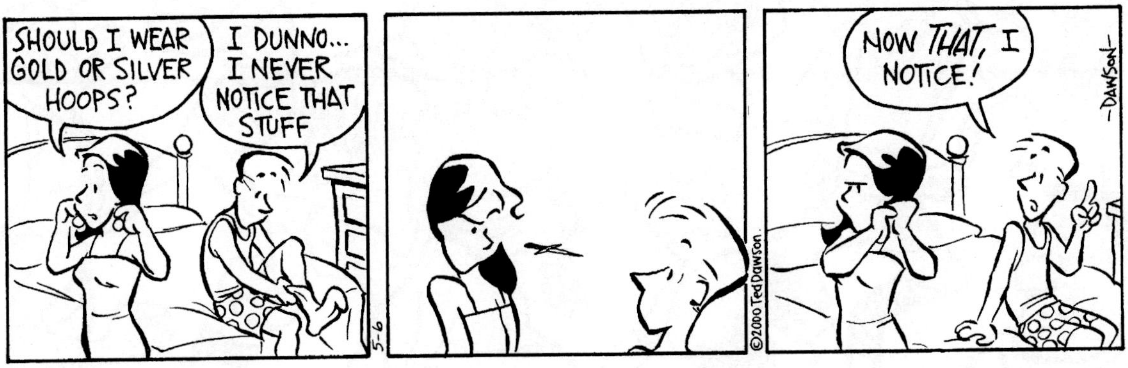
SHOULD I WEAR GOLD OR SILVER HOOPS?
I DUNNO... I NEVER NOTICE THAT STUFF
5-6
©2000 Ted Dawson.
NOW *THAT*, I NOTICE!
-DAWSON-

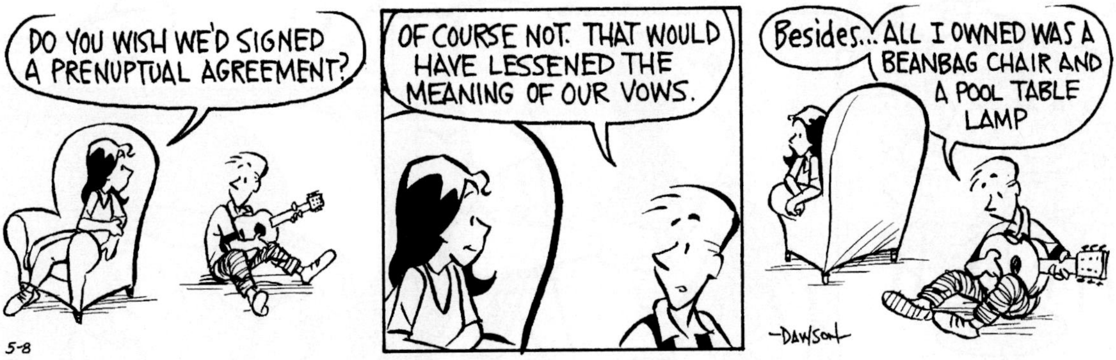
DO YOU WISH WE'D SIGNED A PRENUPTUAL AGREEMENT?
OF COURSE NOT. THAT WOULD HAVE LESSENED THE MEANING OF OUR VOWS.
Besides...
ALL I OWNED WAS A BEANBAG CHAIR AND A POOL TABLE LAMP
-DAWSON-
5-8

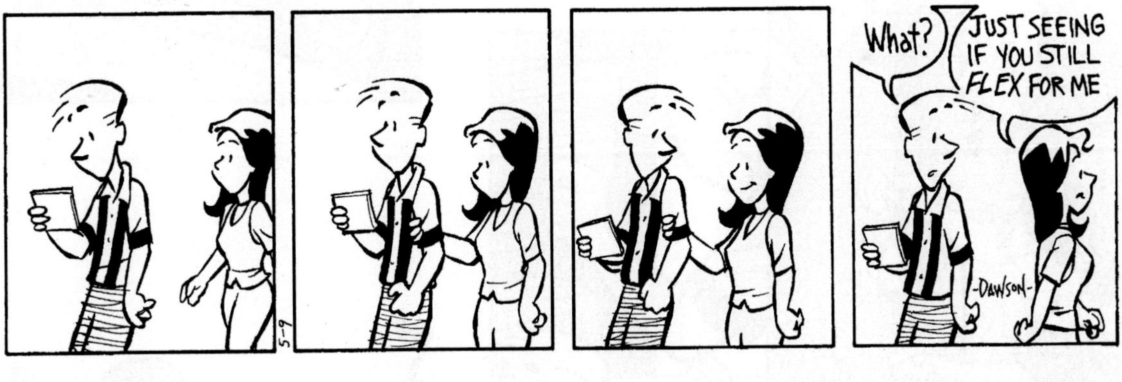
5-9
What?
JUST SEEING IF YOU STILL *FLEX* FOR ME
-DAWSON-

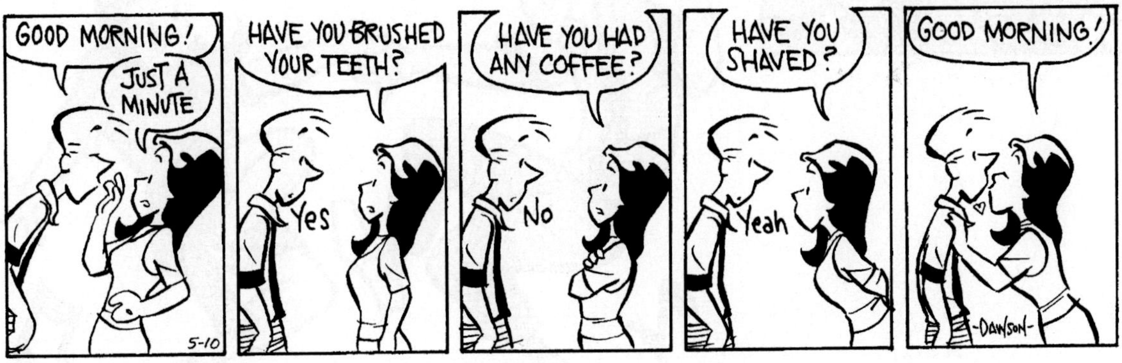
GOOD MORNING!
JUST A MINUTE
5-10
HAVE YOU BRUSHED YOUR TEETH?
Yes
HAVE YOU HAD ANY COFFEE?
No
HAVE YOU SHAVED?
Yeah
GOOD MORNING!
-DAWSON-

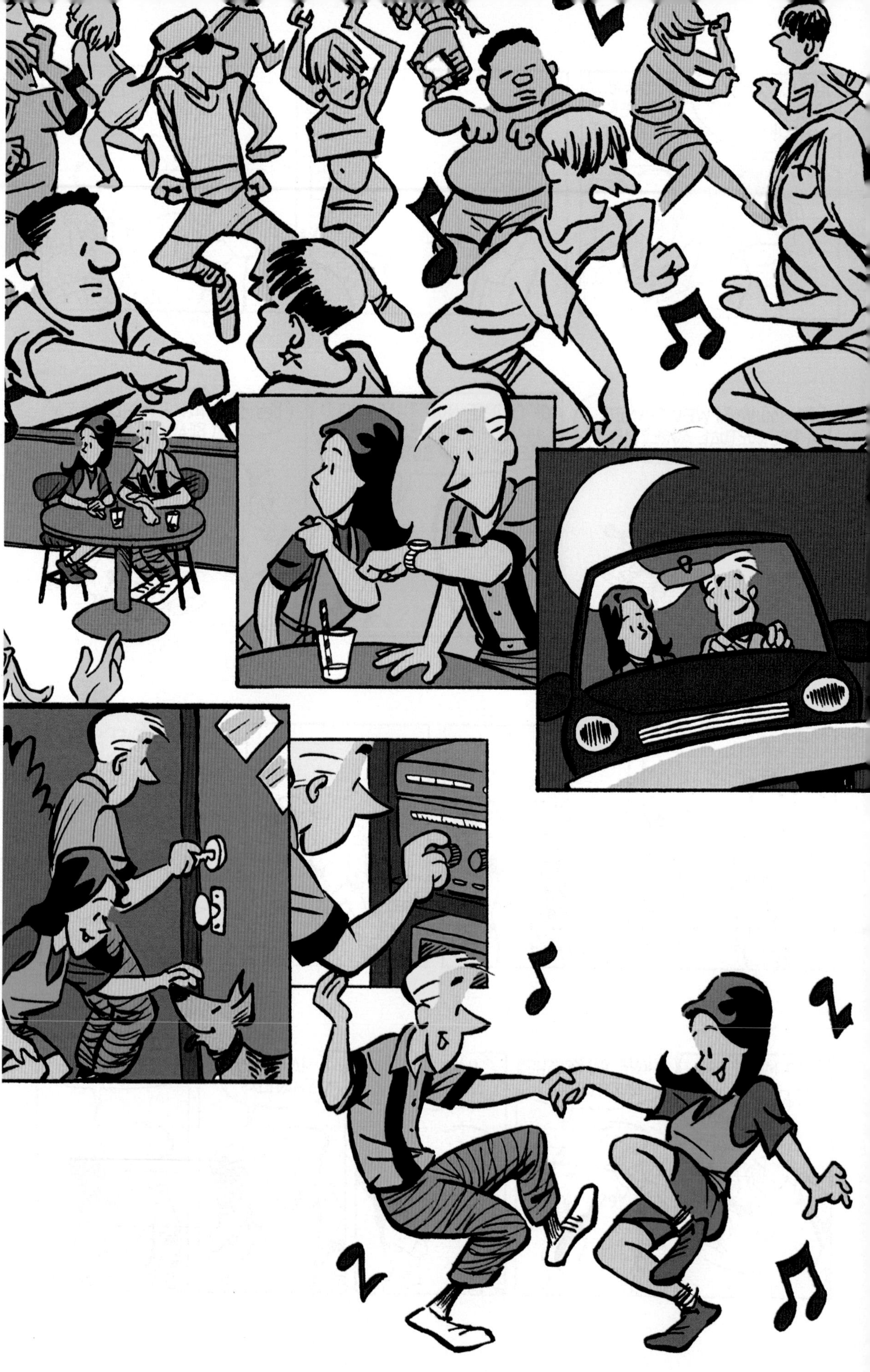

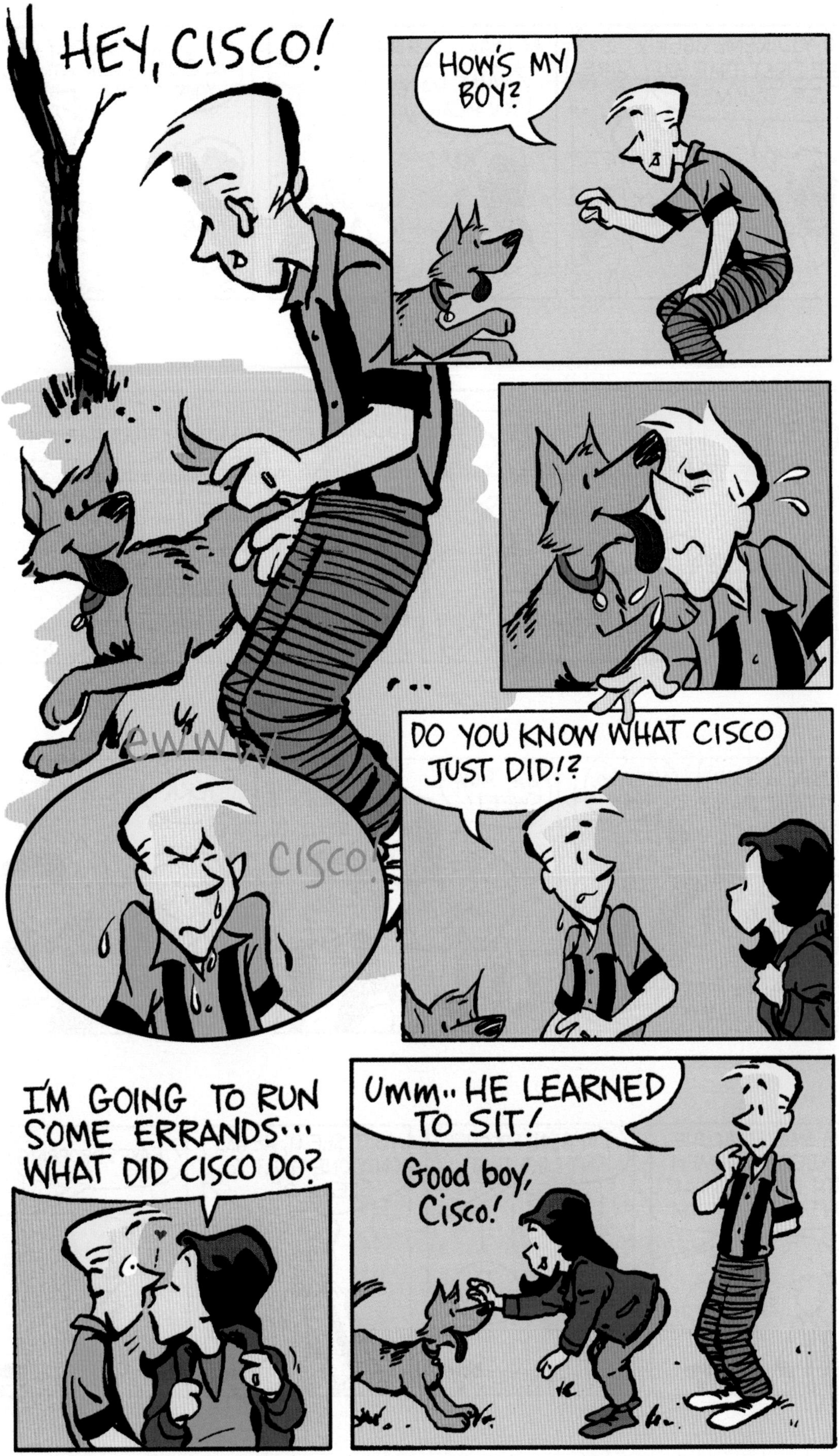
HEY, CISCO!
HOW'S MY BOY?
...
ewww
Cisco!
DO YOU KNOW WHAT CISCO JUST DID!?
I'M GOING TO RUN SOME ERRANDS... WHAT DID CISCO DO?
Umm.. HE LEARNED TO SIT!
Good boy, Cisco!

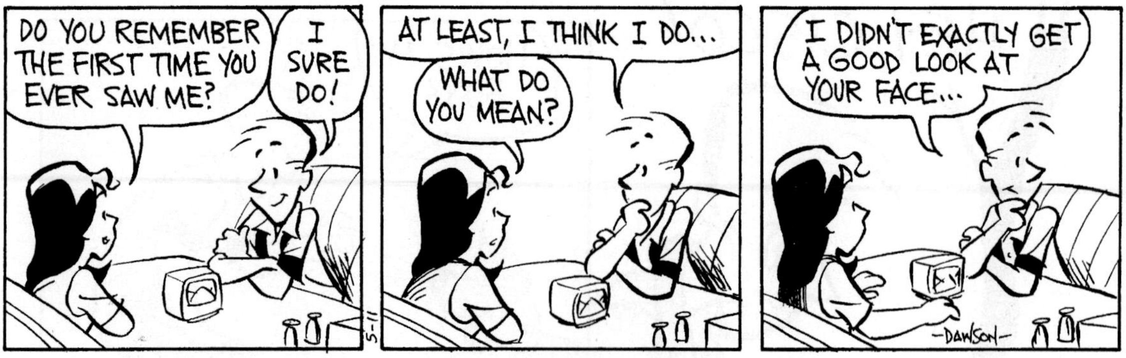
DO YOU REMEMBER THE FIRST TIME YOU EVER SAW ME?
I SURE DO!
5-11
AT LEAST, I THINK I DO...
WHAT DO YOU MEAN?
I DIDN'T EXACTLY GET A GOOD LOOK AT YOUR FACE...
-DAWSON-

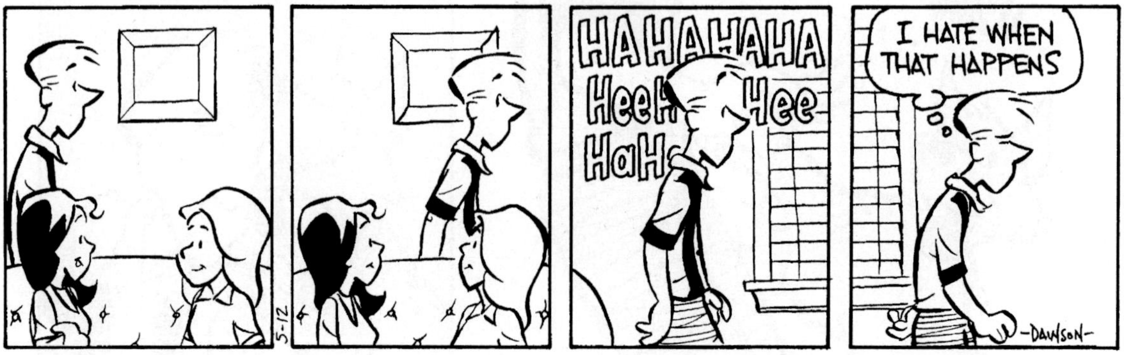
5-12
HAHAHAHA
HeeH Hee
HaH
I HATE WHEN THAT HAPPENS
-DAWSON-

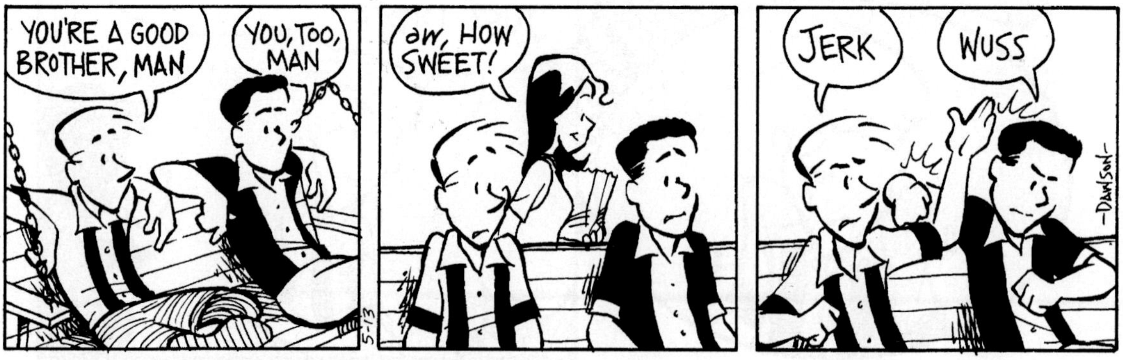
YOU'RE A GOOD BROTHER, MAN
YOU, TOO, MAN
5-13
aw, HOW SWEET!
JERK
WUSS
-DAWSON-

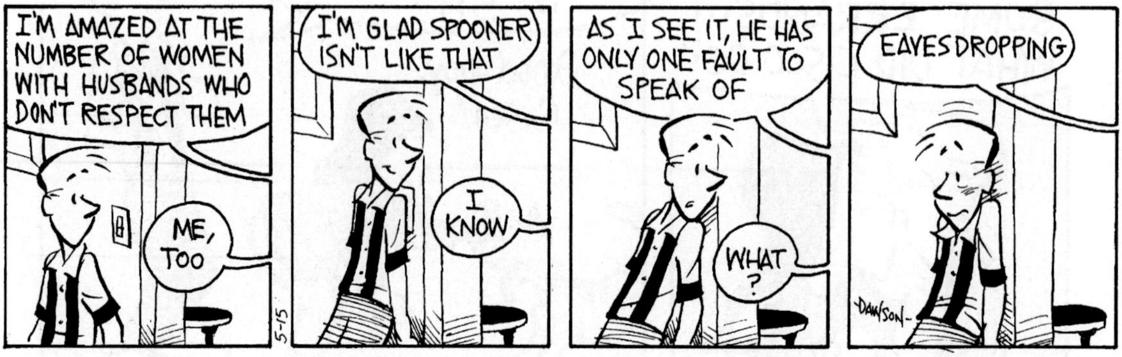
I'M AMAZED AT THE NUMBER OF WOMEN WITH HUSBANDS WHO DON'T RESPECT THEM
ME, TOO
5-15
I'M GLAD SPOONER ISN'T LIKE THAT
I KNOW
AS I SEE IT, HE HAS ONLY ONE FAULT TO SPEAK OF
WHAT?
EAVESDROPPING
-DAWSON-

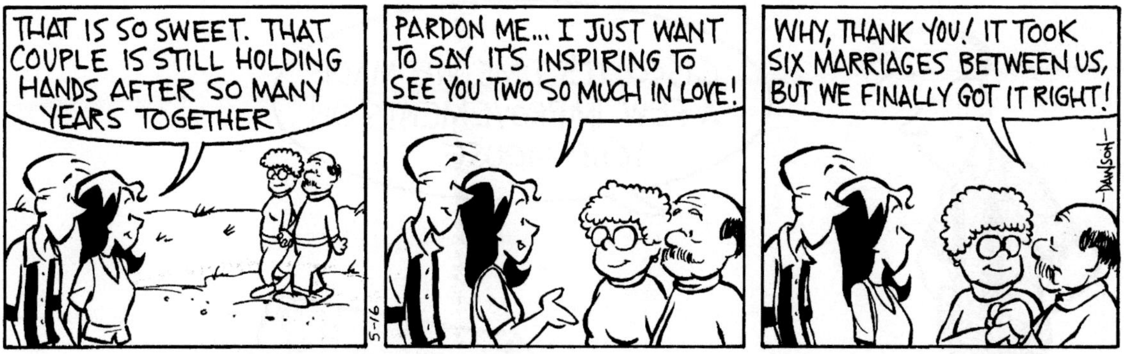
THAT IS SO SWEET. THAT COUPLE IS STILL HOLDING HANDS AFTER SO MANY YEARS TOGETHER
5-16
PARDON ME... I JUST WANT TO SAY IT'S INSPIRING TO SEE YOU TWO SO MUCH IN LOVE!
WHY, THANK YOU! IT TOOK SIX MARRIAGES BETWEEN US, BUT WE FINALLY GOT IT RIGHT!
-DAWSON-

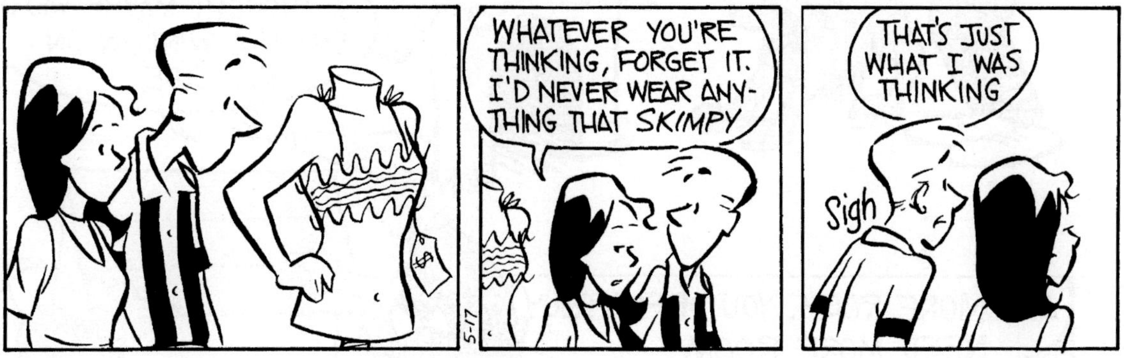
$
5-17
WHATEVER YOU'RE THINKING, FORGET IT. I'D NEVER WEAR ANY-THING THAT *SKIMPY*
THAT'S JUST WHAT I WAS THINKING
Sigh

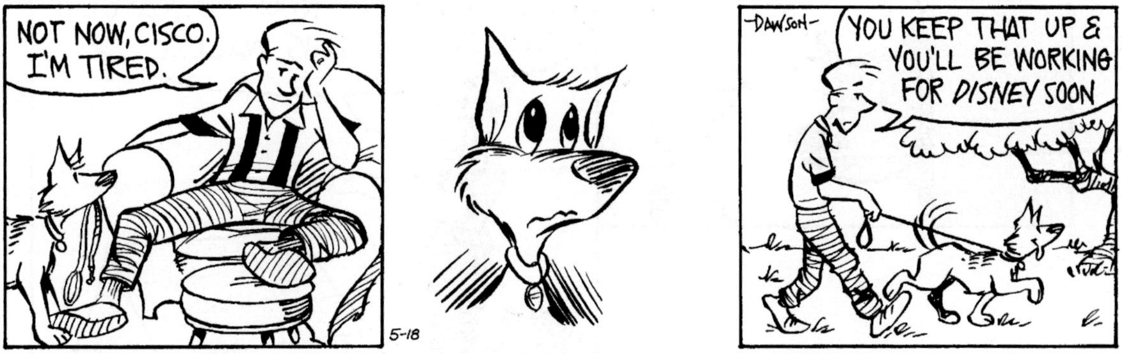
NOT NOW, CISCO. I'M TIRED.
5-18
-DAWSON-
YOU KEEP THAT UP & YOU'LL BE WORKING FOR *DISNEY* SOON

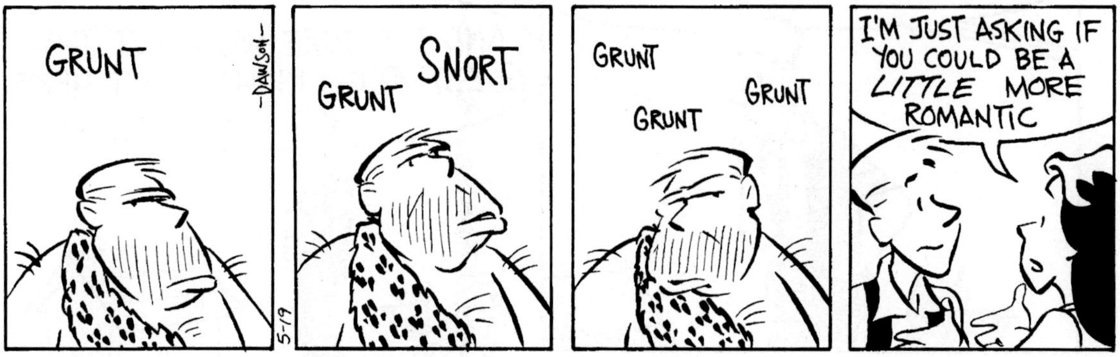
GRUNT
-DAWSON-
5-19
GRUNT
SNORT
GRUNT
GRUNT
GRUNT
I'M JUST ASKING IF YOU COULD BE A *LITTLE* MORE ROMANTIC

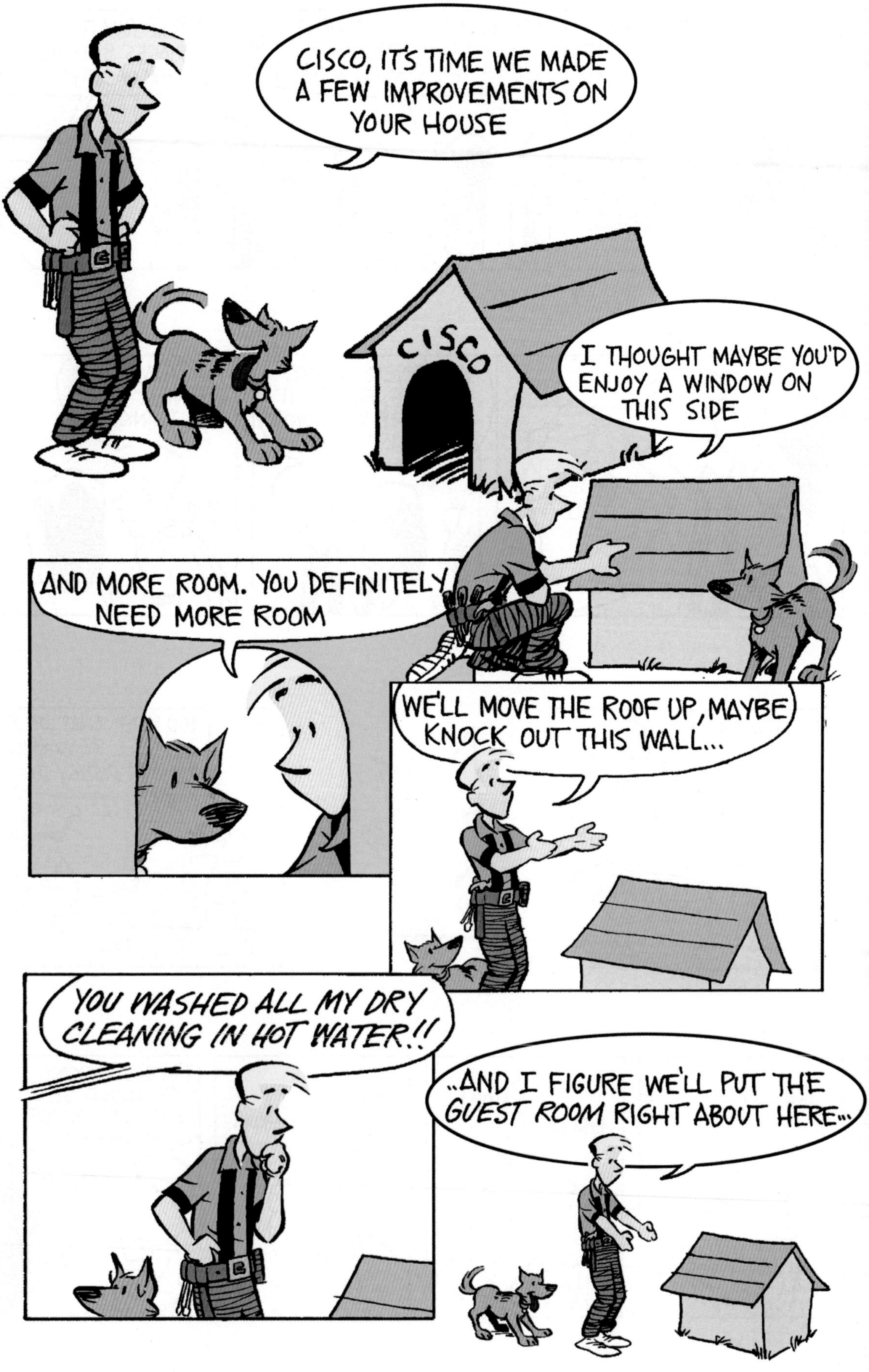
CISCO, IT'S TIME WE MADE A FEW IMPROVEMENTS ON YOUR HOUSE
CISCO
I THOUGHT MAYBE YOU'D ENJOY A WINDOW ON THIS SIDE
AND MORE ROOM. YOU DEFINITELY NEED MORE ROOM
WE'LL MOVE THE ROOF UP, MAYBE KNOCK OUT THIS WALL...
YOU WASHED ALL MY DRY CLEANING IN HOT WATER!!
..AND I FIGURE WE'LL PUT THE GUEST ROOM RIGHT ABOUT HERE...

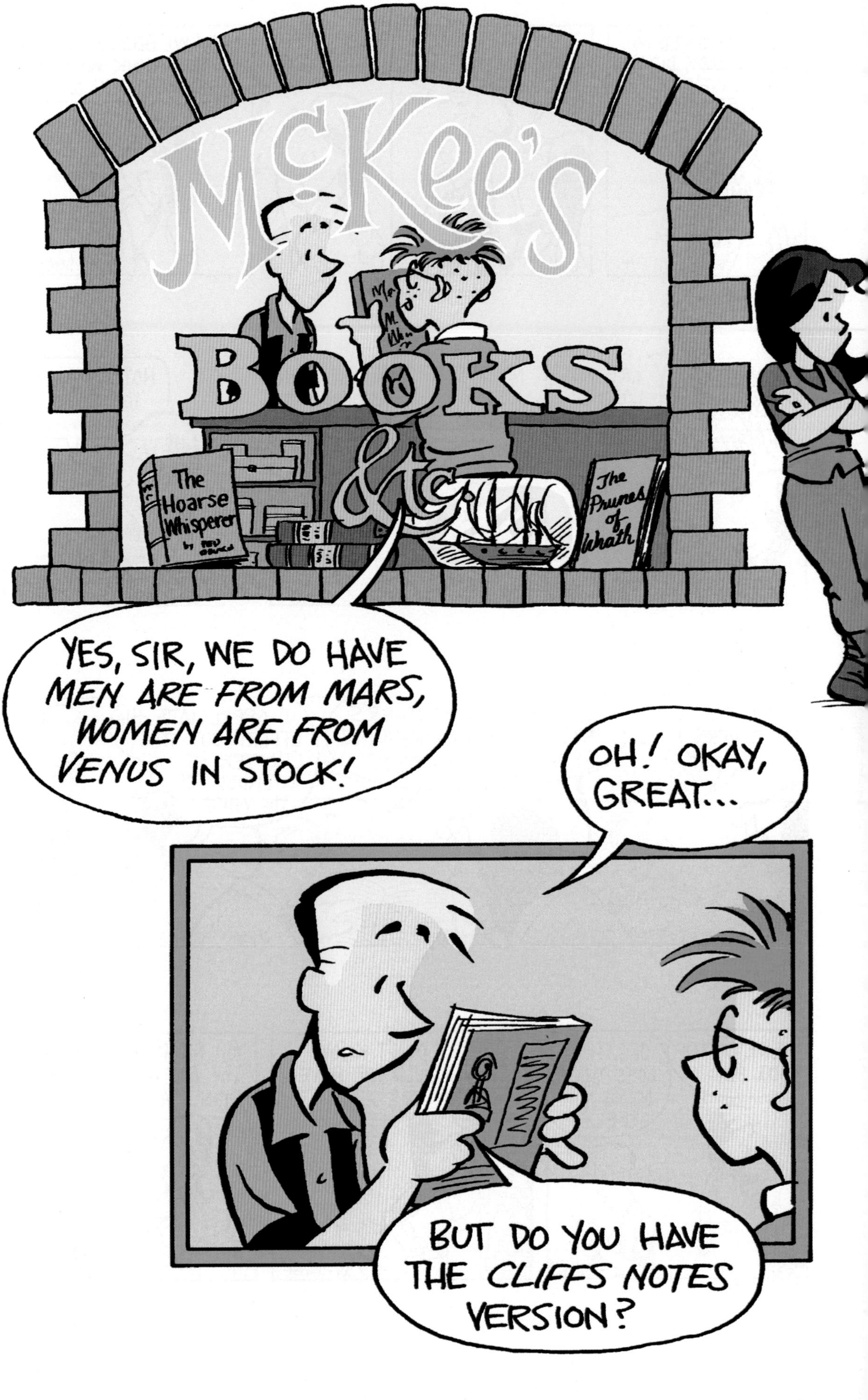
McKee's
BOOKS
&etc.
The Hoarse Whisperer
The Prunes of Whath
YES, SIR, WE DO HAVE *MEN ARE FROM MARS, WOMEN ARE FROM VENUS* IN STOCK!
OH! OKAY, GREAT...
BUT DO YOU HAVE THE *CLIFFS NOTES* VERSION?

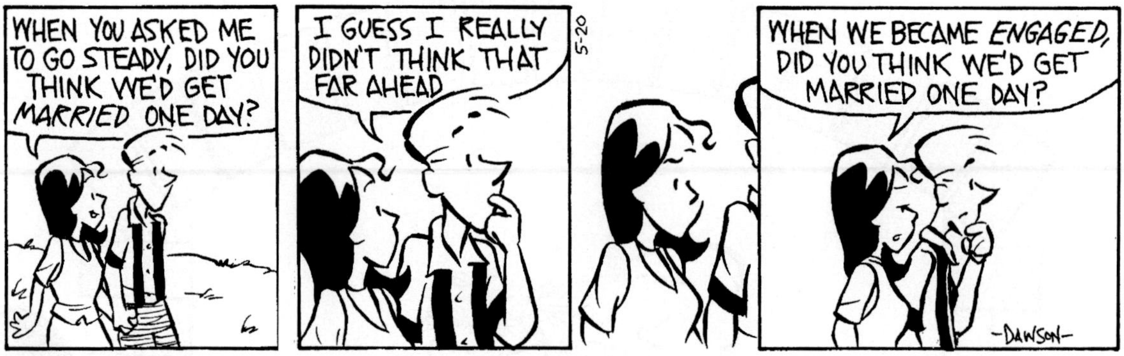
WHEN YOU ASKED ME TO GO STEADY, DID YOU THINK WE'D GET *MARRIED* ONE DAY?
I GUESS I REALLY DIDN'T THINK THAT FAR AHEAD
5-20
WHEN WE BECAME *ENGAGED*, DID YOU THINK WE'D GET MARRIED ONE DAY?
-DAWSON-

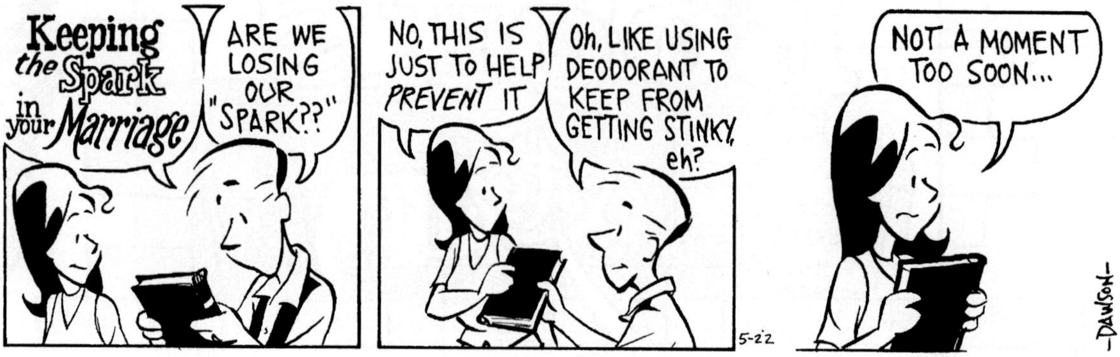
Keeping the Spark in your Marriage
ARE WE LOSING OUR "SPARK??"
NO, THIS IS JUST TO HELP *PREVENT* IT
Oh, LIKE USING DEODORANT TO KEEP FROM GETTING STINKY, eh?
5-22
NOT A MOMENT TOO SOON...
-DAWSON-

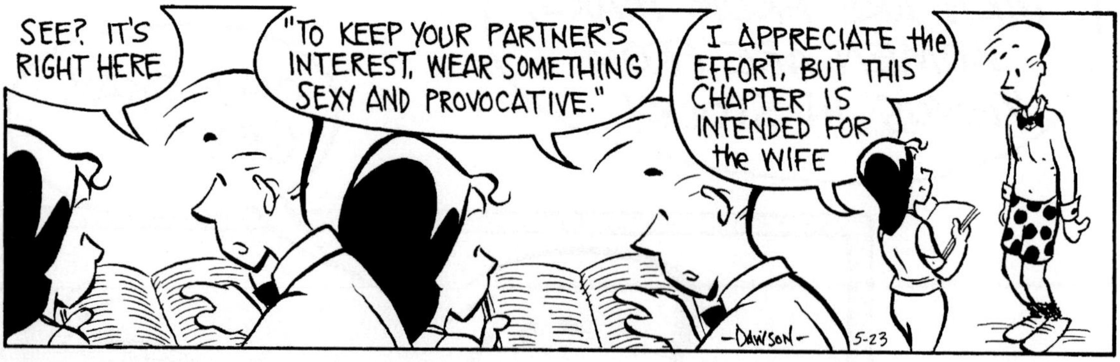
SEE? IT'S RIGHT HERE
"TO KEEP YOUR PARTNER'S INTEREST, WEAR SOMETHING SEXY AND PROVOCATIVE."
I APPRECIATE the EFFORT, BUT THIS CHAPTER IS INTENDED FOR the WIFE
-DAWSON-
5-23

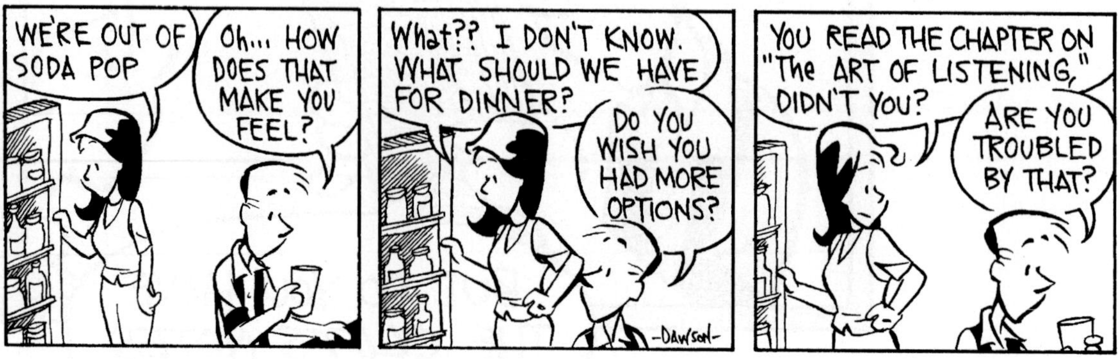
WE'RE OUT OF SODA POP
Oh... HOW DOES THAT MAKE YOU FEEL?
What?? I DON'T KNOW. WHAT SHOULD WE HAVE FOR DINNER?
DO YOU WISH YOU HAD MORE OPTIONS?
-DAWSON-
YOU READ THE CHAPTER ON "The ART OF LISTENING," DIDN'T YOU?
ARE YOU TROUBLED BY THAT?

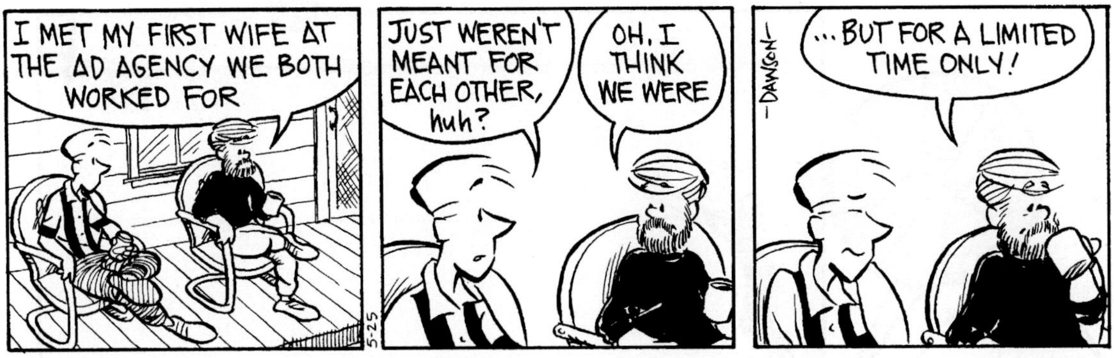
I MET MY FIRST WIFE AT THE AD AGENCY WE BOTH WORKED FOR
5-25
JUST WEREN'T MEANT FOR EACH OTHER, huh?
OH, I THINK WE WERE
—DAWSON—
...BUT FOR A LIMITED TIME ONLY!

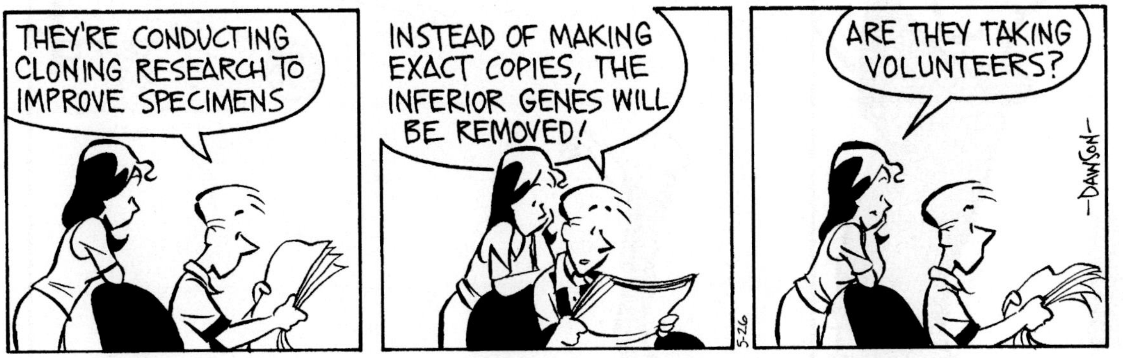
THEY'RE CONDUCTING CLONING RESEARCH TO IMPROVE SPECIMENS
INSTEAD OF MAKING EXACT COPIES, THE INFERIOR GENES WILL BE REMOVED!
5-26
ARE THEY TAKING VOLUNTEERS?
—DAWSON—

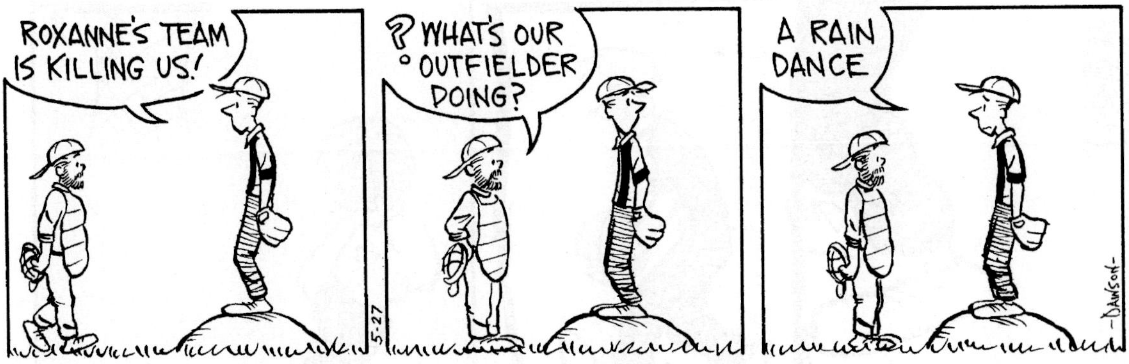
ROXANNE'S TEAM IS KILLING US!
5-27
? WHAT'S OUR OUTFIELDER DOING?
A RAIN DANCE
—DAWSON—

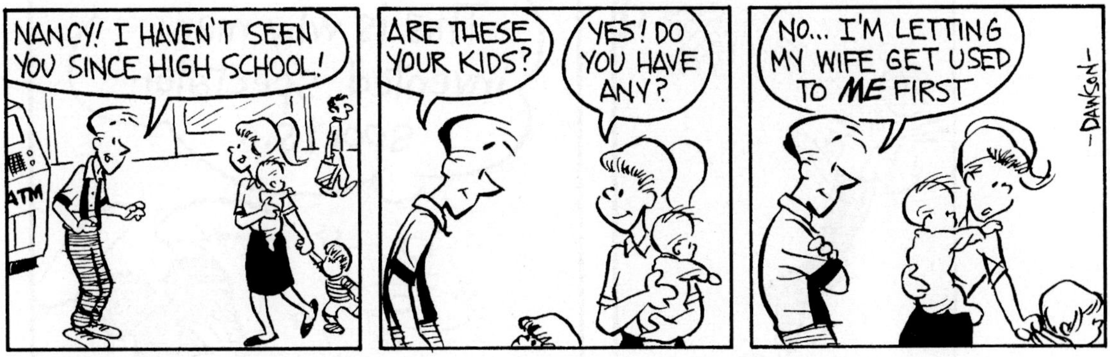
NANCY! I HAVEN'T SEEN YOU SINCE HIGH SCHOOL!
ATM
ARE THESE YOUR KIDS?
YES! DO YOU HAVE ANY?
NO... I'M LETTING MY WIFE GET USED TO ME FIRST
—DAWSON—

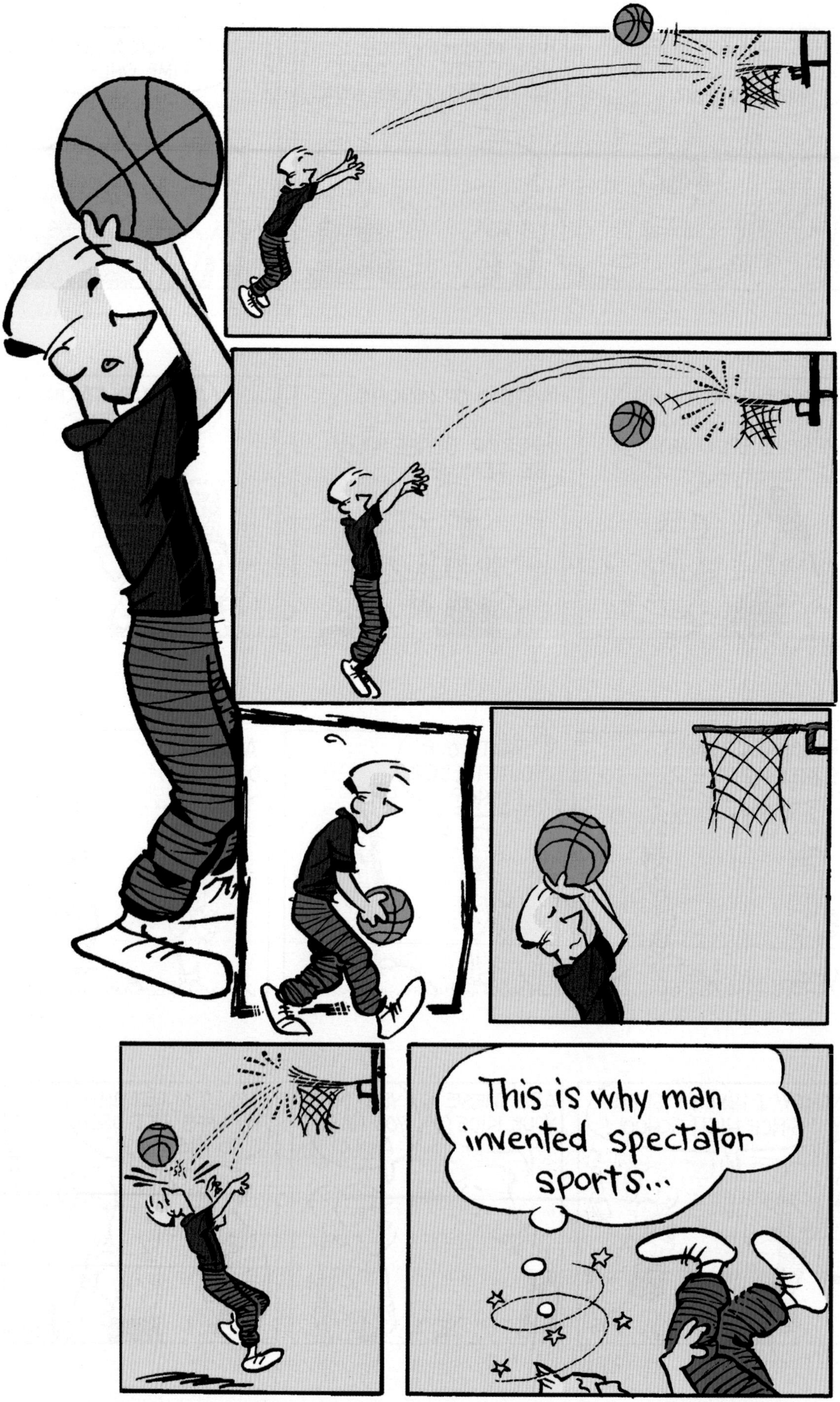
This is why man invented spectator sports...

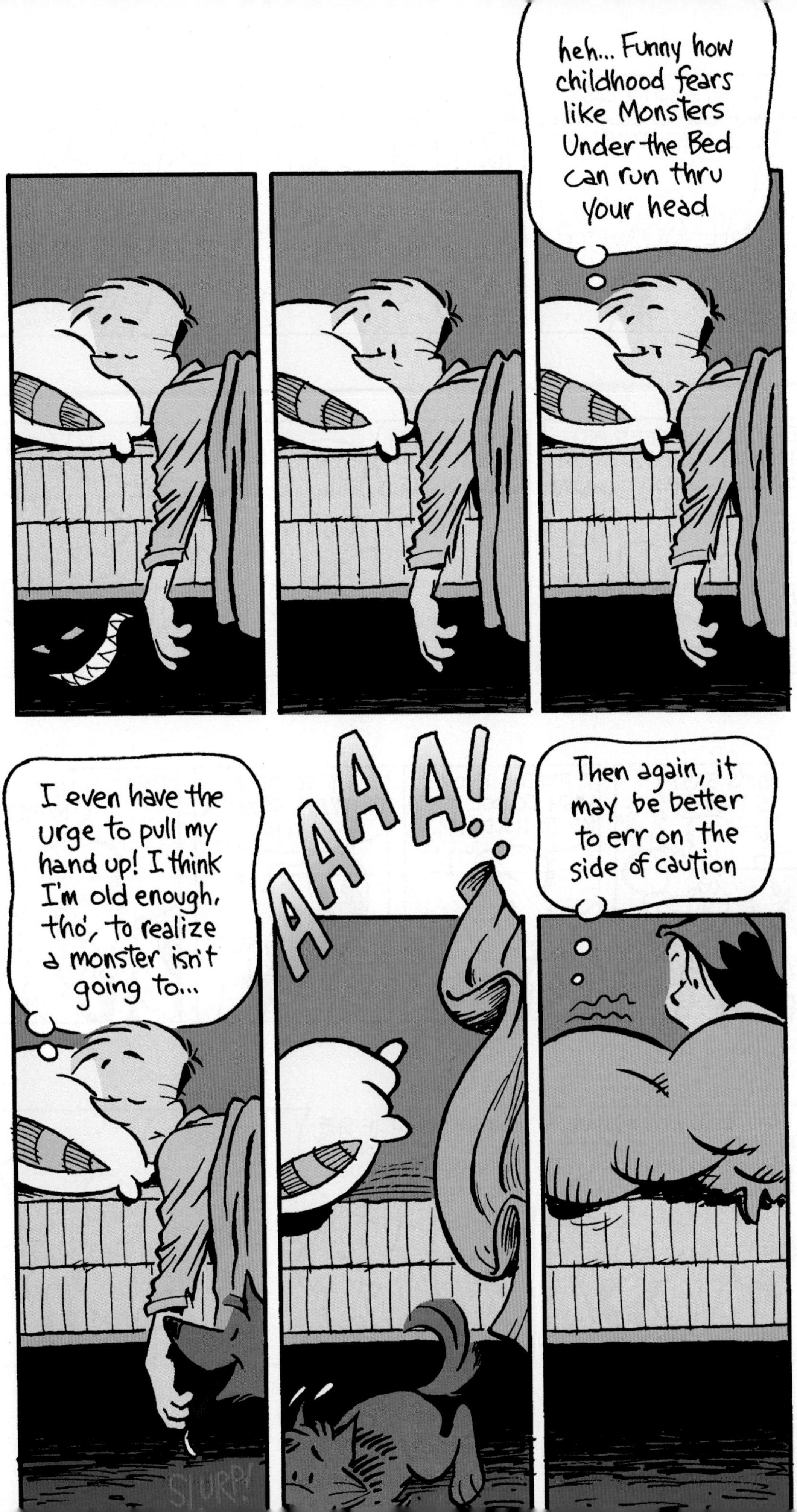

heh... Funny how childhood fears like Monsters Under the Bed can run thru your head
I even have the urge to pull my hand up! I think I'm old enough, tho', to realize a monster isn't going to...
SLURP!
AAAA!!
Then again, it may be better to err on the side of caution

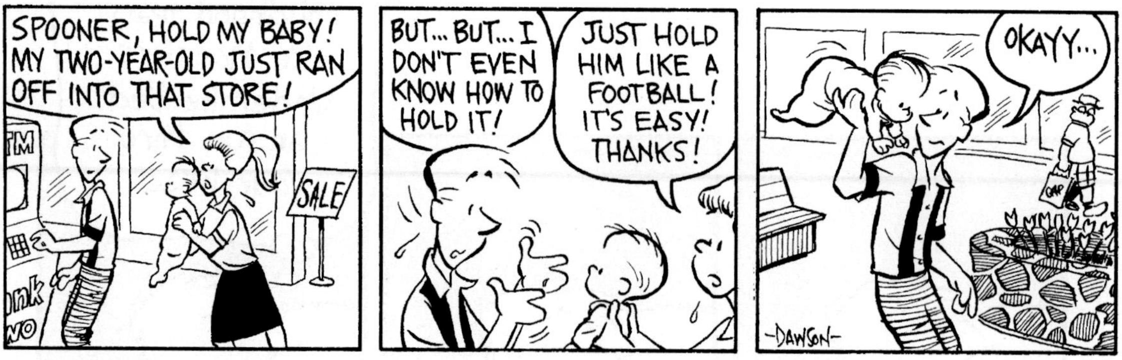
SPOONER, HOLD MY BABY! MY TWO-YEAR-OLD JUST RAN OFF INTO THAT STORE!
SALE
BUT... BUT... I DON'T EVEN KNOW HOW TO HOLD IT!
JUST HOLD HIM LIKE A FOOTBALL! IT'S EASY! THANKS!
OKAYY...
-DAWSON-

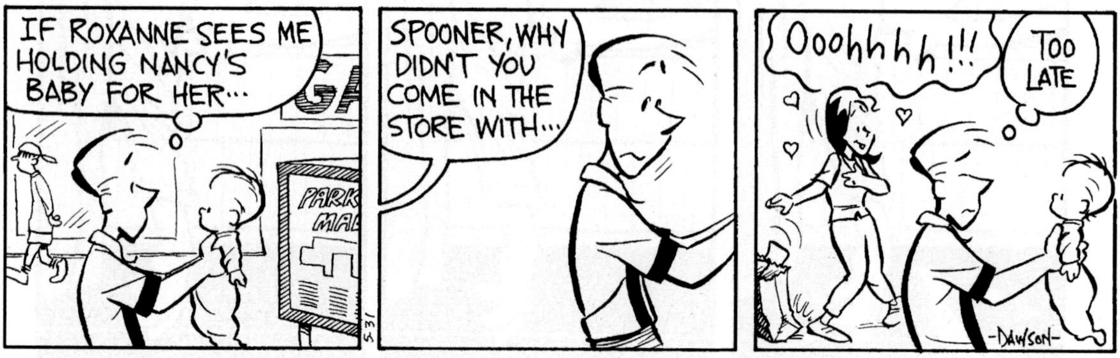
IF ROXANNE SEES ME HOLDING NANCY'S BABY FOR HER...
5-31
SPOONER, WHY DIDN'T YOU COME IN THE STORE WITH...
Ooohhhhh!!!
TOO LATE
-DAWSON-

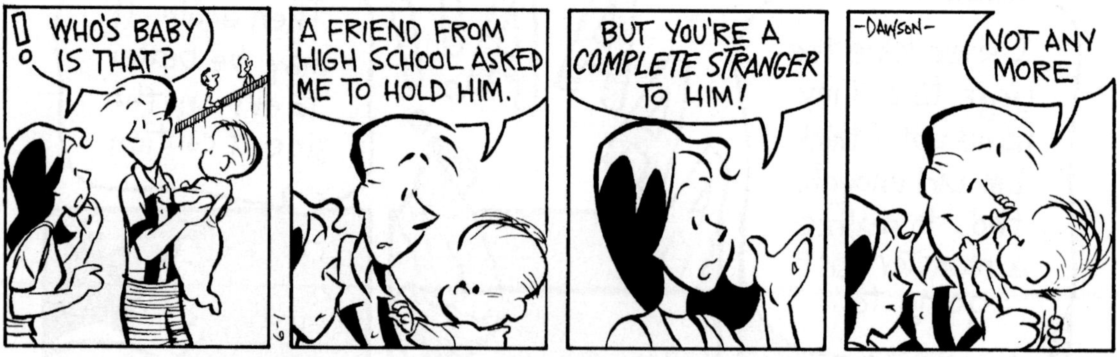
!
WHO'S BABY IS THAT?
6-1
A FRIEND FROM HIGH SCHOOL ASKED ME TO HOLD HIM.
BUT YOU'RE A COMPLETE STRANGER TO HIM!
-DAWSON-
NOT ANY MORE

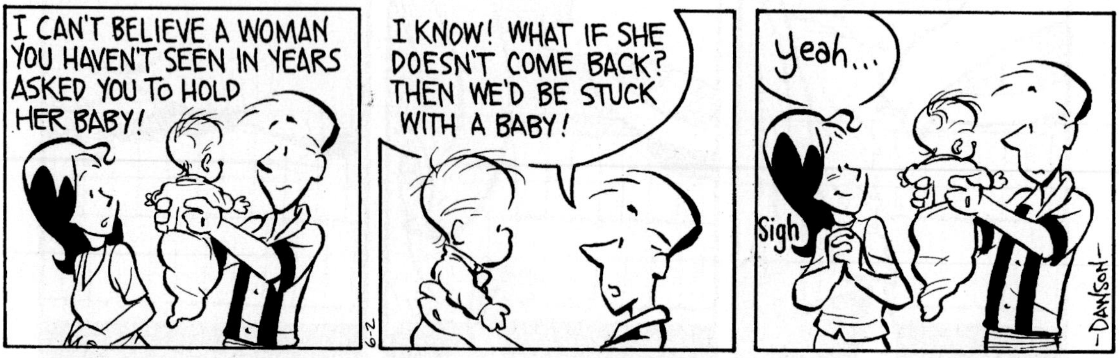
I CAN'T BELIEVE A WOMAN YOU HAVEN'T SEEN IN YEARS ASKED YOU TO HOLD HER BABY!
6-2
I KNOW! WHAT IF SHE DOESN'T COME BACK? THEN WE'D BE STUCK WITH A BABY!
Yeah...
Sigh
-DAWSON-

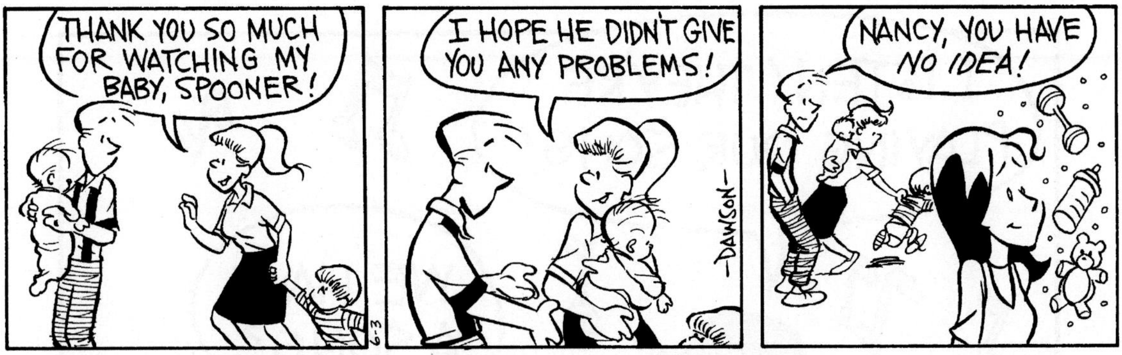
THANK YOU SO MUCH FOR WATCHING MY BABY, SPOONER!
I HOPE HE DIDN'T GIVE YOU ANY PROBLEMS!
NANCY, YOU HAVE *NO IDEA*!
DAWSON
6-3

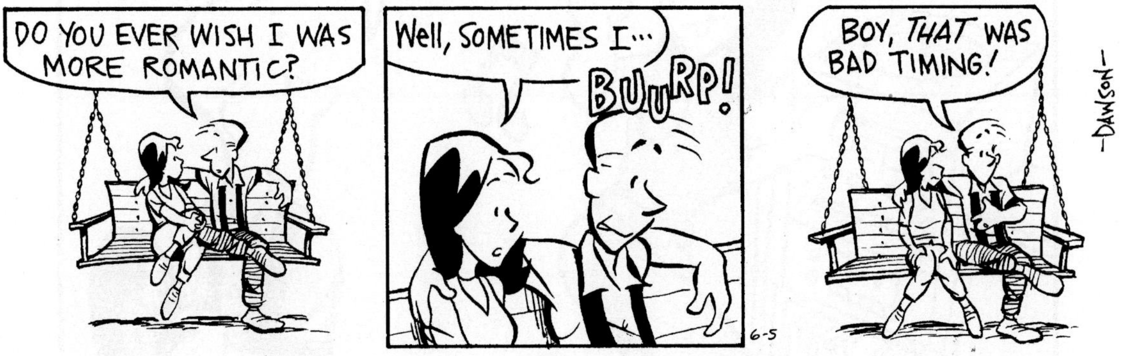
DO YOU EVER WISH I WAS MORE ROMANTIC?
Well, SOMETIMES I...
BUURP!
BOY, *THAT* WAS BAD TIMING!
DAWSON
6-5

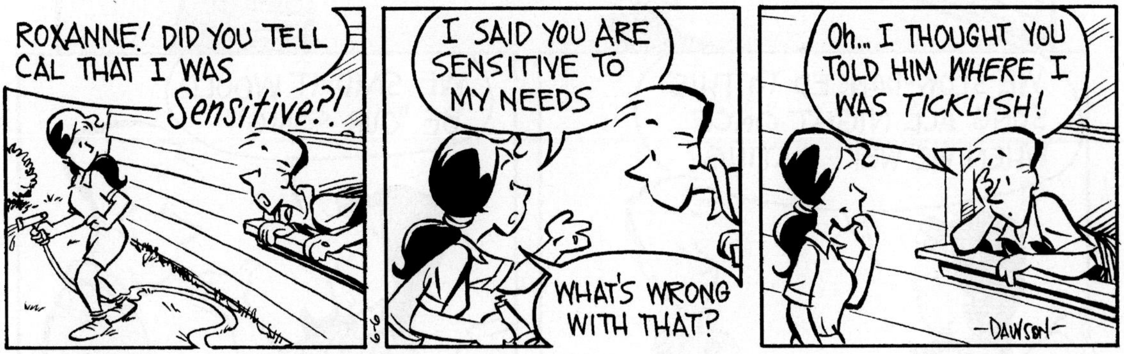
ROXANNE! DID YOU TELL CAL THAT I WAS *Sensitive*?!
I SAID YOU ARE SENSITIVE TO MY NEEDS
WHAT'S WRONG WITH THAT?
Oh... I THOUGHT YOU TOLD HIM *WHERE* I WAS *TICKLISH*!
DAWSON
6-6

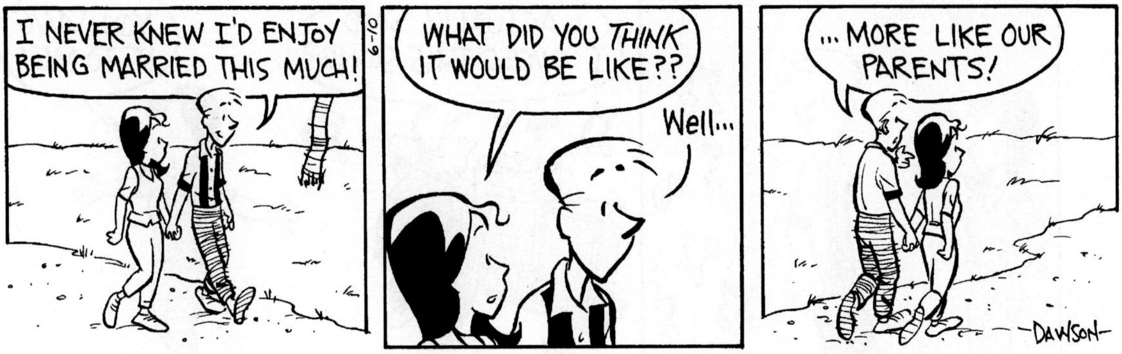
I NEVER KNEW I'D ENJOY BEING MARRIED THIS MUCH!
WHAT DID YOU *THINK* IT WOULD BE LIKE??
Well...
... MORE LIKE OUR PARENTS!
DAWSON
6-10

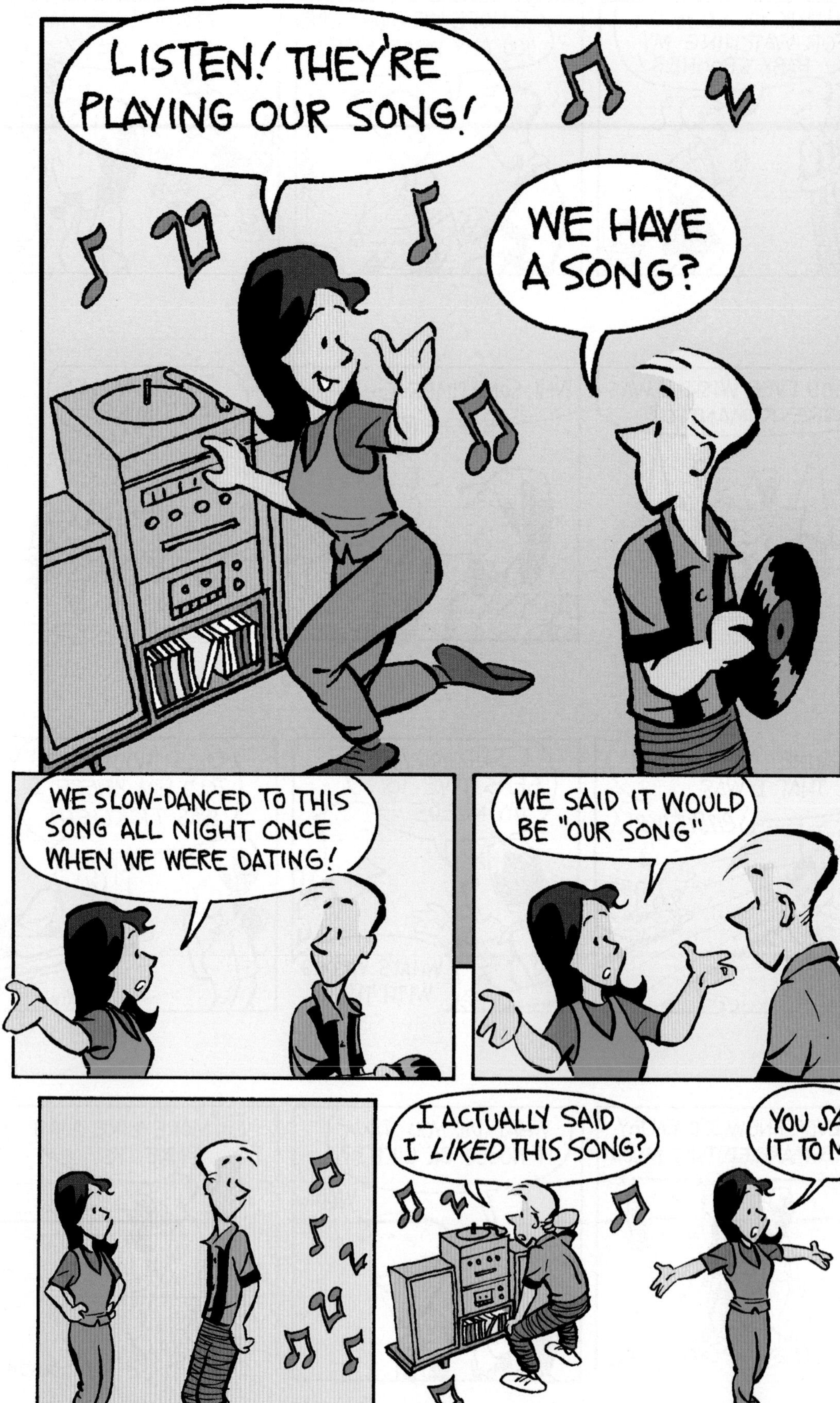
LISTEN! THEY'RE PLAYING OUR SONG!
WE HAVE A SONG?
WE SLOW-DANCED TO THIS SONG ALL NIGHT ONCE WHEN WE WERE DATING!
WE SAID IT WOULD BE "OUR SONG"
I ACTUALLY SAID I *LIKED* THIS SONG?
YOU *SANG* IT TO ME!

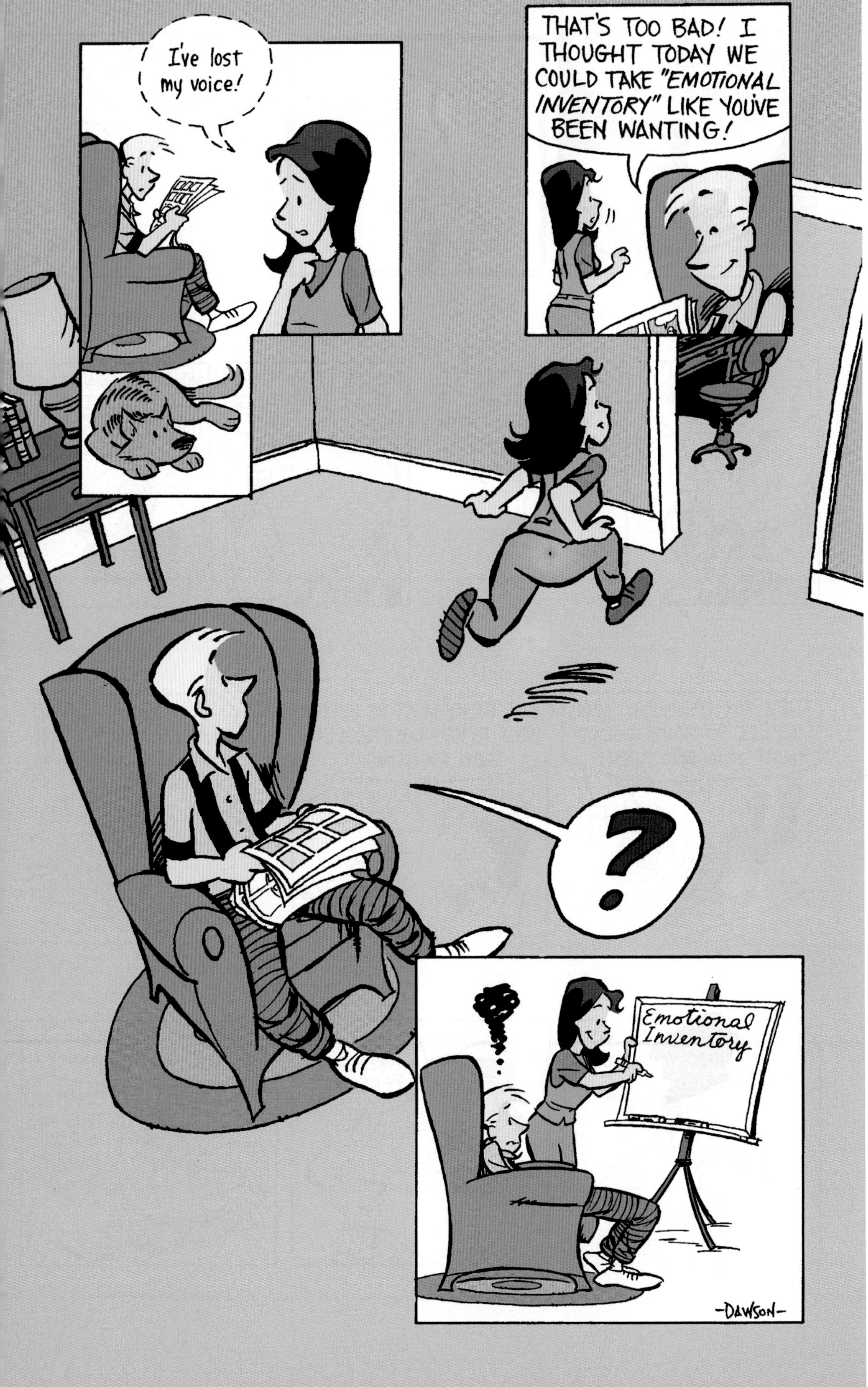
I've lost my voice!
THAT'S TOO BAD! I THOUGHT TODAY WE COULD TAKE "EMOTIONAL INVENTORY" LIKE YOU'VE BEEN WANTING!
?
Emotional Inventory
-DAWSON-

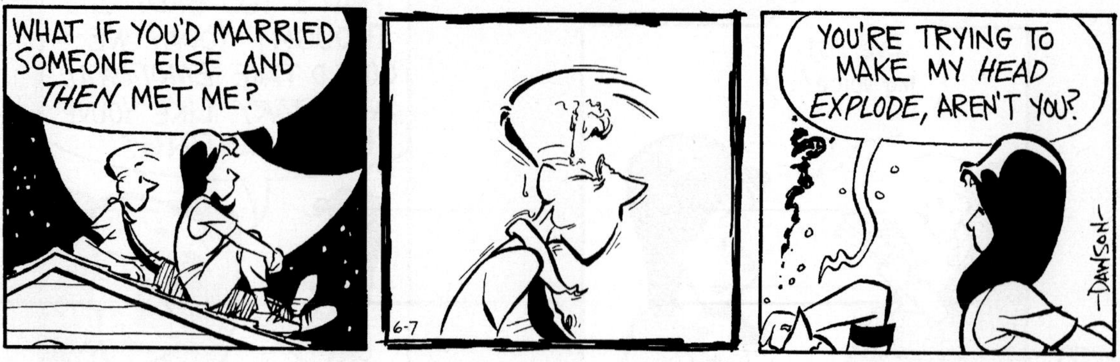
WHAT IF YOU'D MARRIED SOMEONE ELSE AND *THEN* MET ME?
6-7
YOU'RE TRYING TO MAKE MY *HEAD EXPLODE*, AREN'T YOU?
-DAWSON-

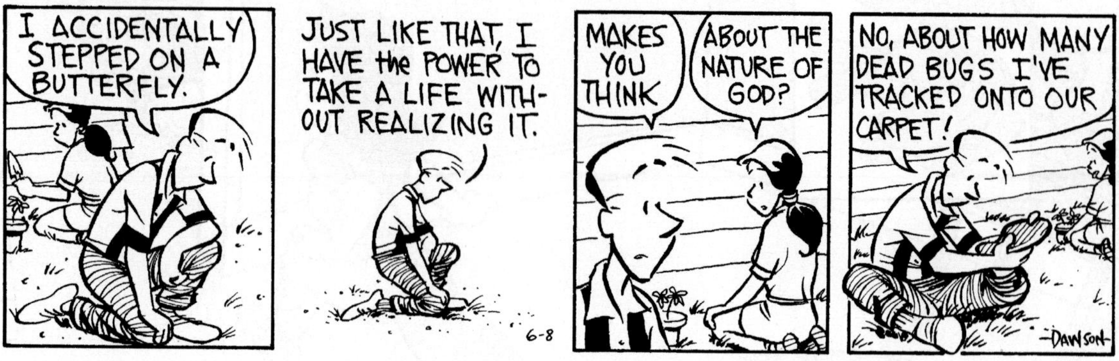
I ACCIDENTALLY STEPPED ON A BUTTERFLY.
JUST LIKE THAT, I HAVE the POWER TO TAKE A LIFE WITHOUT REALIZING IT.
6-8
MAKES YOU THINK
ABOUT THE NATURE OF GOD?
NO, ABOUT HOW MANY DEAD BUGS I'VE TRACKED ONTO OUR CARPET!
-DAWSON-

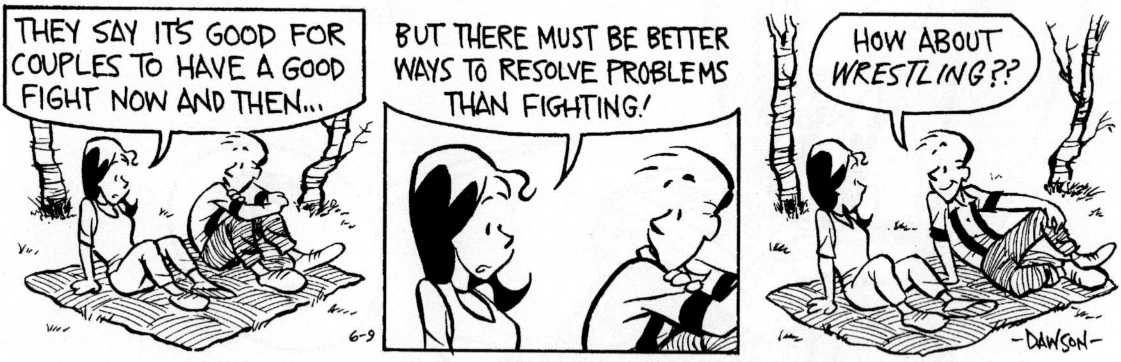
THEY SAY IT'S GOOD FOR COUPLES TO HAVE A GOOD FIGHT NOW AND THEN...
6-9
BUT THERE MUST BE BETTER WAYS TO RESOLVE PROBLEMS THAN FIGHTING!
HOW ABOUT *WRESTLING*??
-DAWSON-

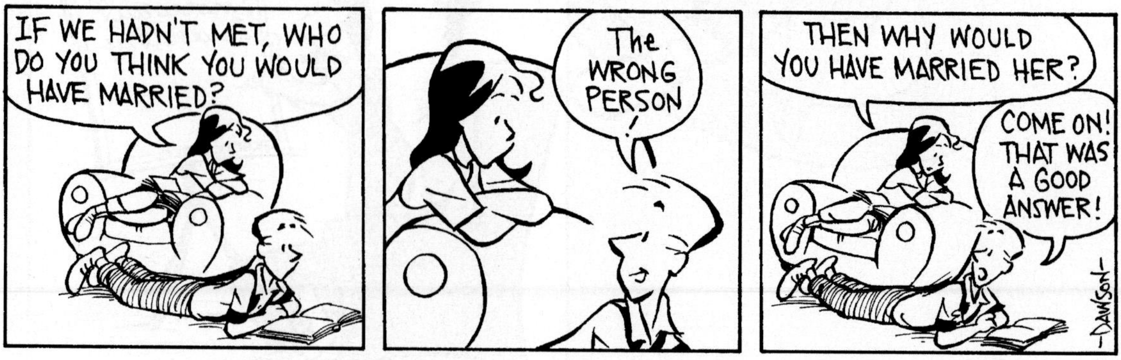
IF WE HADN'T MET, WHO DO YOU THINK YOU WOULD HAVE MARRIED?
The WRONG PERSON!
THEN WHY WOULD YOU HAVE MARRIED HER?
COME ON! THAT WAS A GOOD ANSWER!
-DAWSON-

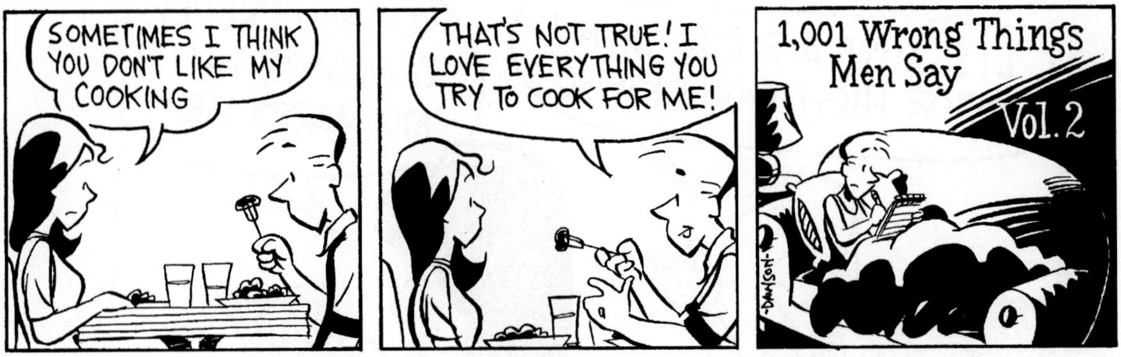
SOMETIMES I THINK YOU DON'T LIKE MY COOKING
THAT'S NOT TRUE! I LOVE EVERYTHING YOU TRY TO COOK FOR ME!
1,001 Wrong Things Men Say
Vol. 2
-DAWSON-

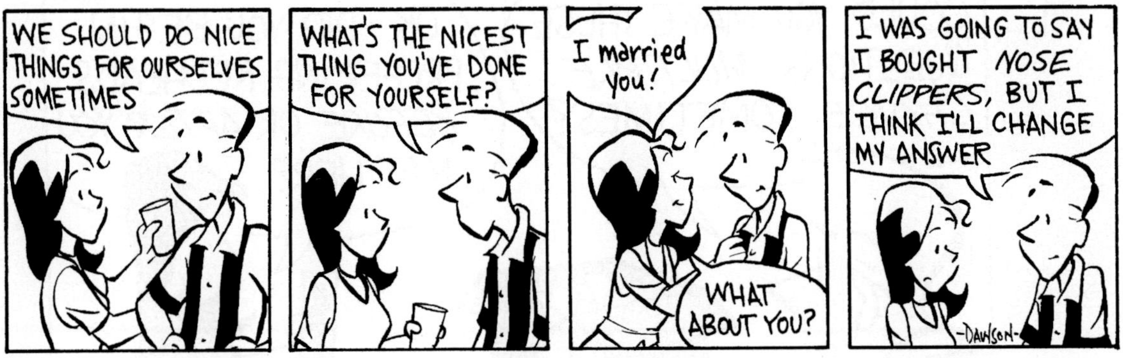
WE SHOULD DO NICE THINGS FOR OURSELVES SOMETIMES
WHAT'S THE NICEST THING YOU'VE DONE FOR YOURSELF?
I married you!
WHAT ABOUT YOU?
I WAS GOING TO SAY I BOUGHT *NOSE CLIPPERS*, BUT I THINK I'LL CHANGE MY ANSWER
-DAWSON-

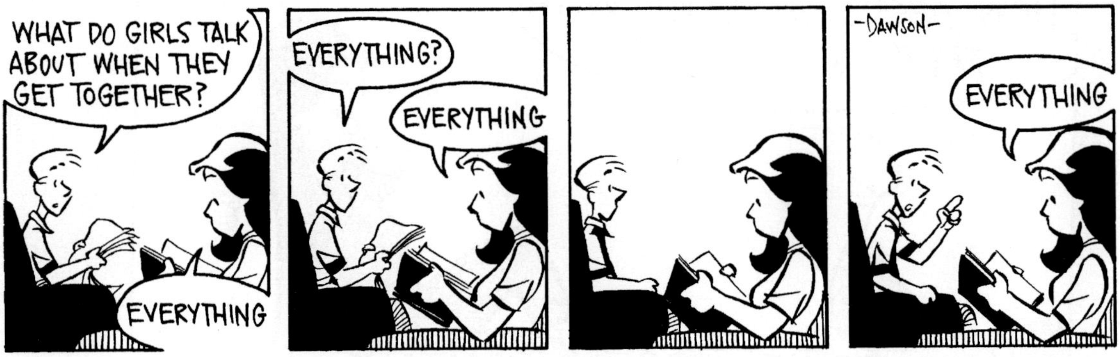
WHAT DO GIRLS TALK ABOUT WHEN THEY GET TOGETHER?
EVERYTHING
EVERYTHING?
EVERYTHING
-DAWSON-
EVERYTHING

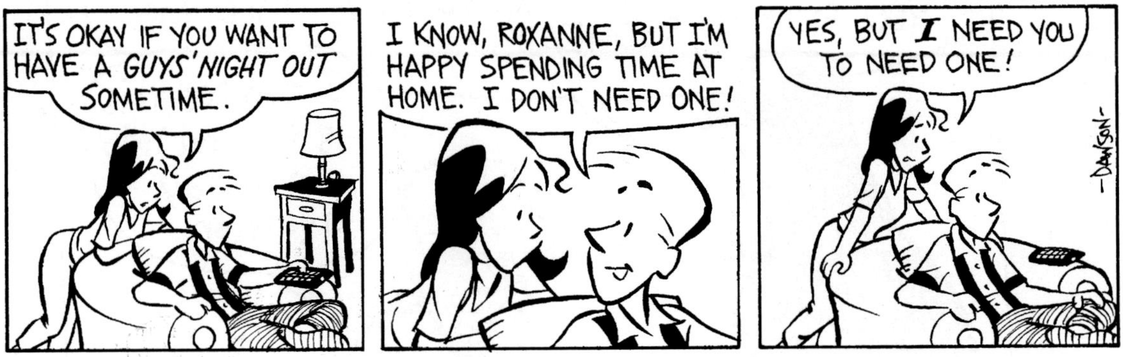
IT'S OKAY IF YOU WANT TO HAVE A *GUYS' NIGHT OUT* SOMETIME.
I KNOW, ROXANNE, BUT I'M HAPPY SPENDING TIME AT HOME. I DON'T NEED ONE!
YES, BUT **I** NEED YOU TO NEED ONE!
-DAWSON-

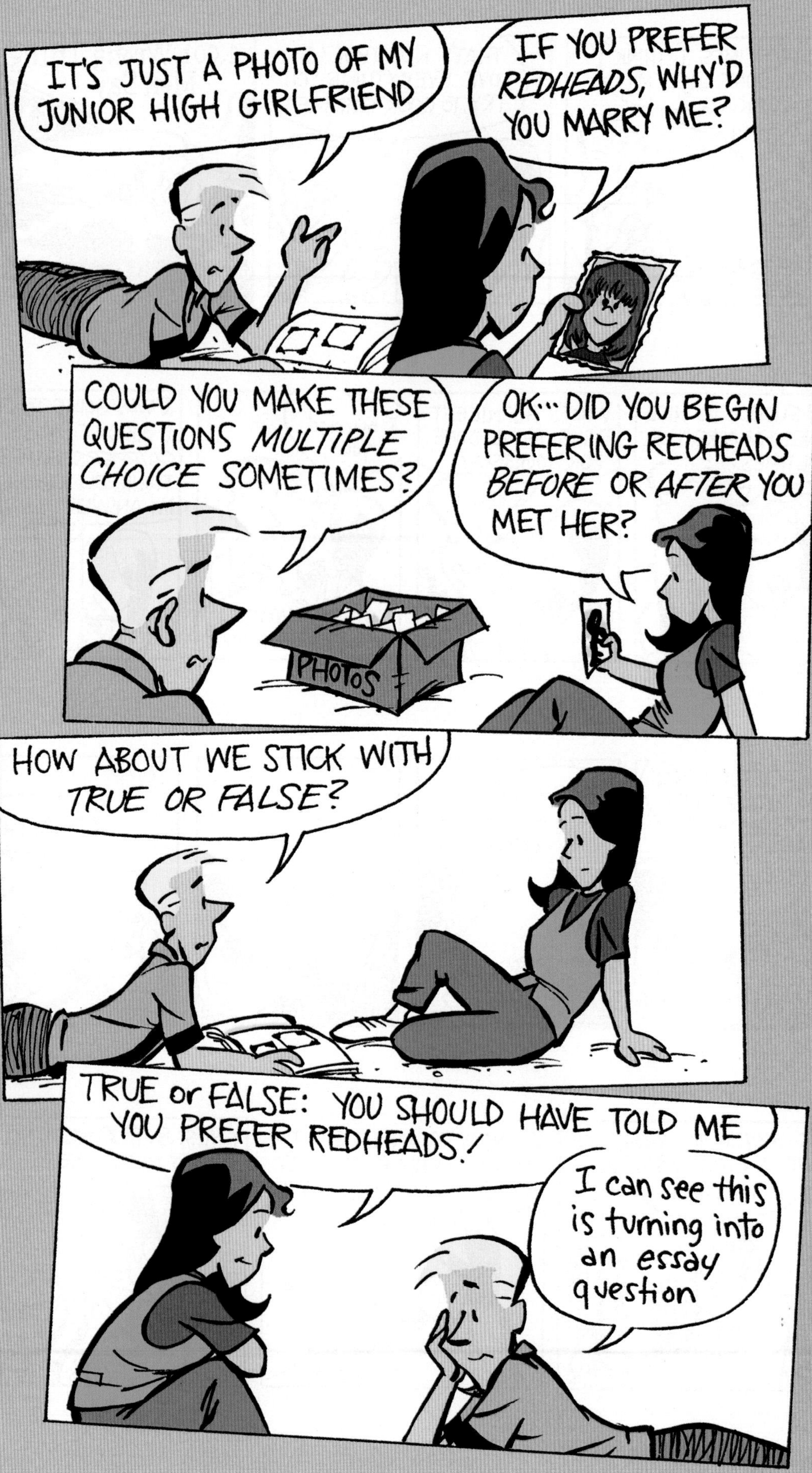
IT'S JUST A PHOTO OF MY JUNIOR HIGH GIRLFRIEND
IF YOU PREFER REDHEADS, WHY'D YOU MARRY ME?
COULD YOU MAKE THESE QUESTIONS MULTIPLE CHOICE SOMETIMES?
OK... DID YOU BEGIN PREFERING REDHEADS BEFORE OR AFTER YOU MET HER?
PHOTOS
HOW ABOUT WE STICK WITH TRUE OR FALSE?
TRUE or FALSE: YOU SHOULD HAVE TOLD ME YOU PREFER REDHEADS!
I can see this is turning into an essay question

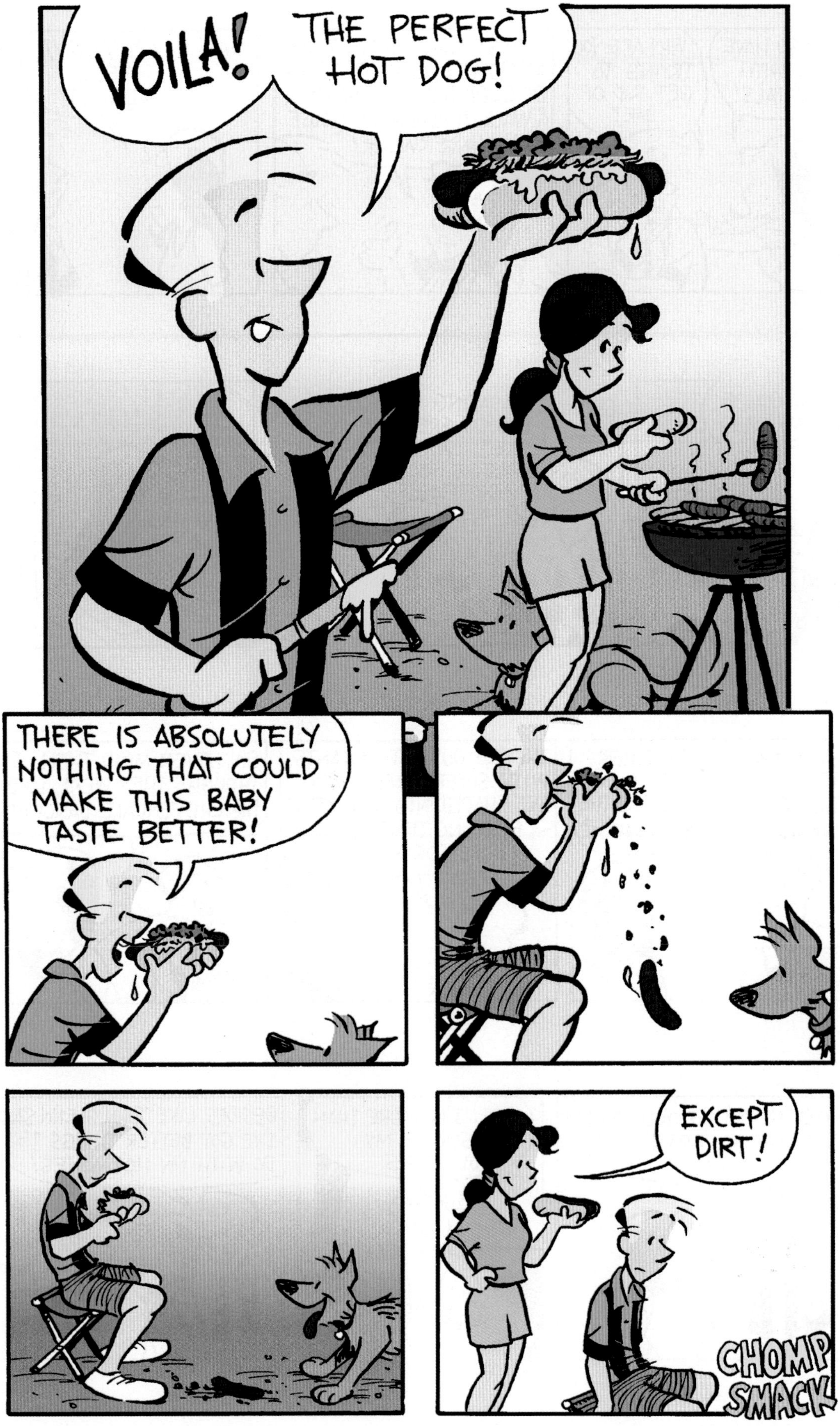
VOILA! THE PERFECT HOT DOG!
THERE IS ABSOLUTELY NOTHING THAT COULD MAKE THIS BABY TASTE BETTER!
EXCEPT DIRT!
CHOMP SMACK

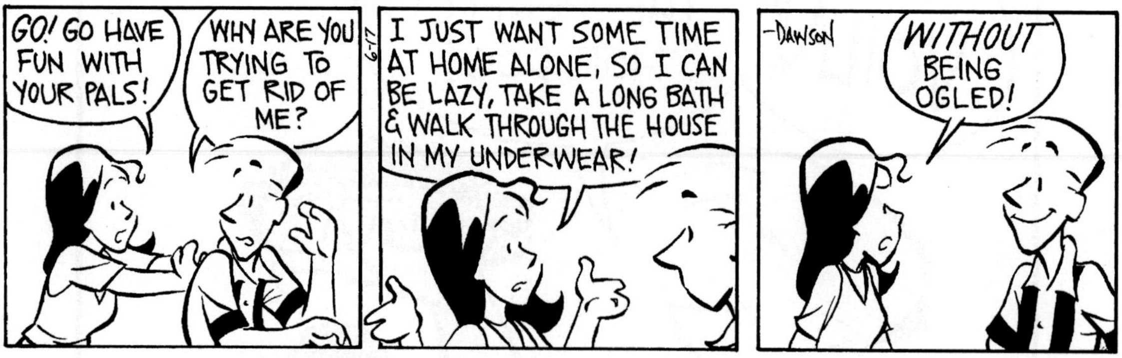
GO! GO HAVE FUN WITH YOUR PALS!
WHY ARE YOU TRYING TO GET RID OF ME?
6-17
I JUST WANT SOME TIME AT HOME ALONE, SO I CAN BE LAZY, TAKE A LONG BATH & WALK THROUGH THE HOUSE IN MY UNDERWEAR!
–DAWSON
WITHOUT BEING OGLED!

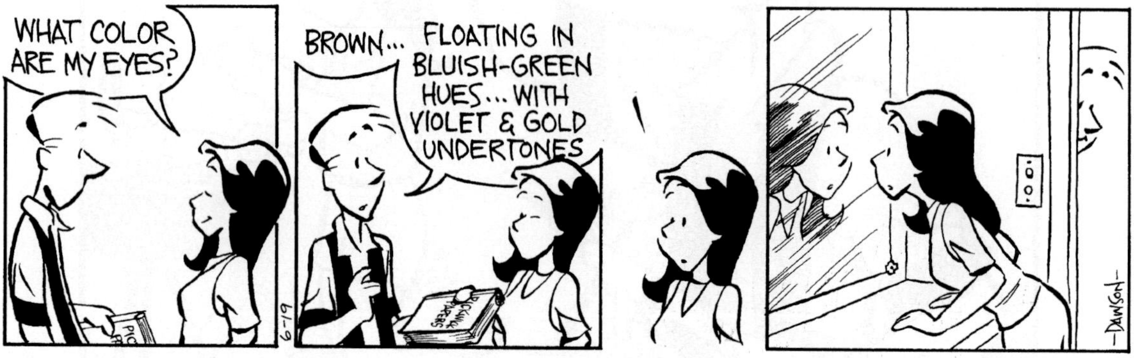
WHAT COLOR ARE MY EYES?
6-19
BROWN... FLOATING IN BLUISH-GREEN HUES... WITH VIOLET & GOLD UNDERTONES
–DAWSON–

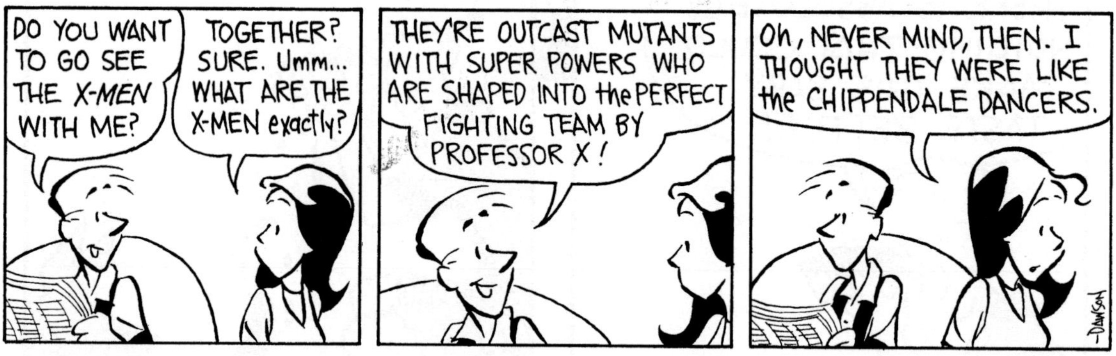
DO YOU WANT TO GO SEE THE *X-MEN* WITH ME?
TOGETHER? SURE. Umm... WHAT ARE THE X-MEN exactly?
THEY'RE OUTCAST MUTANTS WITH SUPER POWERS WHO ARE SHAPED INTO the PERFECT FIGHTING TEAM BY PROFESSOR X!
Oh, NEVER MIND, THEN. I THOUGHT THEY WERE LIKE the CHIPPENDALE DANCERS.
–DAWSON

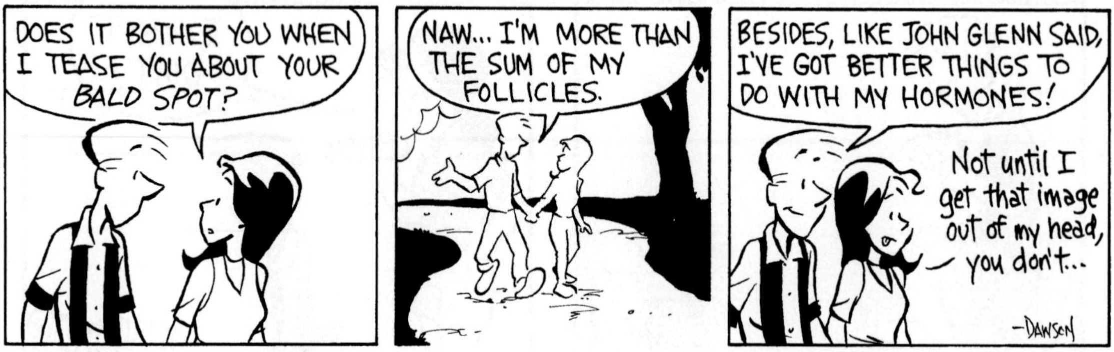
DOES IT BOTHER YOU WHEN I TEASE YOU ABOUT YOUR *BALD SPOT*?
NAW... I'M MORE THAN THE SUM OF MY FOLLICLES.
BESIDES, LIKE JOHN GLENN SAID, I'VE GOT BETTER THINGS TO DO WITH MY HORMONES!
Not until I get that image out of my head, you don't..
–DAWSON

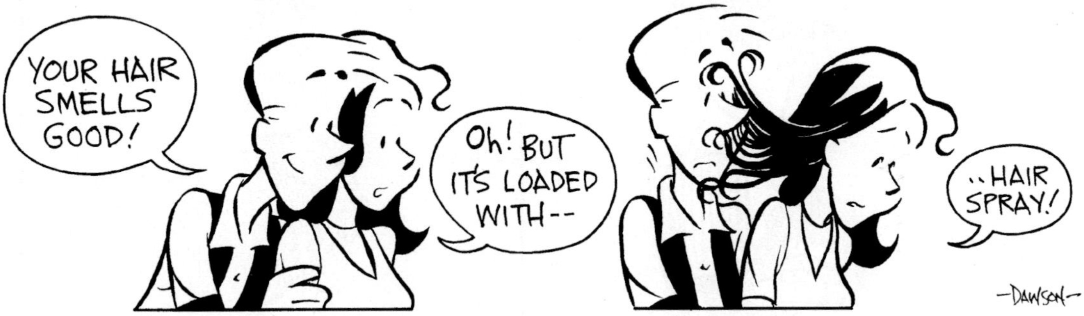
YOUR HAIR SMELLS GOOD!
Oh! BUT IT'S LOADED WITH--
..HAIR SPRAY!
-DAWSON-

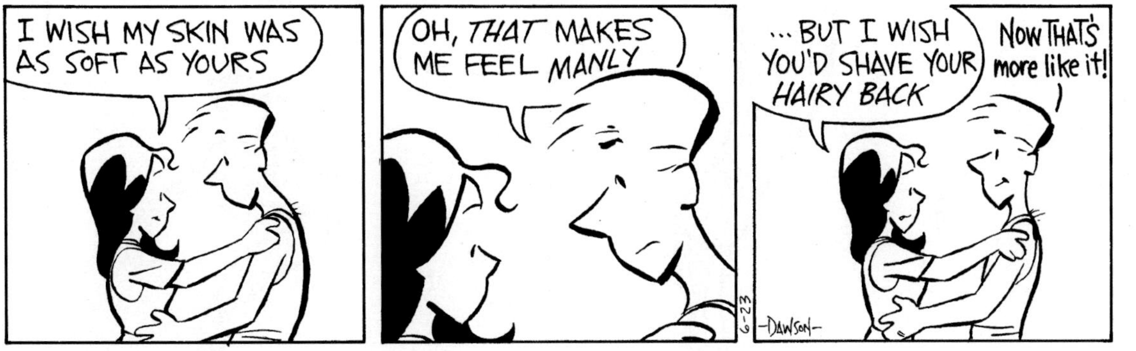
I WISH MY SKIN WAS AS SOFT AS YOURS
OH, *THAT* MAKES ME FEEL *MANLY*
6-23
...BUT I WISH YOU'D SHAVE YOUR *HAIRY BACK*
Now THAT'S more like it!
-DAWSON-

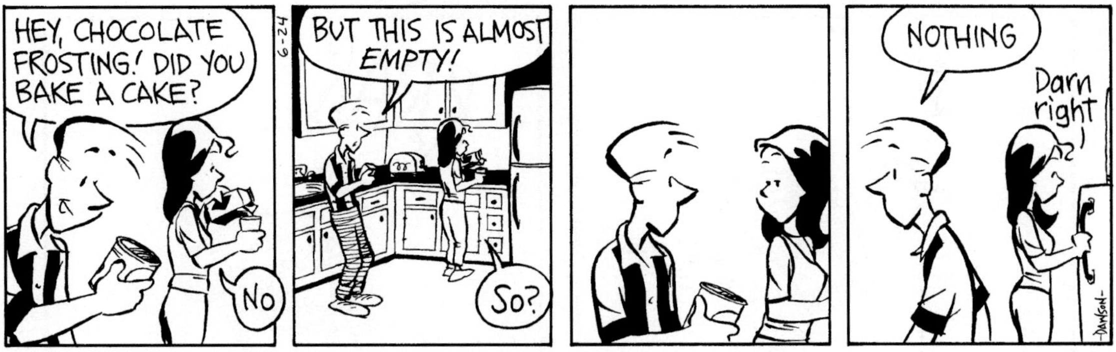
HEY, CHOCOLATE FROSTING! DID YOU BAKE A CAKE?
No
6-24
BUT THIS IS ALMOST *EMPTY!*
So?
NOTHING
Darn right
-DAWSON-

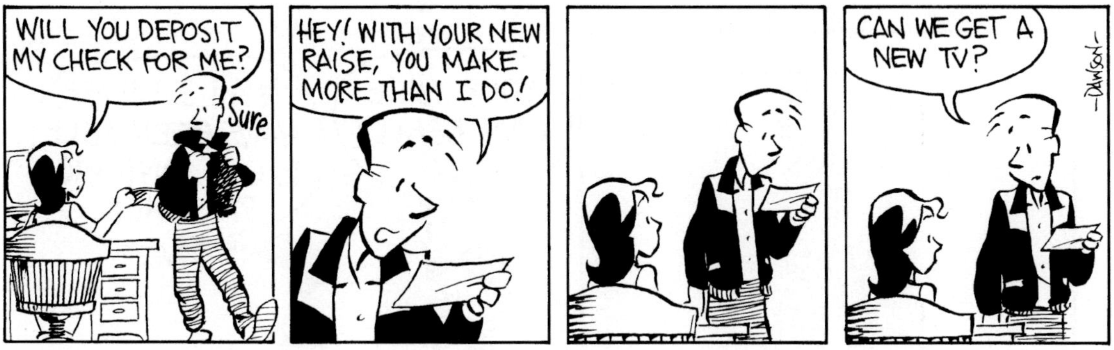
WILL YOU DEPOSIT MY CHECK FOR ME?
Sure
HEY! WITH YOUR NEW RAISE, YOU MAKE MORE THAN I DO!
CAN WE GET A NEW TV?
-DAWSON-

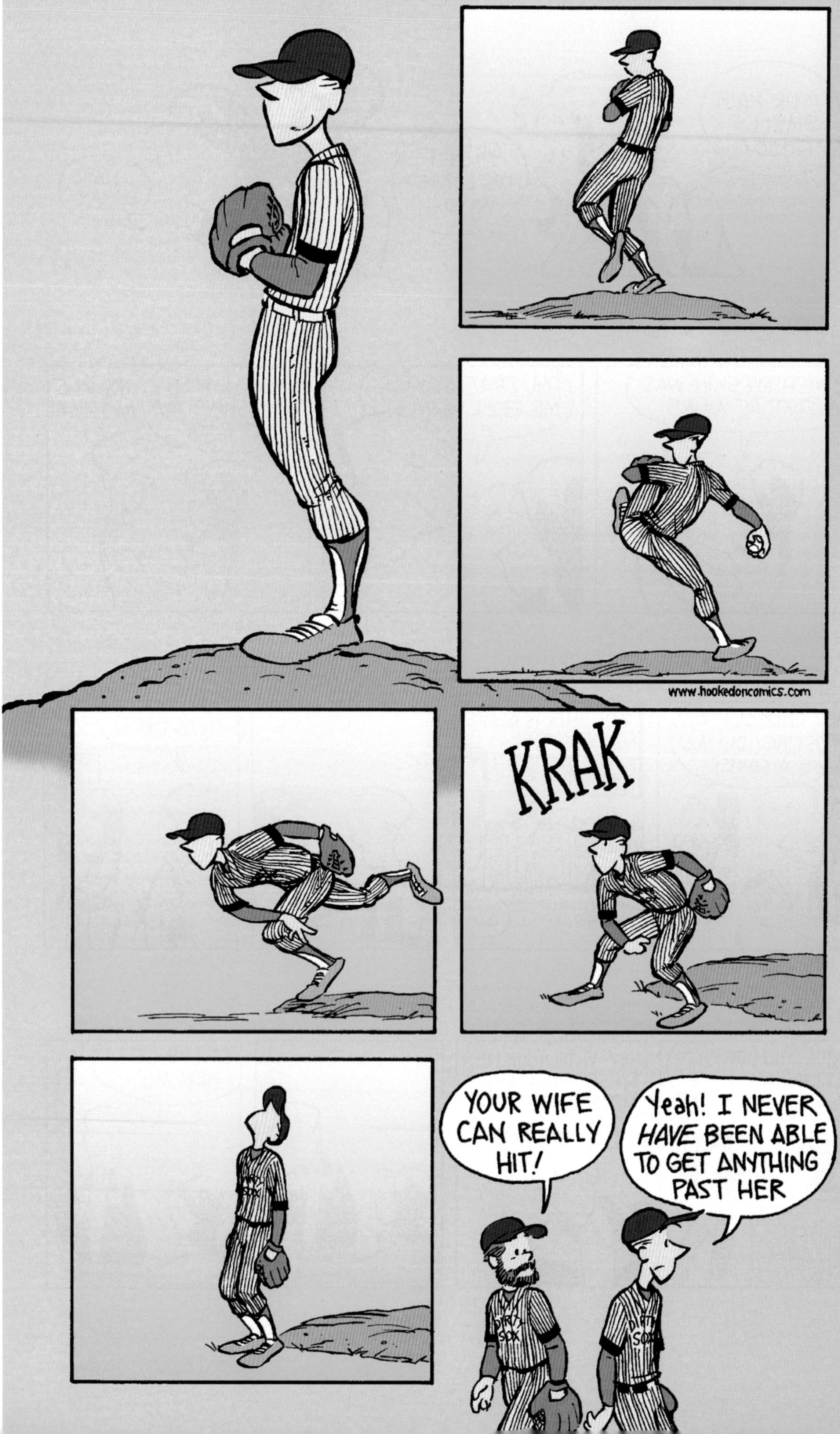
www.hookedoncomics.com
KRAK
YOUR WIFE CAN REALLY HIT!
Yeah! I NEVER HAVE BEEN ABLE TO GET ANYTHING PAST HER

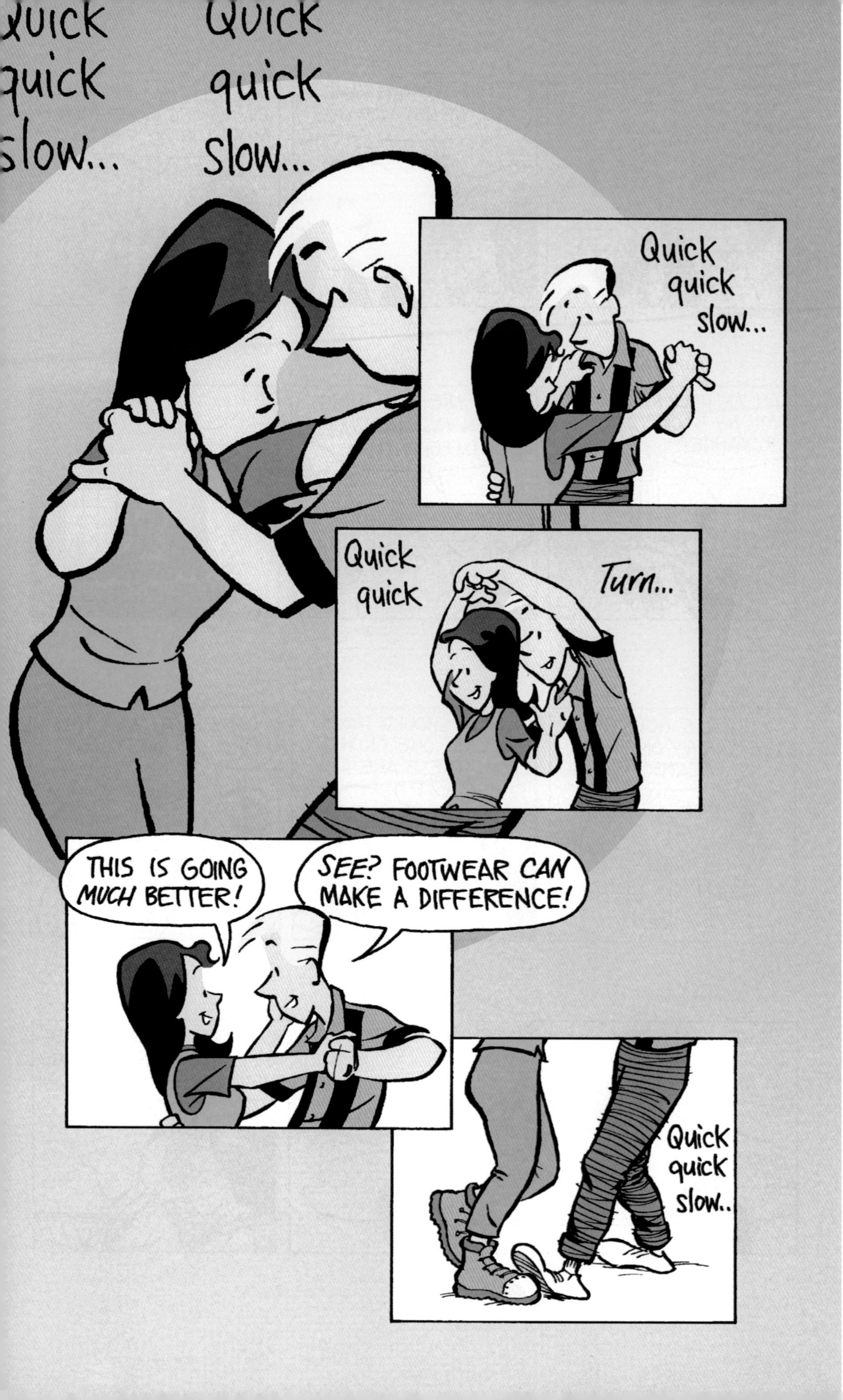
Quick quick slow...
Quick quick slow...
Quick quick slow...
Quick quick
Turn...
THIS IS GOING MUCH BETTER!
SEE? FOOTWEAR CAN MAKE A DIFFERENCE!
Quick quick slow..

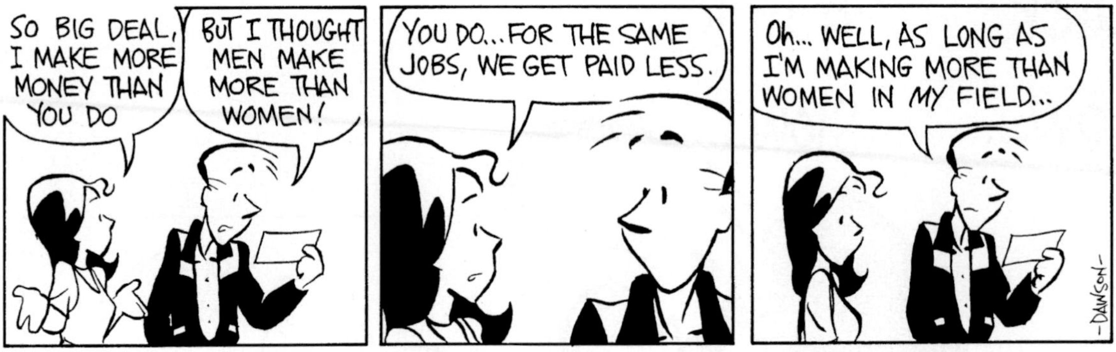
SO BIG DEAL, I MAKE MORE MONEY THAN YOU DO
BUT I THOUGHT MEN MAKE MORE THAN WOMEN!
YOU DO...FOR THE SAME JOBS, WE GET PAID LESS.
Oh... WELL, AS LONG AS I'M MAKING MORE THAN WOMEN IN MY FIELD...
-DAWSON-

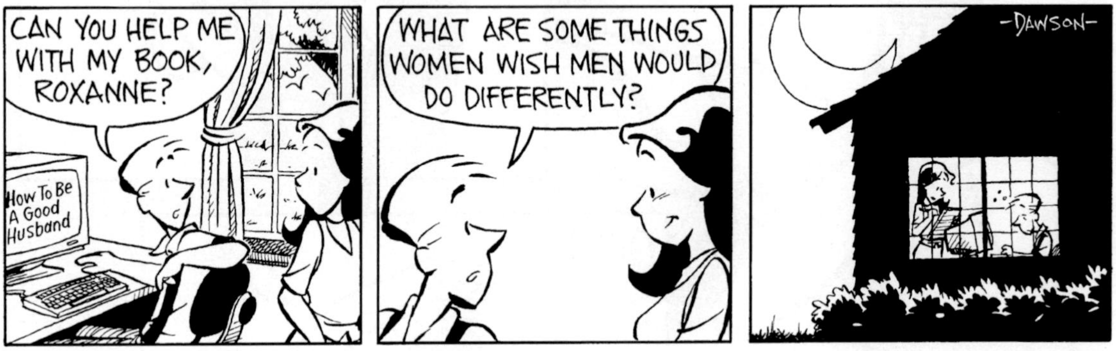
CAN YOU HELP ME WITH MY BOOK, ROXANNE?
How To Be A Good Husband
WHAT ARE SOME THINGS WOMEN WISH MEN WOULD DO DIFFERENTLY?
-DAWSON-

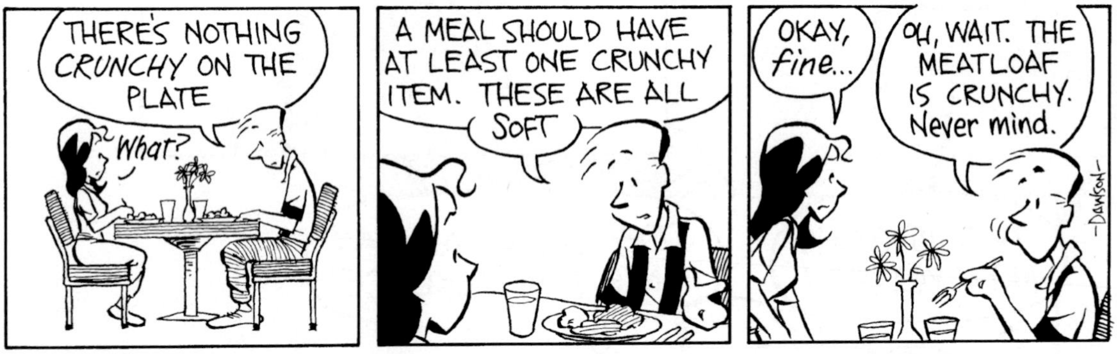
THERE'S NOTHING CRUNCHY ON THE PLATE
What?
A MEAL SHOULD HAVE AT LEAST ONE CRUNCHY ITEM. THESE ARE ALL
SOFT
OKAY, fine...
OH, WAIT. THE MEATLOAF IS CRUNCHY. Never mind.
-DAWSON-

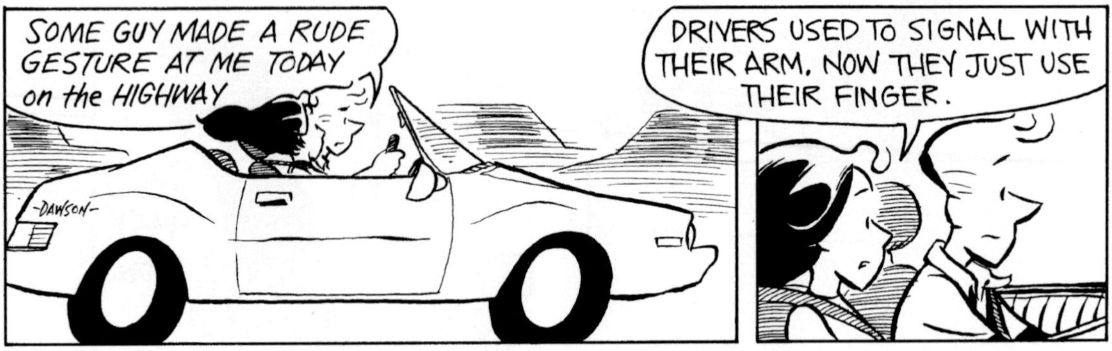
SOME GUY MADE A RUDE GESTURE AT ME TODAY on the HIGHWAY
-DAWSON-
DRIVERS USED TO SIGNAL WITH THEIR ARM. NOW THEY JUST USE THEIR FINGER.

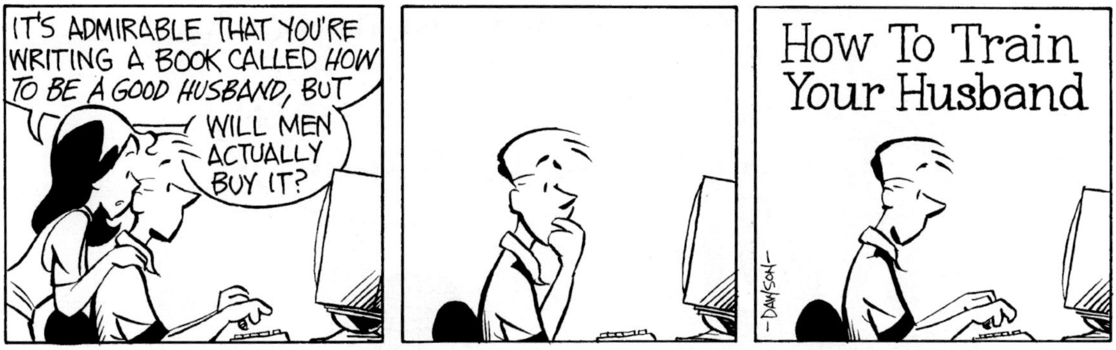
IT'S ADMIRABLE THAT YOU'RE WRITING A BOOK CALLED *HOW TO BE A GOOD HUSBAND*, BUT
WILL MEN ACTUALLY BUY IT?
How To Train Your Husband
-DAWSON-

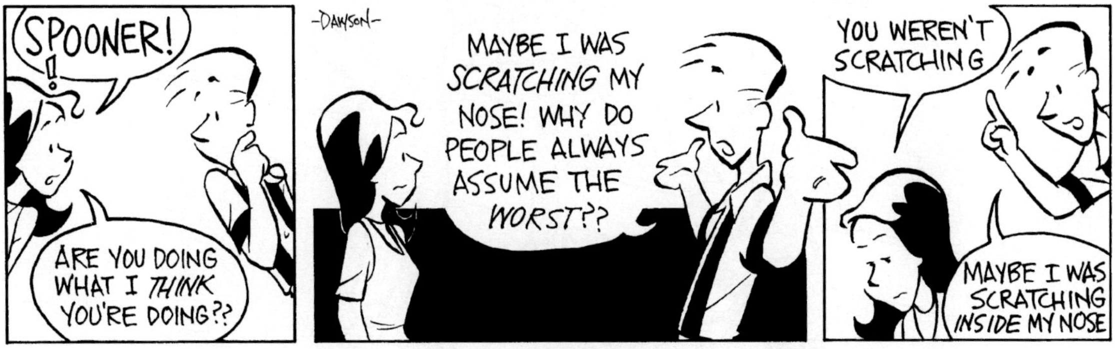
SPOONER!
ARE YOU DOING WHAT I *THINK* YOU'RE DOING??
-DAWSON-
MAYBE I WAS *SCRATCHING* MY NOSE! WHY DO PEOPLE ALWAYS ASSUME THE *WORST*??
YOU WEREN'T SCRATCHING
MAYBE I WAS SCRATCHING *INSIDE* MY NOSE

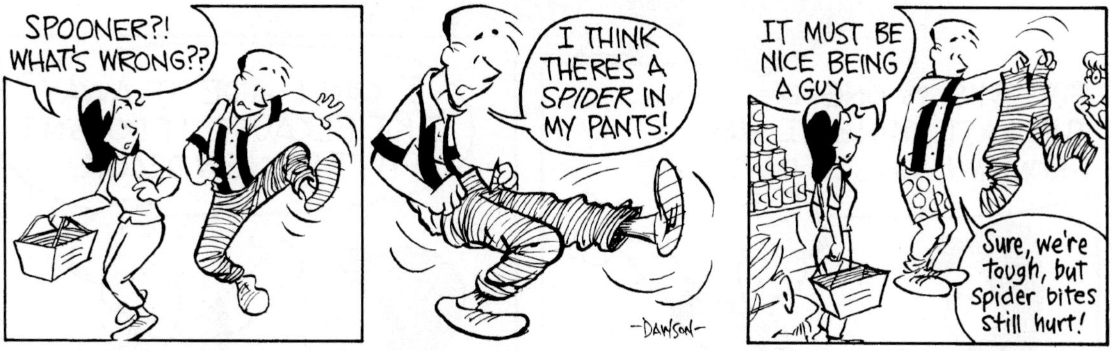
SPOONER?! WHAT'S WRONG??
I THINK THERE'S A *SPIDER* IN MY PANTS!
-DAWSON-
IT MUST BE NICE BEING A GUY
Sure, we're tough, but spider bites still hurt!

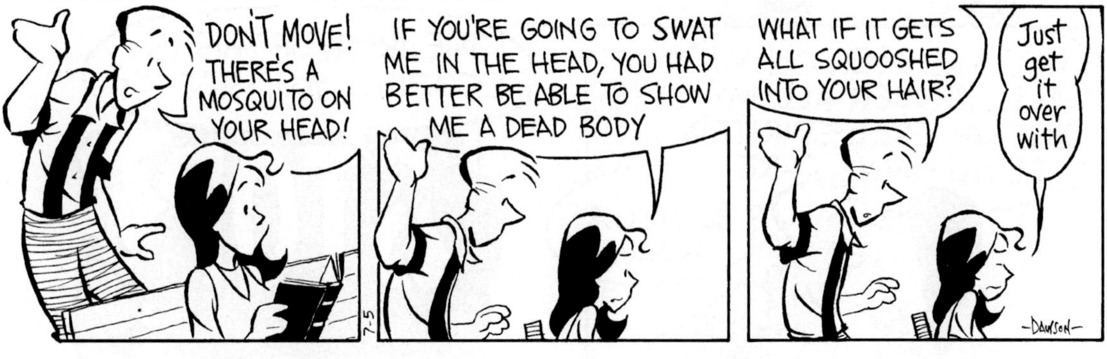
DON'T MOVE! THERE'S A MOSQUITO ON YOUR HEAD!
IF YOU'RE GOING TO SWAT ME IN THE HEAD, YOU HAD BETTER BE ABLE TO SHOW ME A DEAD BODY
WHAT IF IT GETS ALL SQUOOSHED INTO YOUR HAIR?
Just get it over with
-DAWSON-

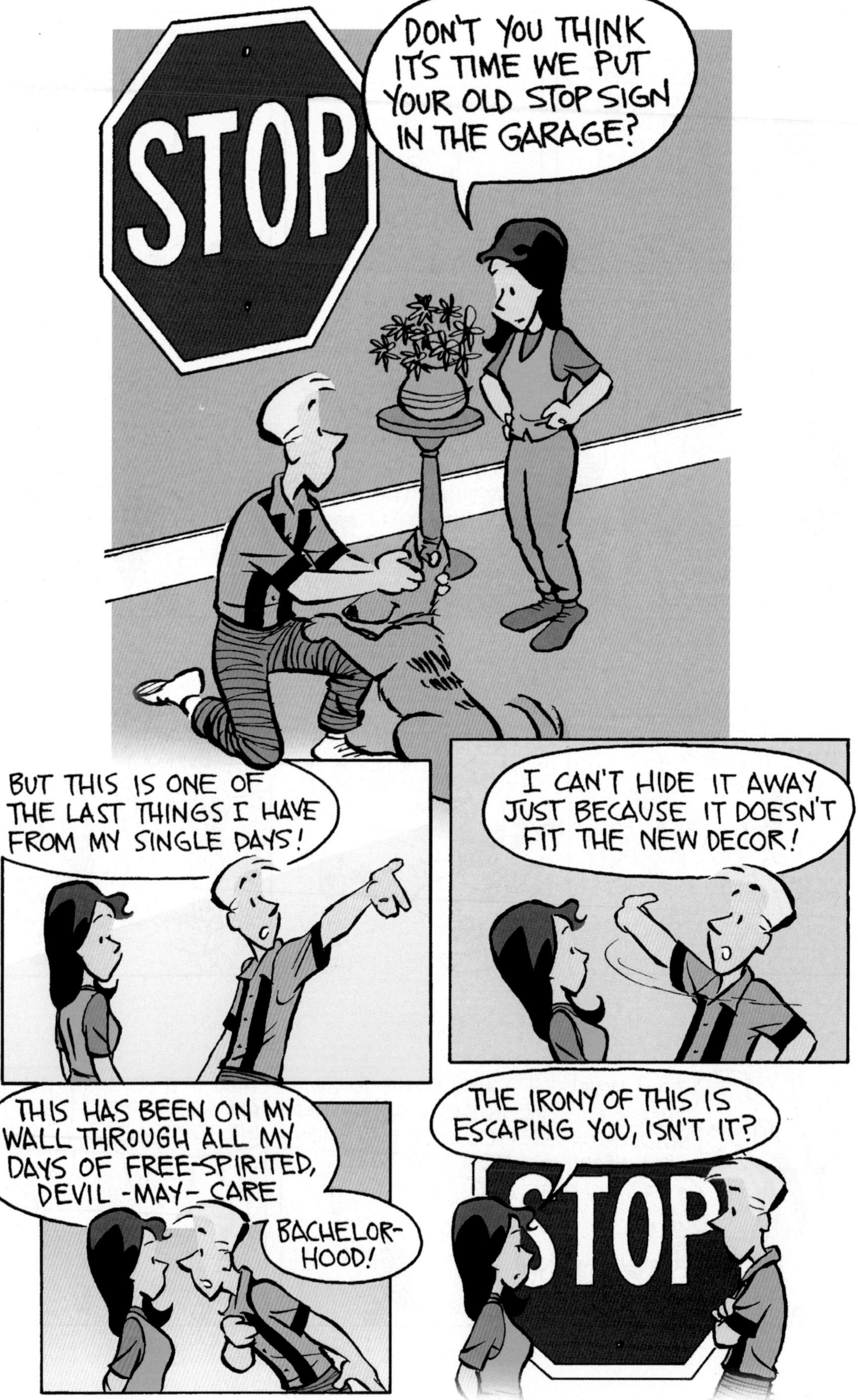
STOP
DON'T YOU THINK IT'S TIME WE PUT YOUR OLD STOP SIGN IN THE GARAGE?
BUT THIS IS ONE OF THE LAST THINGS I HAVE FROM MY SINGLE DAYS!
I CAN'T HIDE IT AWAY JUST BECAUSE IT DOESN'T FIT THE NEW DECOR!
THIS HAS BEEN ON MY WALL THROUGH ALL MY DAYS OF FREE-SPIRITED, DEVIL-MAY-CARE
BACHELORHOOD!
THE IRONY OF THIS IS ESCAPING YOU, ISN'T IT?
STOP

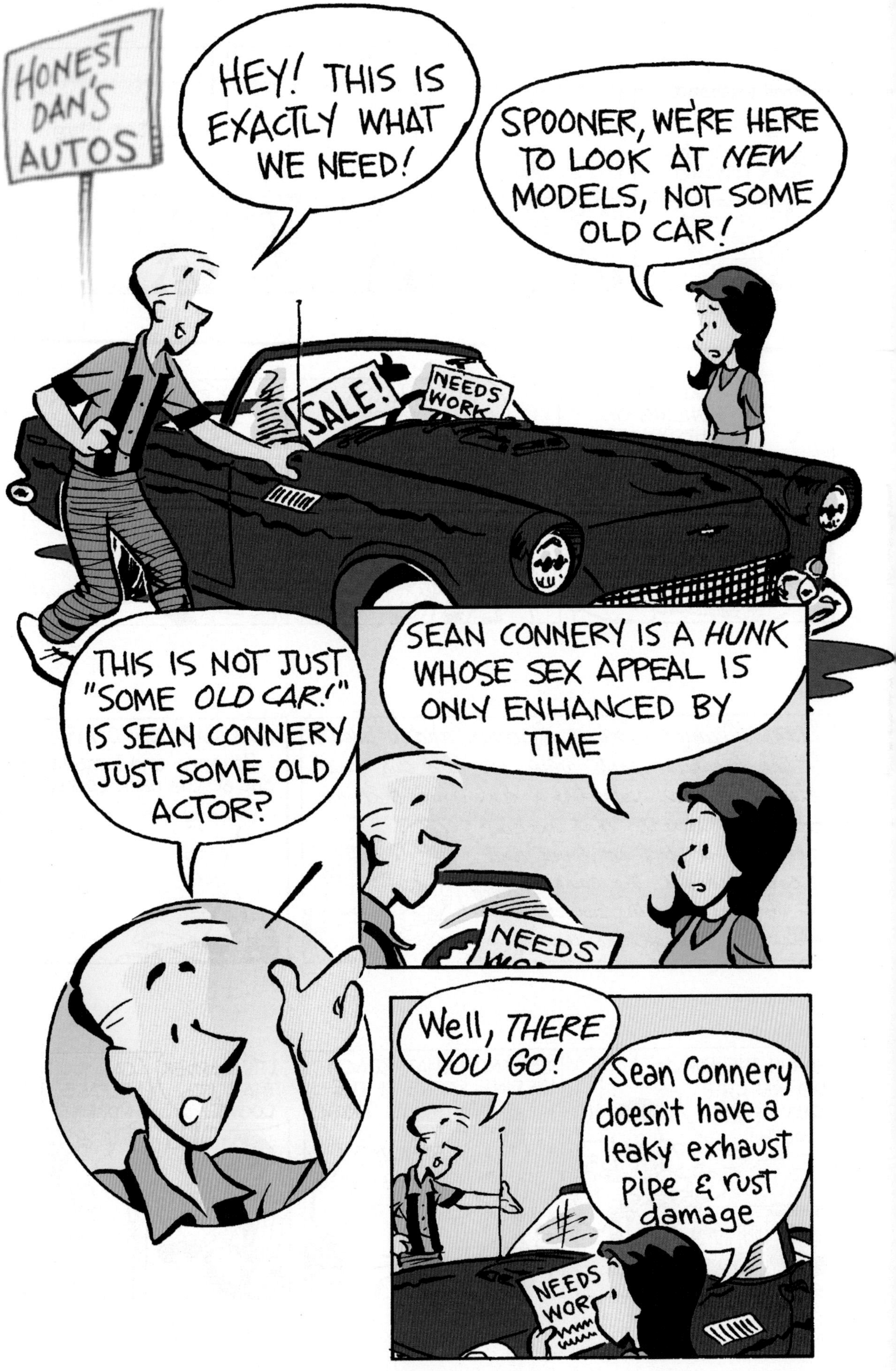
HONEST DAN'S AUTOS
HEY! THIS IS EXACTLY WHAT WE NEED!
SPOONER, WE'RE HERE TO LOOK AT *NEW* MODELS, NOT SOME OLD CAR!
SALE!
NEEDS WORK
THIS IS NOT JUST "SOME *OLD CAR!*" IS SEAN CONNERY JUST SOME OLD ACTOR?
SEAN CONNERY IS A *HUNK* WHOSE SEX APPEAL IS ONLY ENHANCED BY TIME
Well, *THERE YOU GO!*
Sean Connery doesn't have a leaky exhaust pipe & rust damage

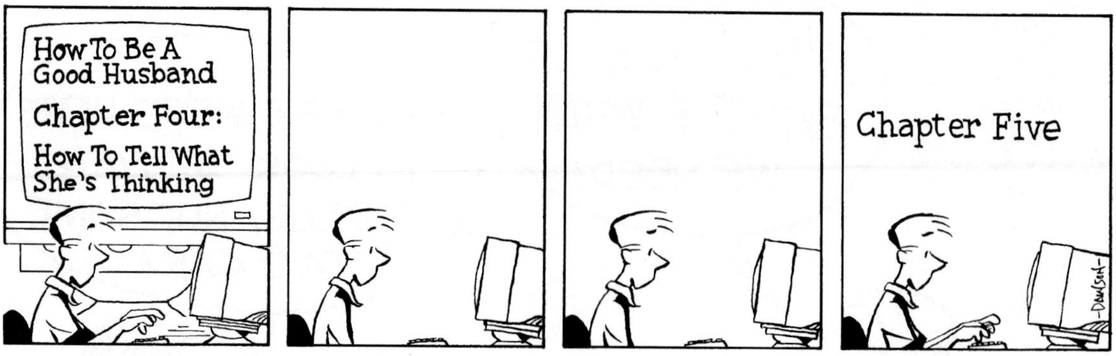
How To Be A Good Husband
Chapter Four:
How To Tell What She's Thinking
Chapter Five
-DAWSON-

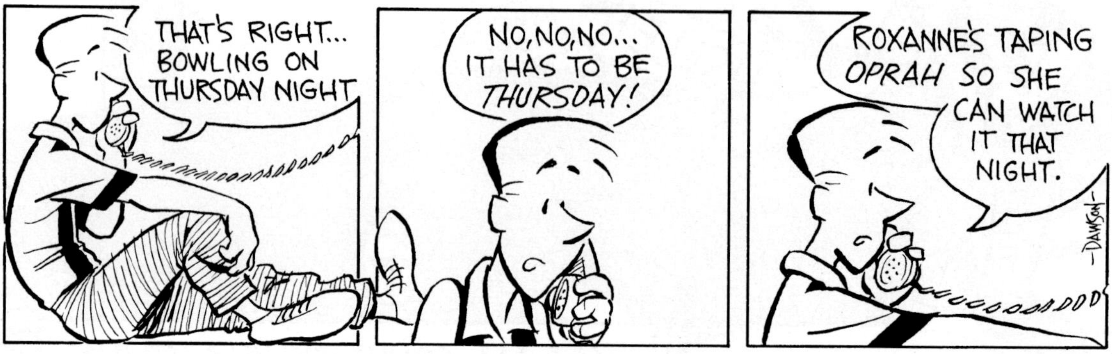
THAT'S RIGHT... BOWLING ON THURSDAY NIGHT
NO, NO, NO... IT HAS TO BE THURSDAY!
ROXANNE'S TAPING OPRAH SO SHE CAN WATCH IT THAT NIGHT.
-DAWSON-

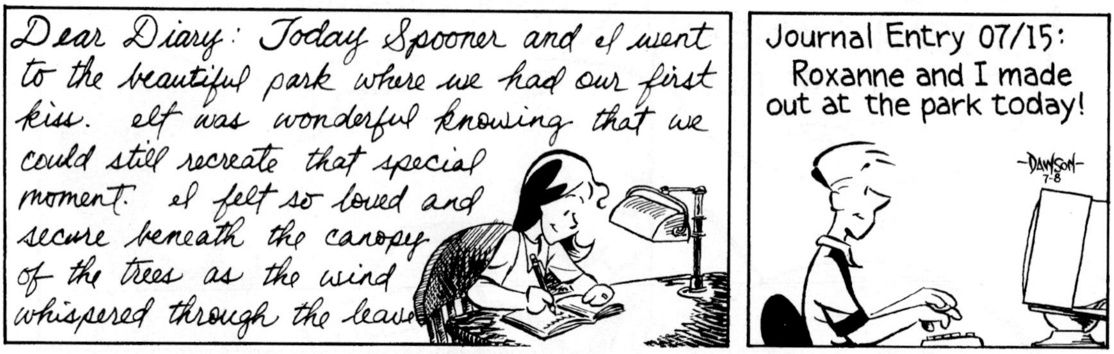
Dear Diary: Today Spooner and I went to the beautiful park where we had our first kiss. It was wonderful knowing that we could still recreate that special moment. I felt so loved and secure beneath the canopy of the trees as the wind whispered through the leave
Journal Entry 07/15: Roxanne and I made out at the park today!
-DAWSON- 7-8

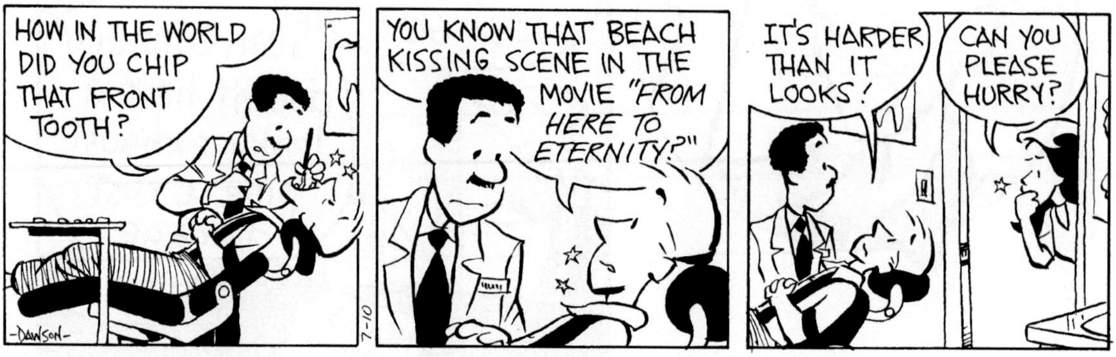
HOW IN THE WORLD DID YOU CHIP THAT FRONT TOOTH?
-DAWSON-
7-10
YOU KNOW THAT BEACH KISSING SCENE IN THE MOVIE "FROM HERE TO ETERNITY?"
IT'S HARDER THAN IT LOOKS!
CAN YOU PLEASE HURRY?

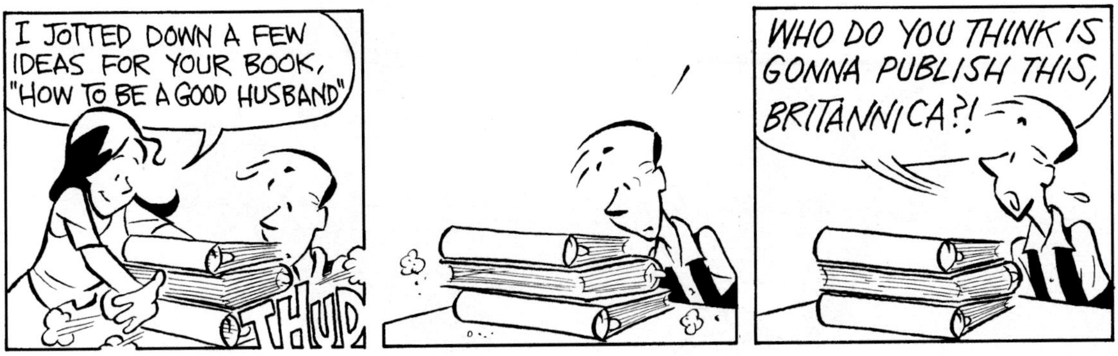

I JOTTED DOWN A FEW IDEAS FOR YOUR BOOK, "HOW TO BE A GOOD HUSBAND"
THUD
WHO DO YOU THINK IS GONNA PUBLISH THIS, BRITANNICA?!

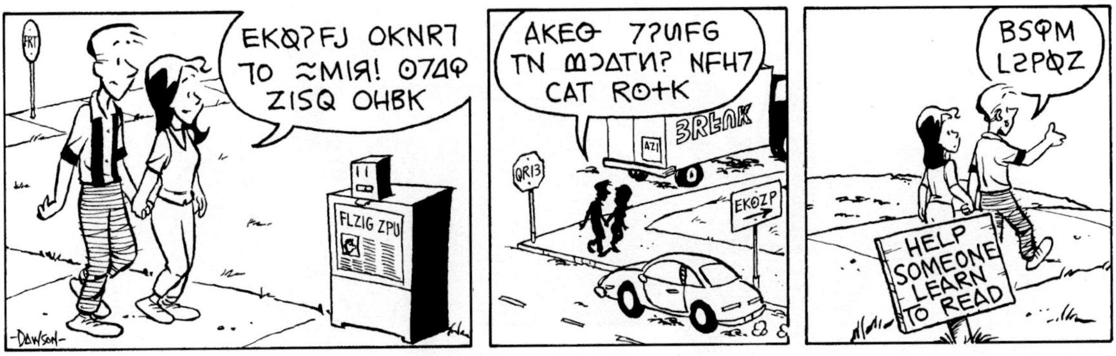

FRT
EKQ?FJ OKNR7 TO ≈MIЯ! 074Φ ZISQ OHBK
FLZIG ZPU
-DAWSON-
AKEG 7?UFG TN ꟿDATN? NFH7 CAT ROtK
AZI
QR13
EKOZP
BSΦM L2PQZ
HELP SOMEONE LEARN TO READ

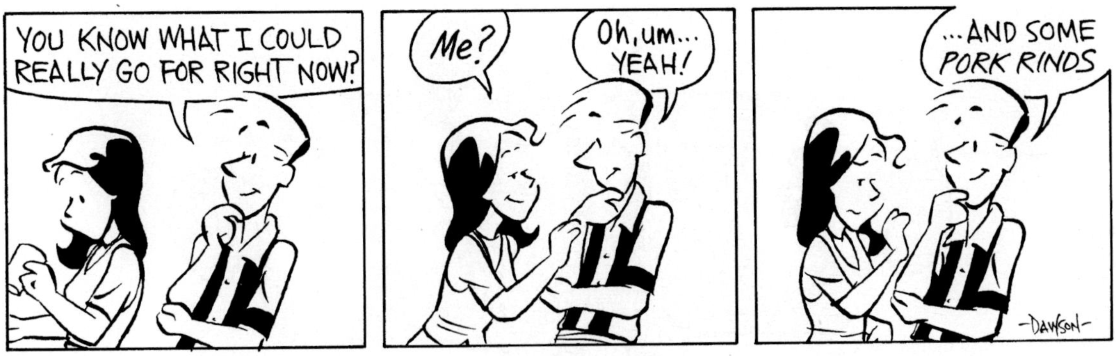

YOU KNOW WHAT I COULD REALLY GO FOR RIGHT NOW?
Me?
Oh, um... YEAH!
...AND SOME PORK RINDS
-DAWSON-

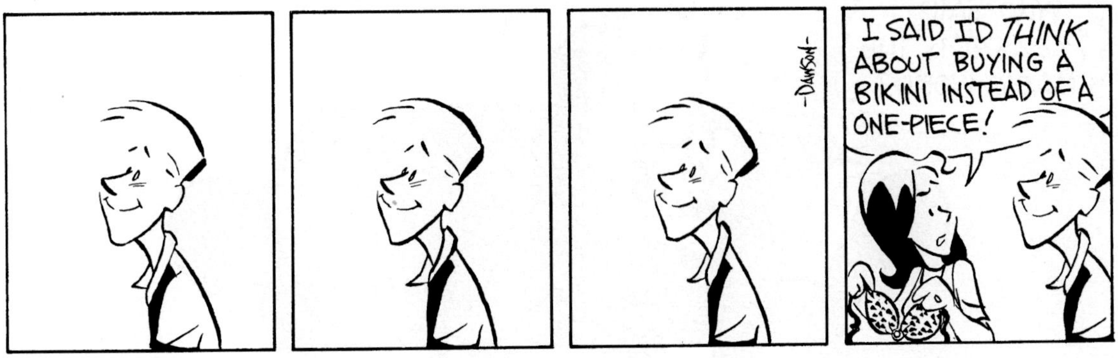

-DAWSON-
I SAID I'D THINK ABOUT BUYING A BIKINI INSTEAD OF A ONE-PIECE!

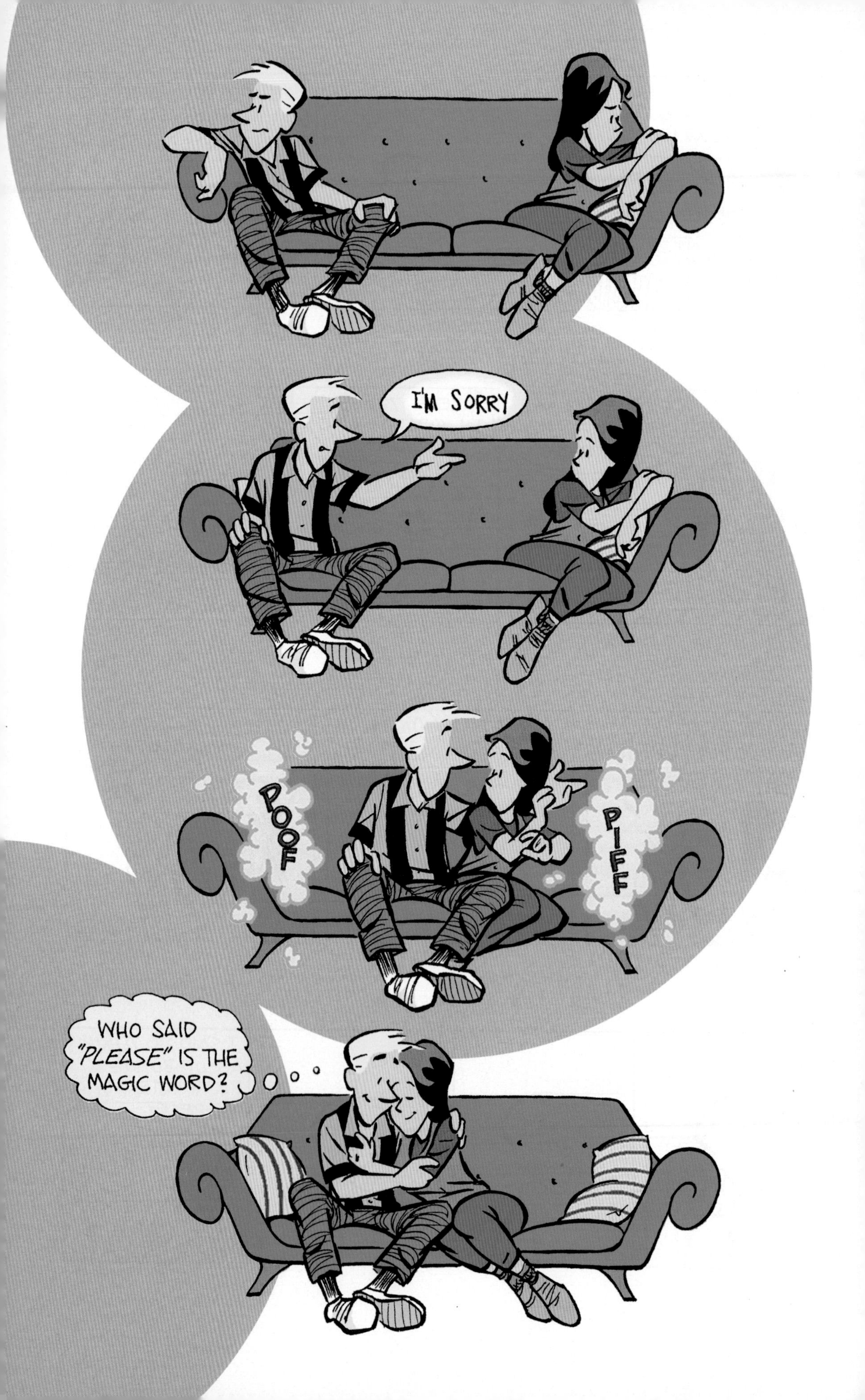

I'M SORRY
POOF
PIFF
WHO SAID "PLEASE" IS THE MAGIC WORD?

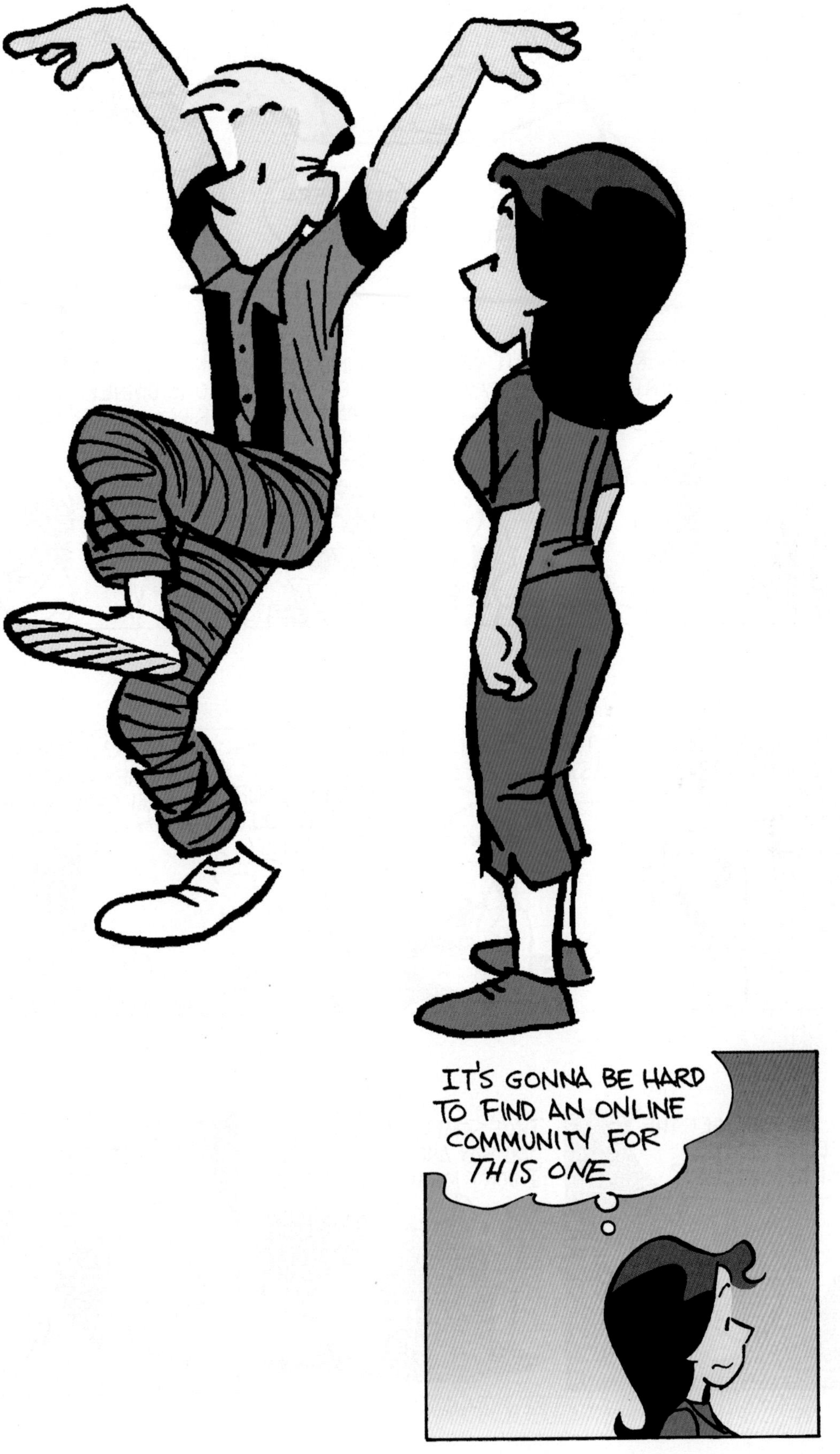
IT'S GONNA BE HARD TO FIND AN ONLINE COMMUNITY FOR THIS ONE

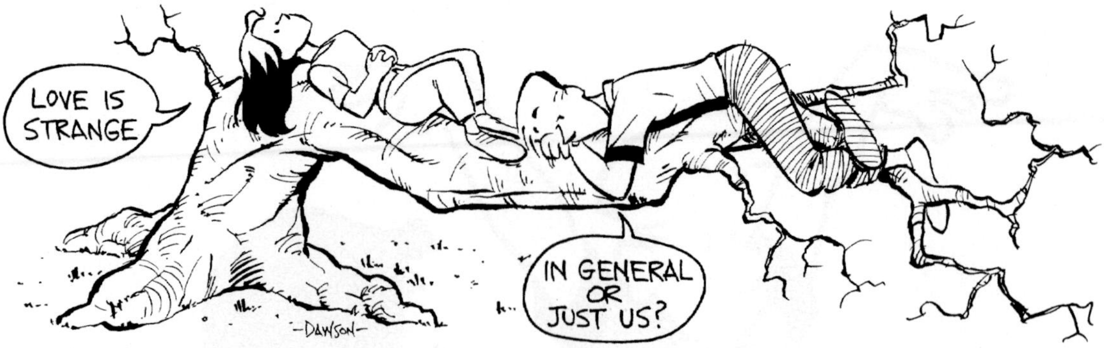
LOVE IS STRANGE
IN GENERAL OR JUST US?
-DAWSON-

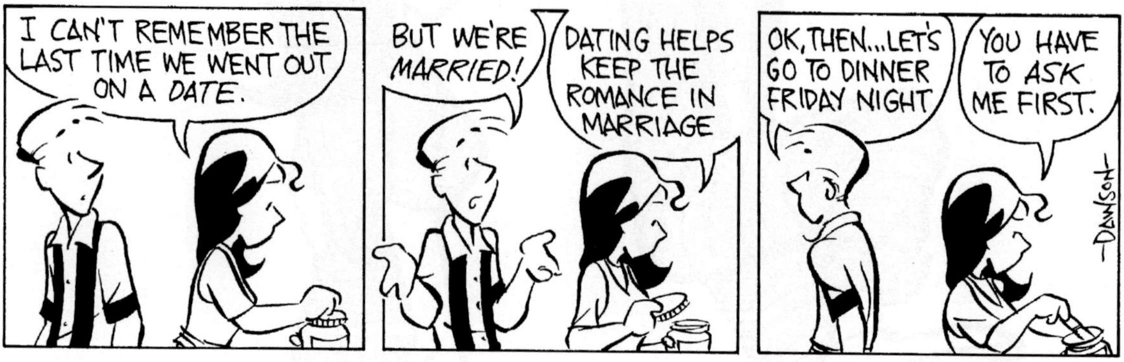
I CAN'T REMEMBER THE LAST TIME WE WENT OUT ON A *DATE*.
BUT WE'RE *MARRIED!*
DATING HELPS KEEP THE ROMANCE IN MARRIAGE
OK, THEN...LET'S GO TO DINNER FRIDAY NIGHT
YOU HAVE TO *ASK* ME FIRST.
-DAWSON-

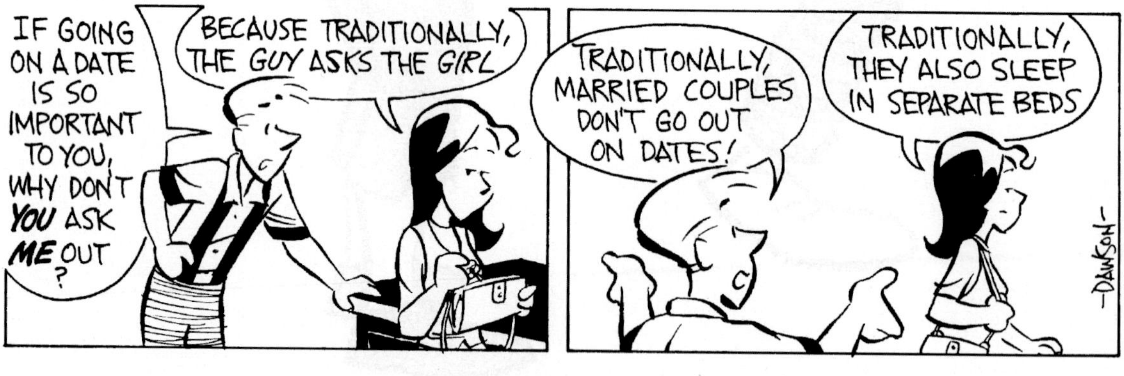
IF GOING ON A DATE IS SO IMPORTANT TO YOU, WHY DON'T **YOU** ASK **ME** OUT?
BECAUSE TRADITIONALLY, THE *GUY* ASKS THE *GIRL*
TRADITIONALLY, MARRIED COUPLES DON'T GO OUT ON DATES!
TRADITIONALLY, THEY ALSO SLEEP IN SEPARATE BEDS
-DAWSON-

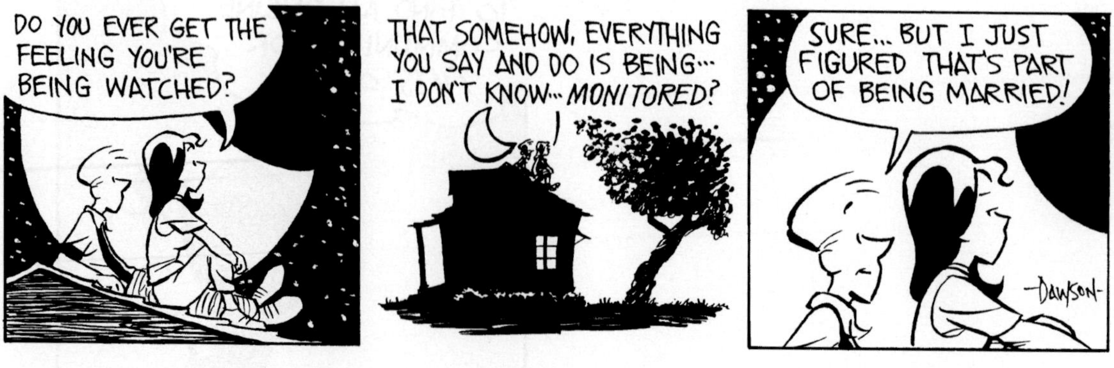
DO YOU EVER GET THE FEELING YOU'RE BEING WATCHED?
THAT SOMEHOW, EVERYTHING YOU SAY AND DO IS BEING... I DON'T KNOW... *MONITORED?*
SURE... BUT I JUST FIGURED THAT'S PART OF BEING MARRIED!
-DAWSON-

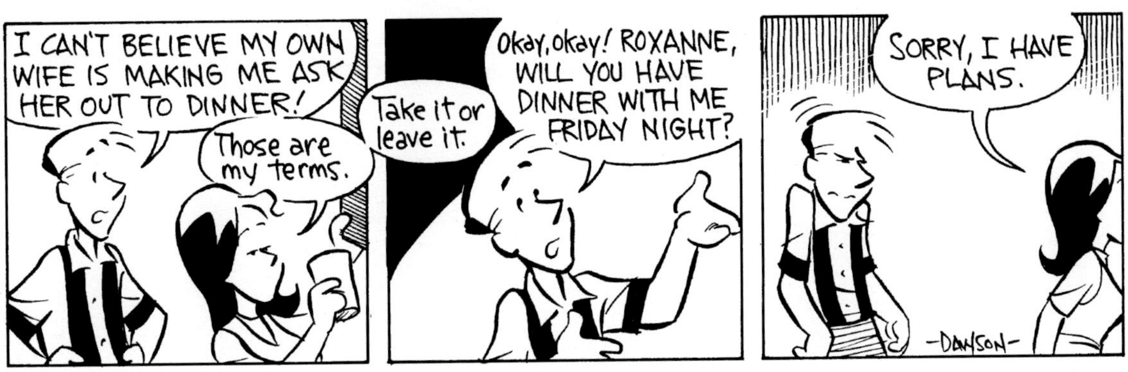
I CAN'T BELIEVE MY OWN WIFE IS MAKING ME ASK HER OUT TO DINNER!
Those are my terms.
Take it or leave it.
Okay, okay! ROXANNE, WILL YOU HAVE DINNER WITH ME FRIDAY NIGHT?
SORRY, I HAVE PLANS.
-DAWSON-

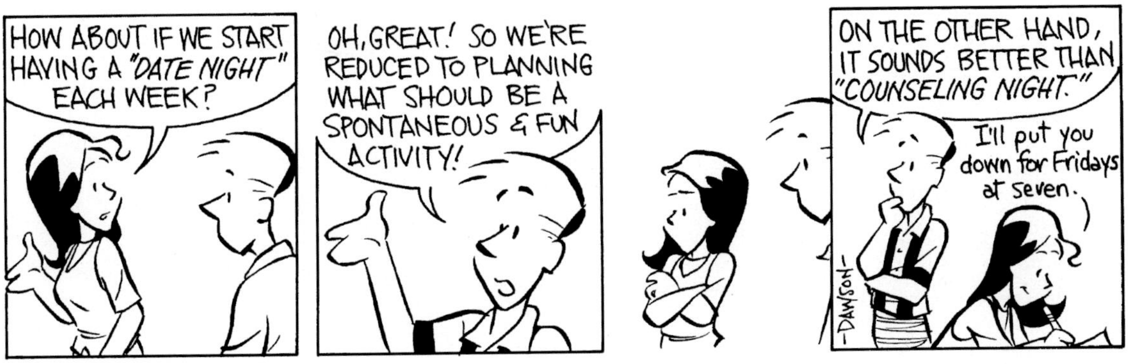
HOW ABOUT IF WE START HAVING A "DATE NIGHT" EACH WEEK?
OH, GREAT! SO WE'RE REDUCED TO PLANNING WHAT SHOULD BE A SPONTANEOUS & FUN ACTIVITY!
ON THE OTHER HAND, IT SOUNDS BETTER THAN "COUNSELING NIGHT."
I'll put you down for Fridays at seven.
-DAWSON-

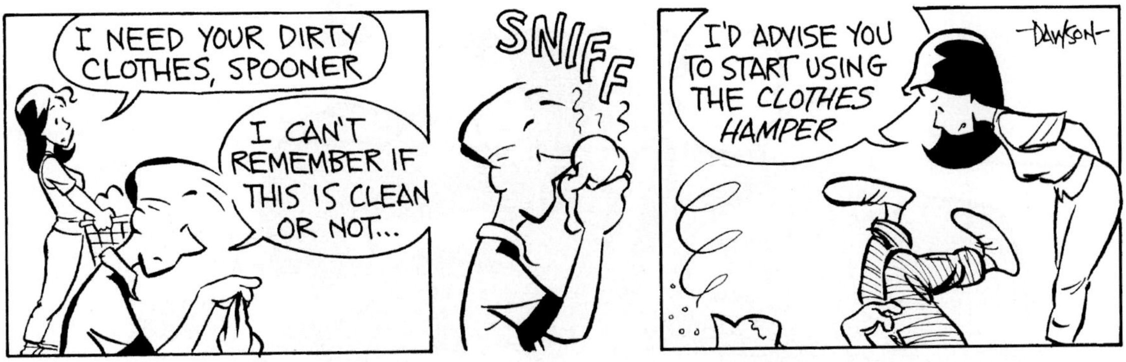
I NEED YOUR DIRTY CLOTHES, SPOONER
I CAN'T REMEMBER IF THIS IS CLEAN OR NOT...
SNIFF
I'D ADVISE YOU TO START USING THE CLOTHES HAMPER
-DAWSON-

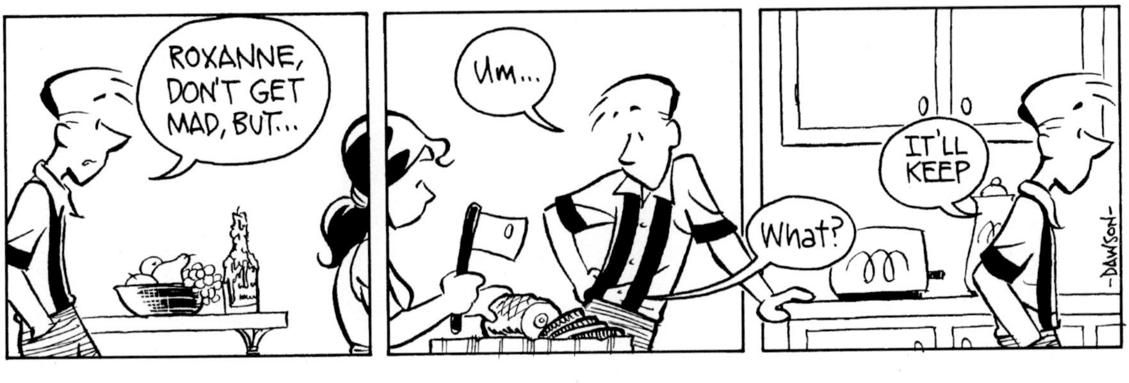
ROXANNE, DON'T GET MAD, BUT...
Um...
What?
IT'LL KEEP
-DAWSON-

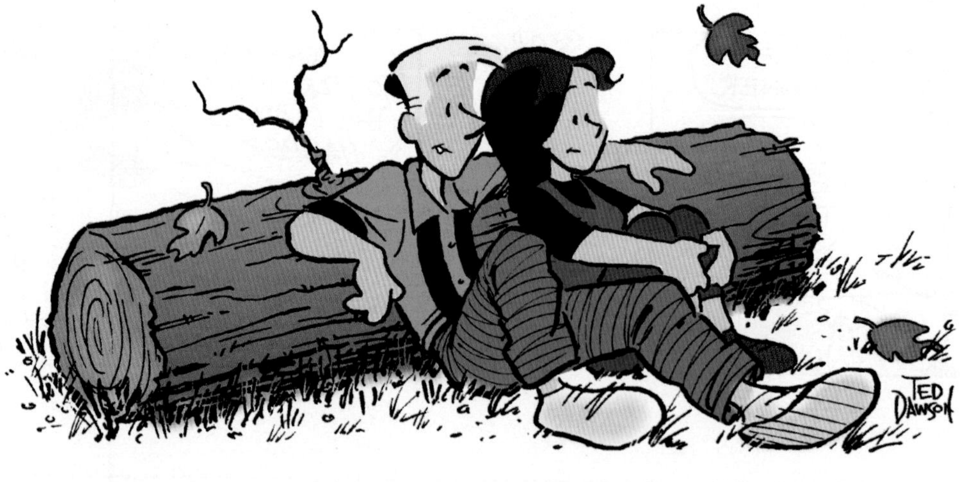
TED
DAWSON

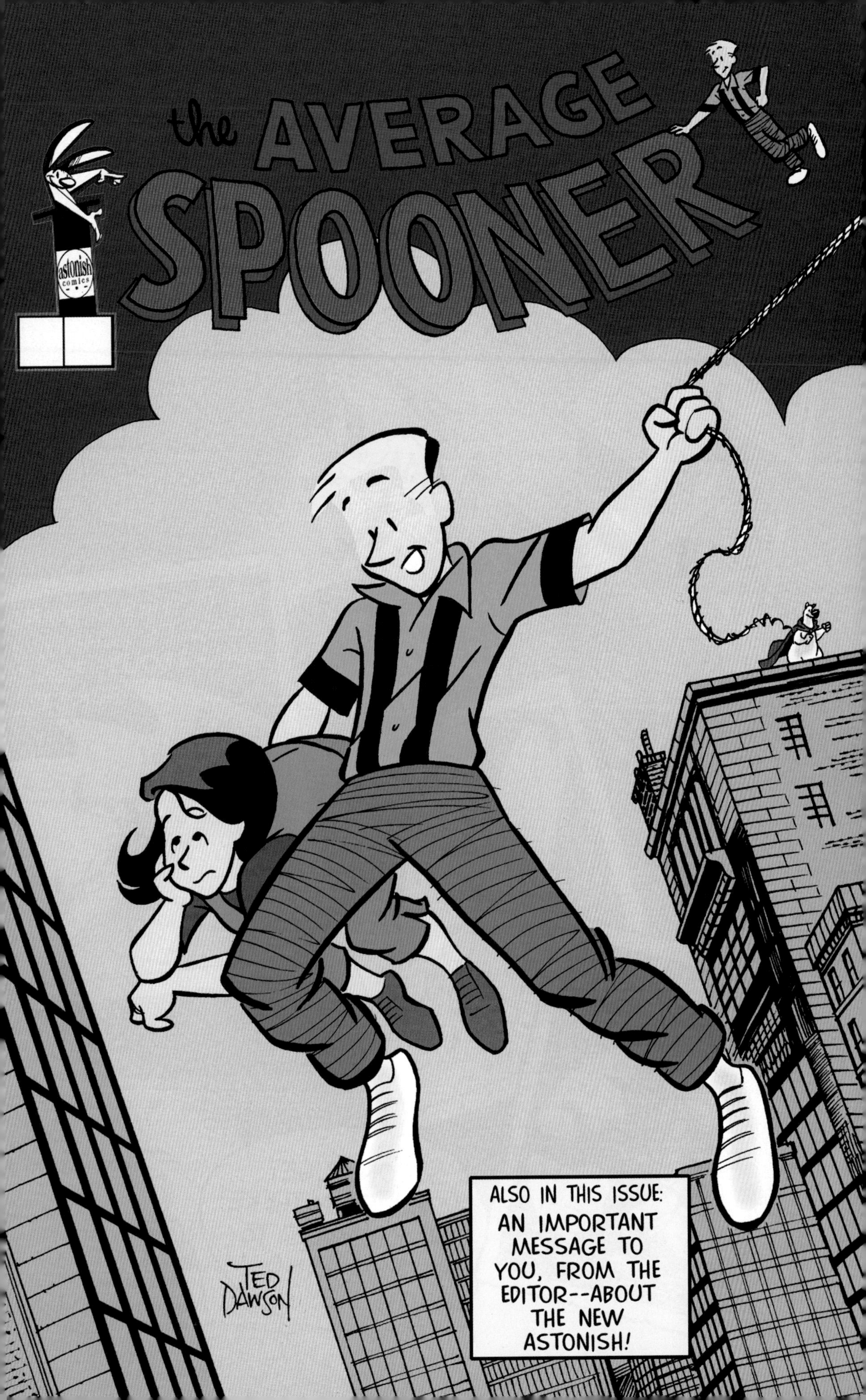
the AVERAGE SPOONER
astonish comics
TED DAWSON
ALSO IN THIS ISSUE:
AN IMPORTANT MESSAGE TO YOU, FROM THE EDITOR--ABOUT THE NEW ASTONISH!

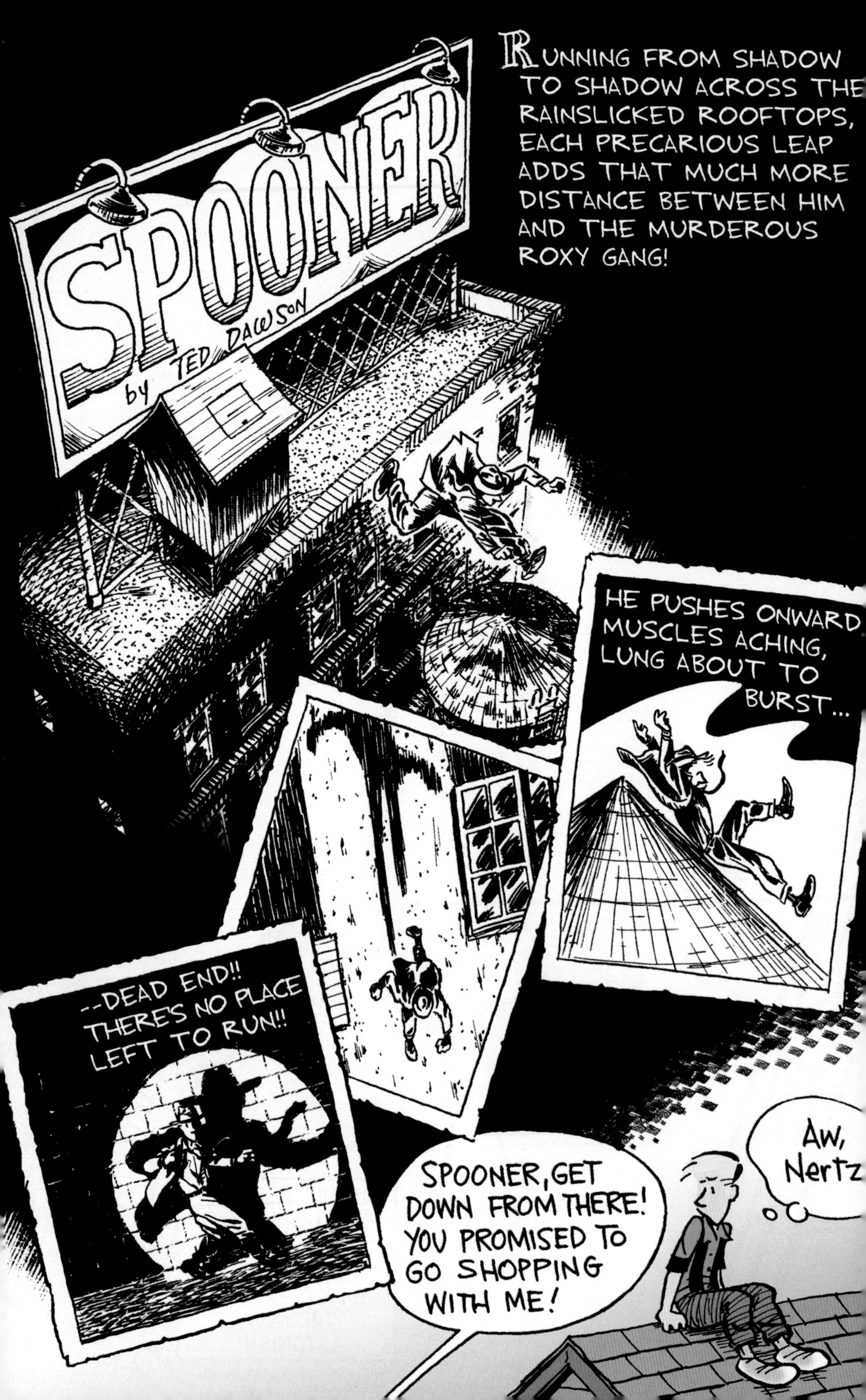
SPOONER
by TED DAWSON
RUNNING FROM SHADOW TO SHADOW ACROSS THE RAINSLICKED ROOFTOPS, EACH PRECARIOUS LEAP ADDS THAT MUCH MORE DISTANCE BETWEEN HIM AND THE MURDEROUS ROXY GANG!
HE PUSHES ONWARD MUSCLES ACHING, LUNG ABOUT TO BURST...
--DEAD END!! THERE'S NO PLACE LEFT TO RUN!!
SPOONER, GET DOWN FROM THERE! YOU PROMISED TO GO SHOPPING WITH ME!
AW, Nertz

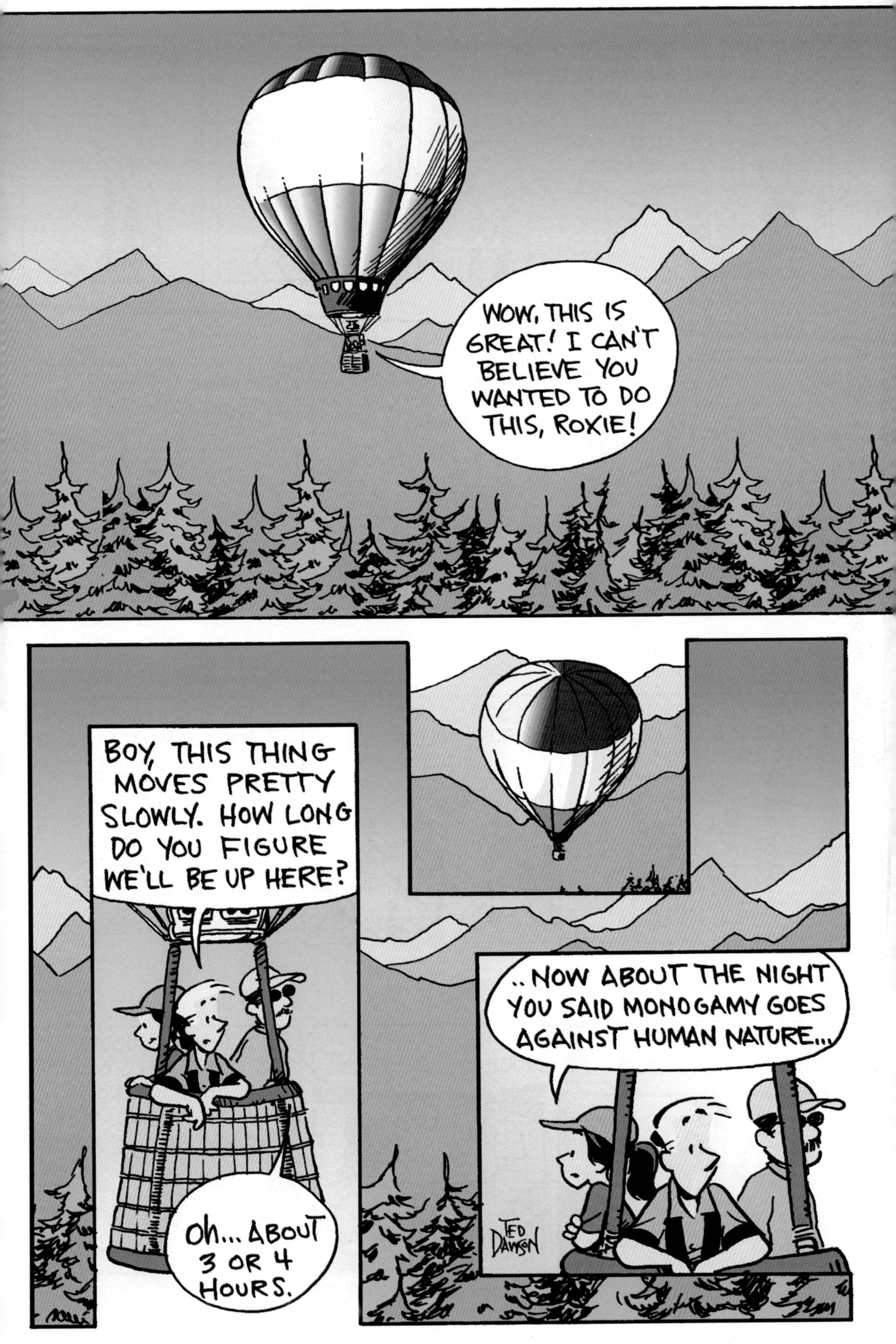
WOW, THIS IS GREAT! I CAN'T BELIEVE YOU WANTED TO DO THIS, ROXIE!
BOY, THIS THING MOVES PRETTY SLOWLY. HOW LONG DO YOU FIGURE WE'LL BE UP HERE?
Oh... ABOUT 3 OR 4 HOURS.
..NOW ABOUT THE NIGHT YOU SAID MONOGAMY GOES AGAINST HUMAN NATURE...
TED DAWSON

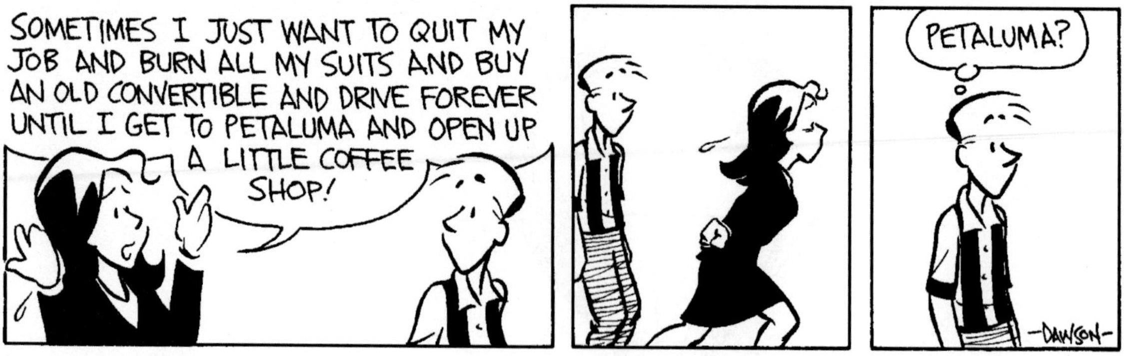
SOMETIMES I JUST WANT TO QUIT MY JOB AND BURN ALL MY SUITS AND BUY AN OLD CONVERTIBLE AND DRIVE FOREVER UNTIL I GET TO PETALUMA AND OPEN UP A LITTLE COFFEE SHOP!
PETALUMA?
-DAWSON-

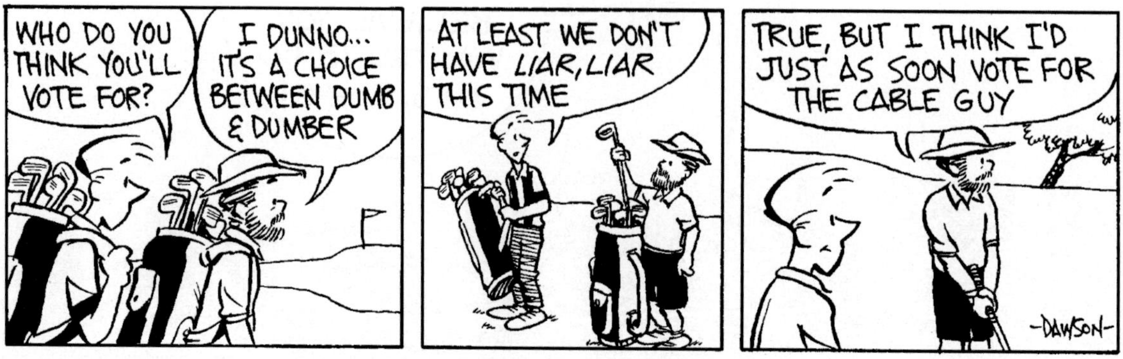
WHO DO YOU THINK YOU'LL VOTE FOR?
I DUNNO... IT'S A CHOICE BETWEEN DUMB & DUMBER
AT LEAST WE DON'T HAVE *LIAR, LIAR* THIS TIME
TRUE, BUT I THINK I'D JUST AS SOON VOTE FOR THE CABLE GUY
-DAWSON-

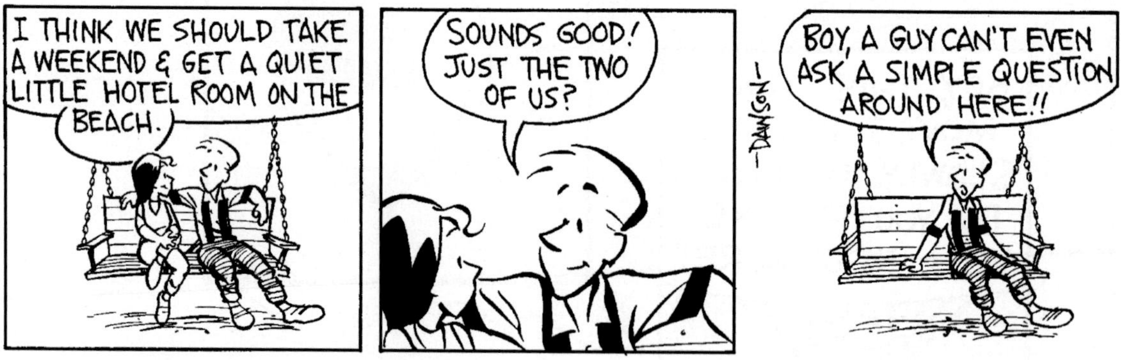
I THINK WE SHOULD TAKE A WEEKEND & GET A QUIET LITTLE HOTEL ROOM ON THE BEACH.
SOUNDS GOOD! JUST THE TWO OF US?
-DAWSON-
BOY, A GUY CAN'T EVEN ASK A SIMPLE QUESTION AROUND HERE!!

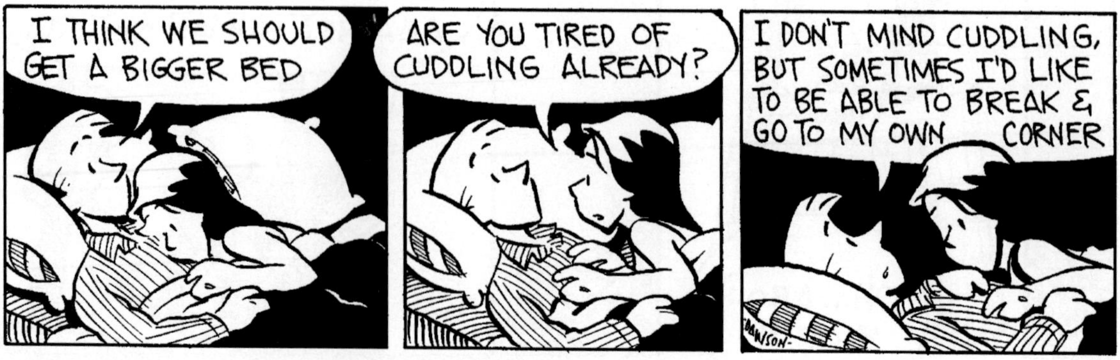
I THINK WE SHOULD GET A BIGGER BED
ARE YOU TIRED OF CUDDLING ALREADY?
I DON'T MIND CUDDLING, BUT SOMETIMES I'D LIKE TO BE ABLE TO BREAK & GO TO MY OWN CORNER
-DAWSON-

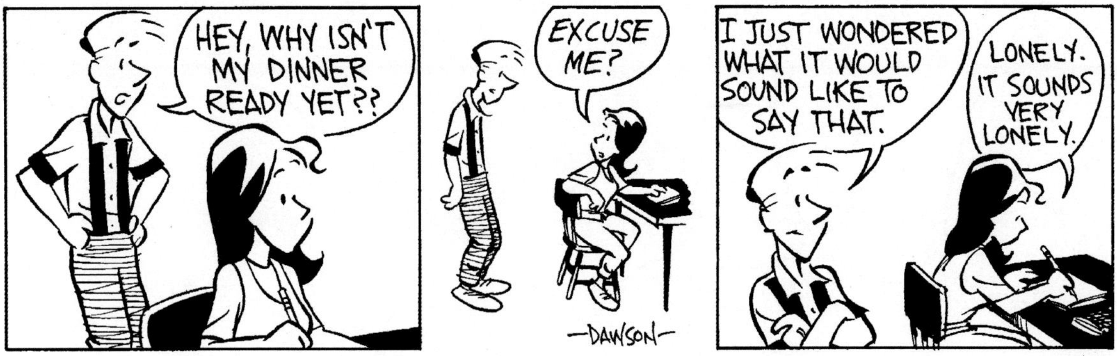
HEY, WHY ISN'T MY DINNER READY YET??
EXCUSE ME?
—DAWSON—
I JUST WONDERED WHAT IT WOULD SOUND LIKE TO SAY THAT.
LONELY. IT SOUNDS VERY LONELY.

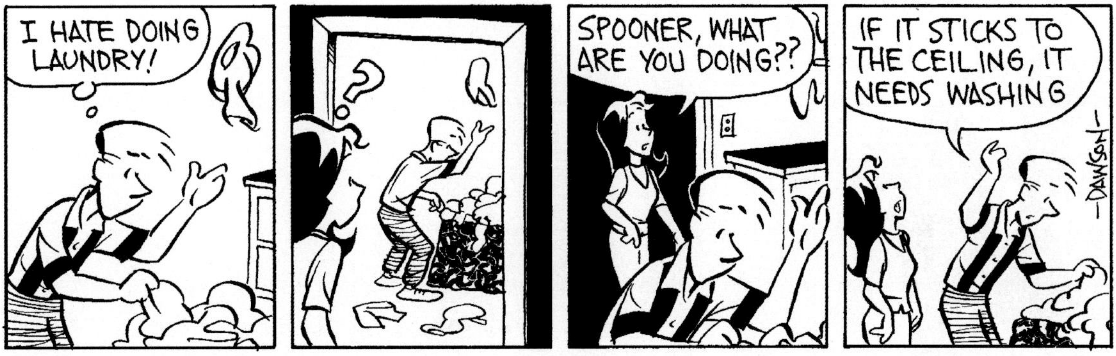
I HATE DOING LAUNDRY!
?
SPOONER, WHAT ARE YOU DOING??
IF IT STICKS TO THE CEILING, IT NEEDS WASHING
—DAWSON—

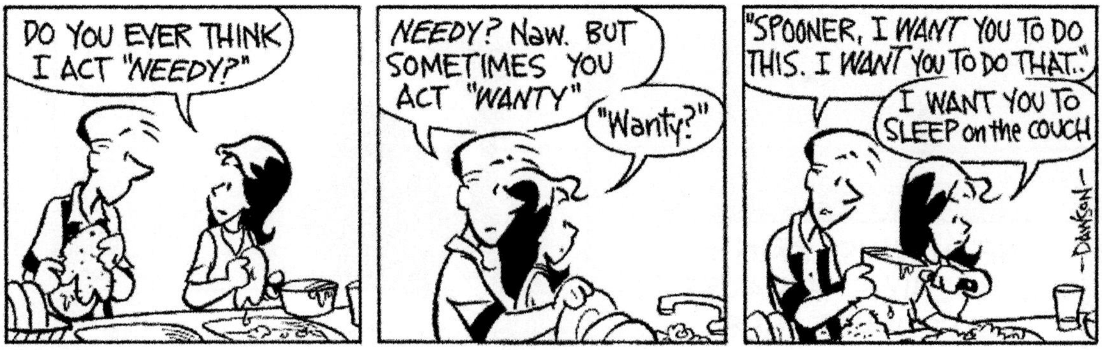
DO YOU EVER THINK I ACT "NEEDY?"
NEEDY? Naw. BUT SOMETIMES YOU ACT "WANTY"
"Wanty?"
"SPOONER, I WANT YOU TO DO THIS. I WANT YOU TO DO THAT."
I WANT YOU TO SLEEP on the COUCH
—DAWSON—

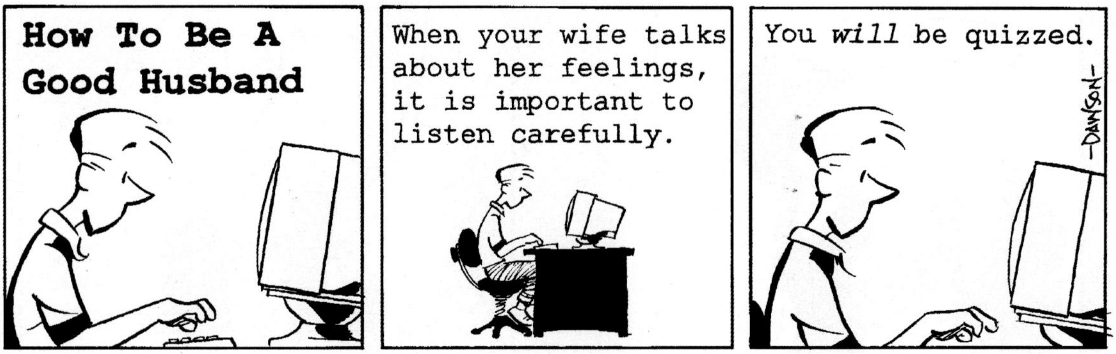
How To Be A Good Husband
When your wife talks about her feelings, it is important to listen carefully.
You will be quizzed.
—DAWSON—

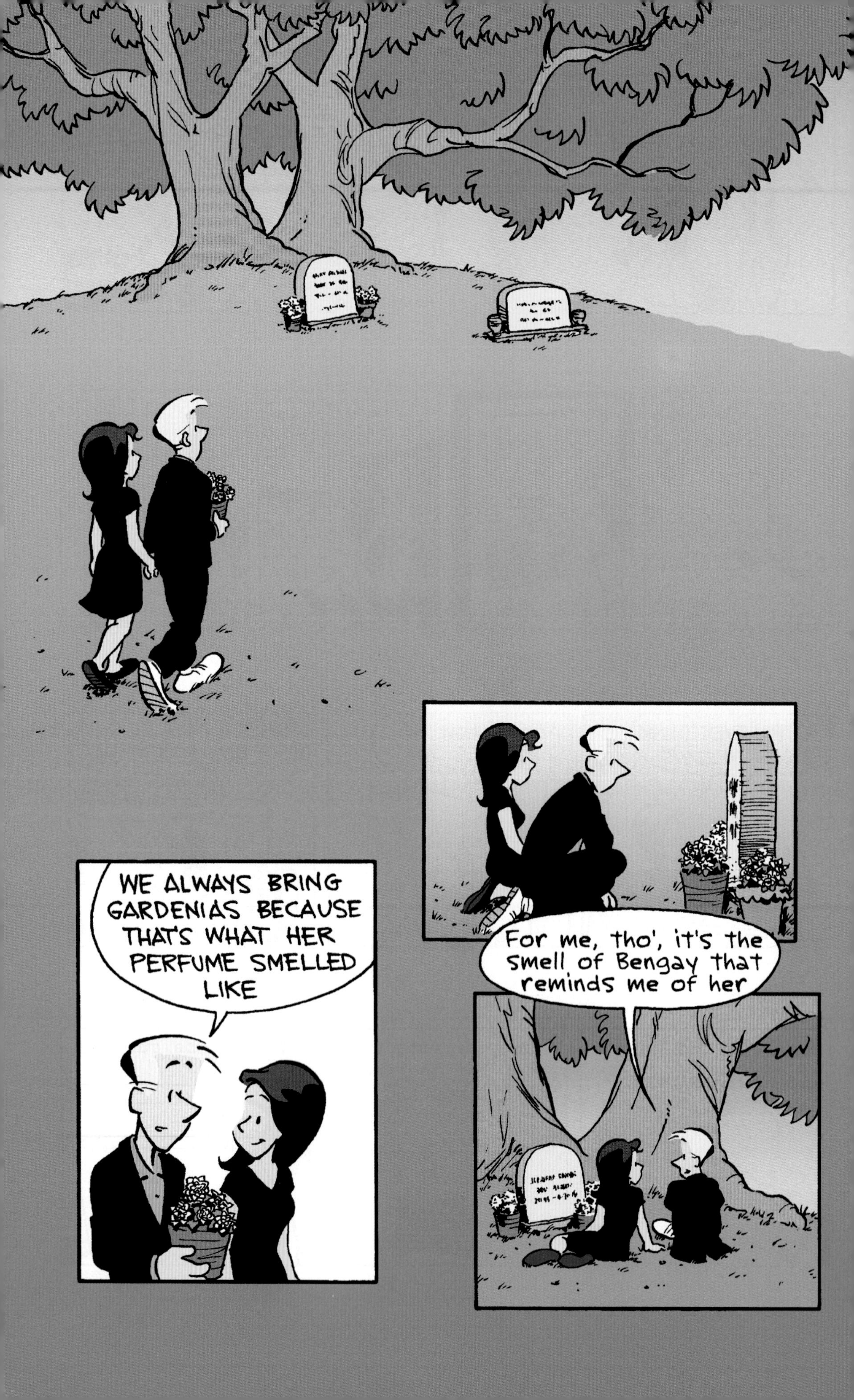
WE ALWAYS BRING GARDENIAS BECAUSE THAT'S WHAT HER PERFUME SMELLED LIKE
For me, tho', it's the smell of Bengay that reminds me of her

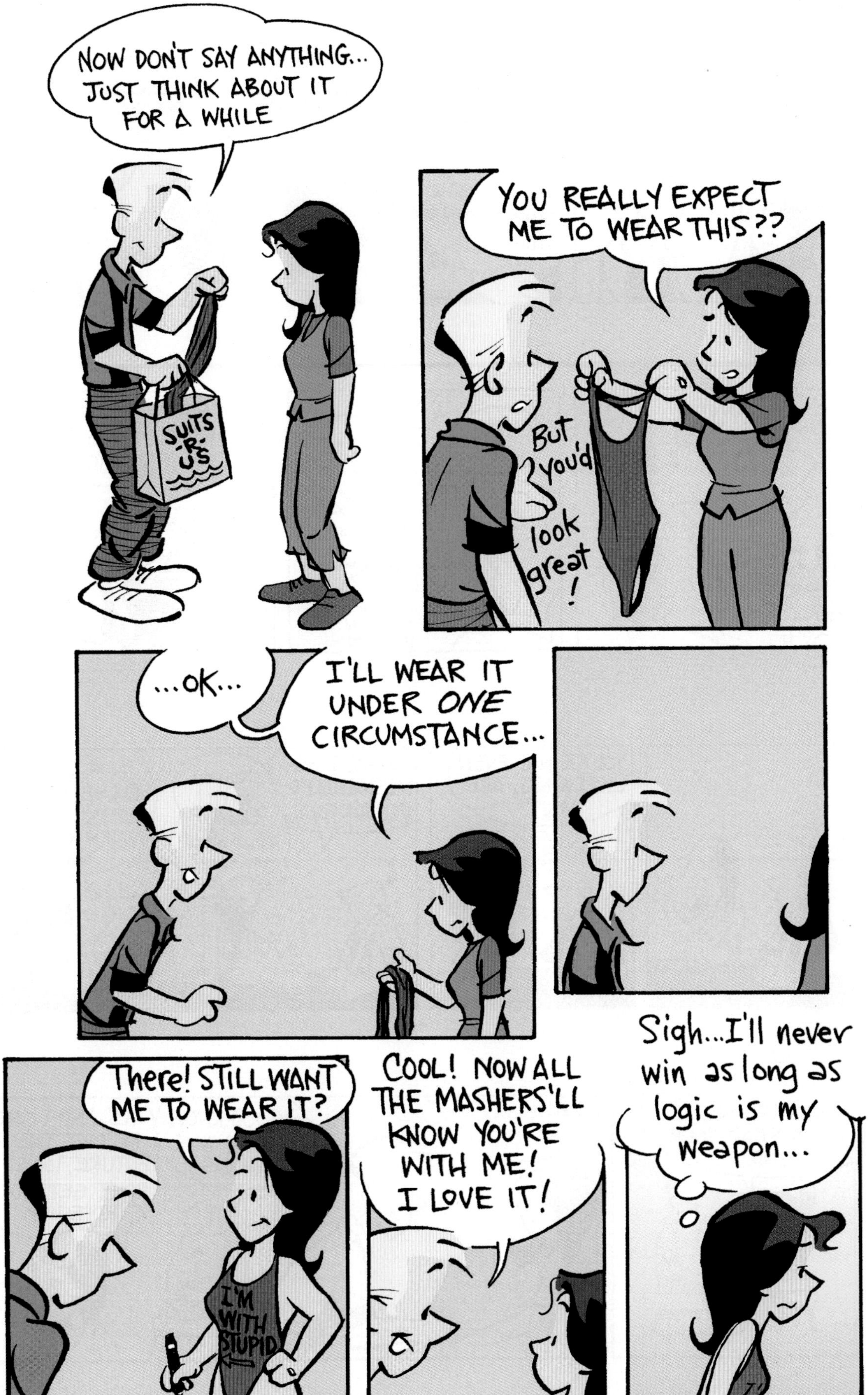
NOW DON'T SAY ANYTHING... JUST THINK ABOUT IT FOR A WHILE
SUITS -R- US
YOU REALLY EXPECT ME TO WEAR THIS??
But you'd look great!
...OK...
I'LL WEAR IT UNDER *ONE* CIRCUMSTANCE...
There! STILL WANT ME TO WEAR IT?
I'M WITH STUPID
COOL! NOW ALL THE MASHERS'LL KNOW YOU'RE WITH ME! I LOVE IT!
Sigh...I'll never win as long as logic is my weapon...

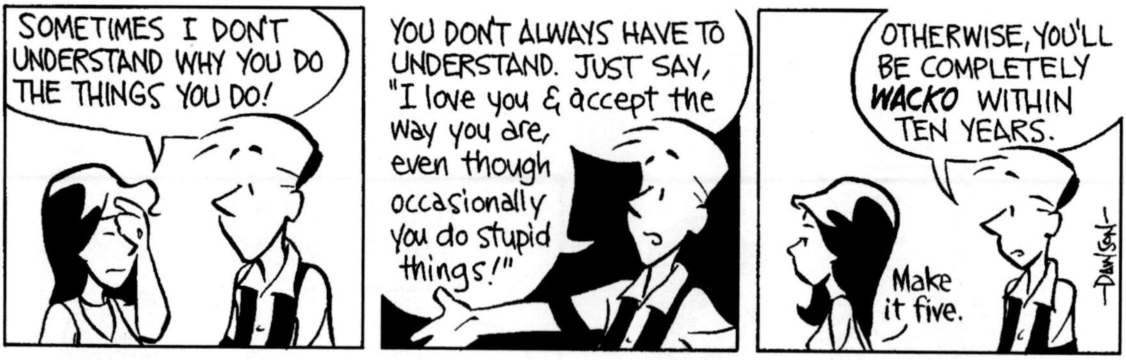
SOMETIMES I DON'T UNDERSTAND WHY YOU DO THE THINGS YOU DO!
YOU DON'T ALWAYS HAVE TO UNDERSTAND. JUST SAY, "I love you & accept the way you are, even though occasionally you do stupid things!"
OTHERWISE, YOU'LL BE COMPLETELY WACKO WITHIN TEN YEARS.
Make it five.
DAWSON

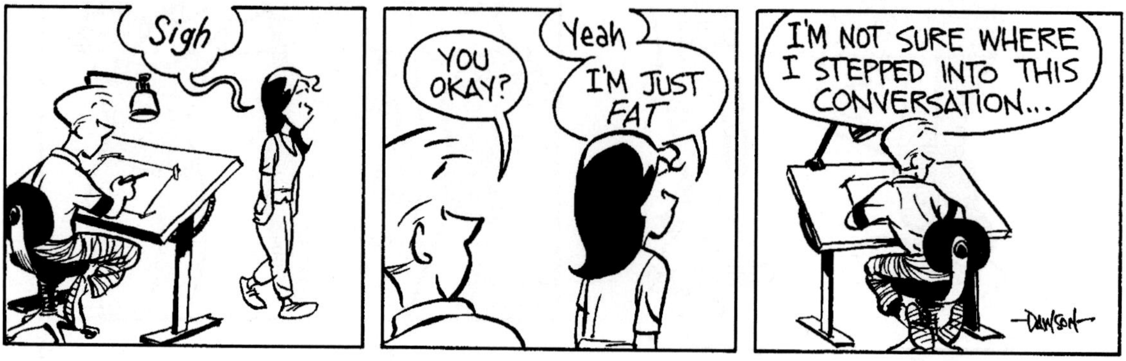
Sigh
YOU OKAY?
Yeah
I'M JUST FAT
I'M NOT SURE WHERE I STEPPED INTO THIS CONVERSATION...
DAWSON

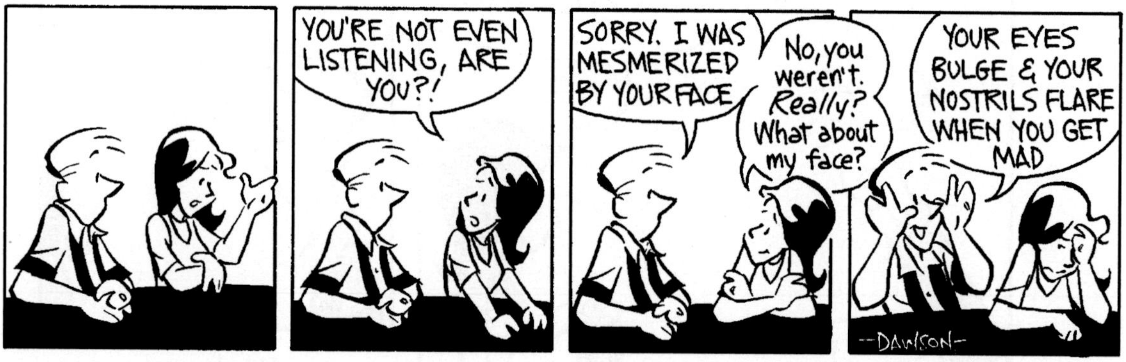
YOU'RE NOT EVEN LISTENING, ARE YOU?!
SORRY. I WAS MESMERIZED BY YOUR FACE
No, you weren't. Really? What about my face?
YOUR EYES BULGE & YOUR NOSTRILS FLARE WHEN YOU GET MAD
DAWSON

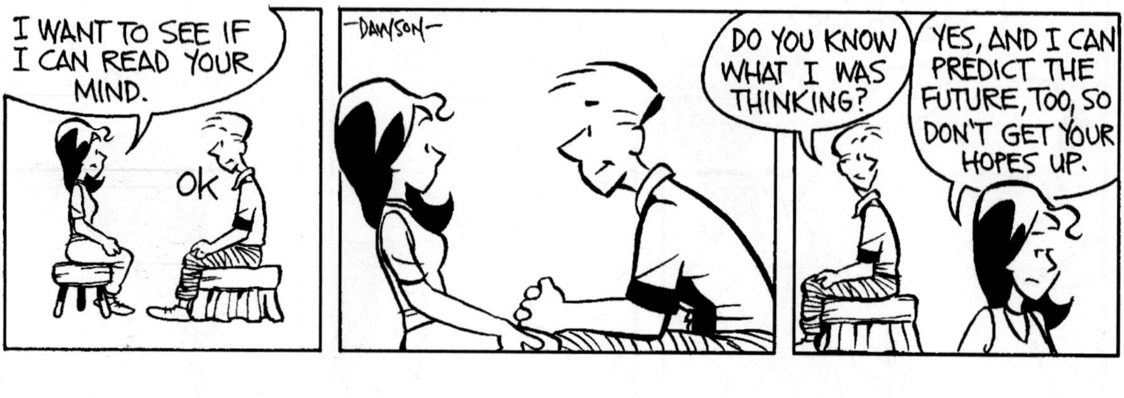
I WANT TO SEE IF I CAN READ YOUR MIND.
OK
DAWSON
DO YOU KNOW WHAT I WAS THINKING?
YES, AND I CAN PREDICT THE FUTURE, TOO, SO DON'T GET YOUR HOPES UP.

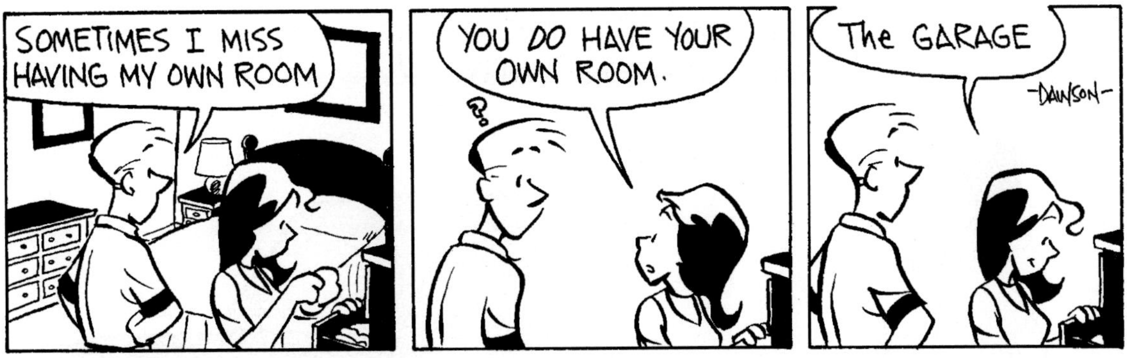
SOMETIMES I MISS HAVING MY OWN ROOM
?
YOU *DO* HAVE YOUR OWN ROOM.
The GARAGE
-DAWSON-

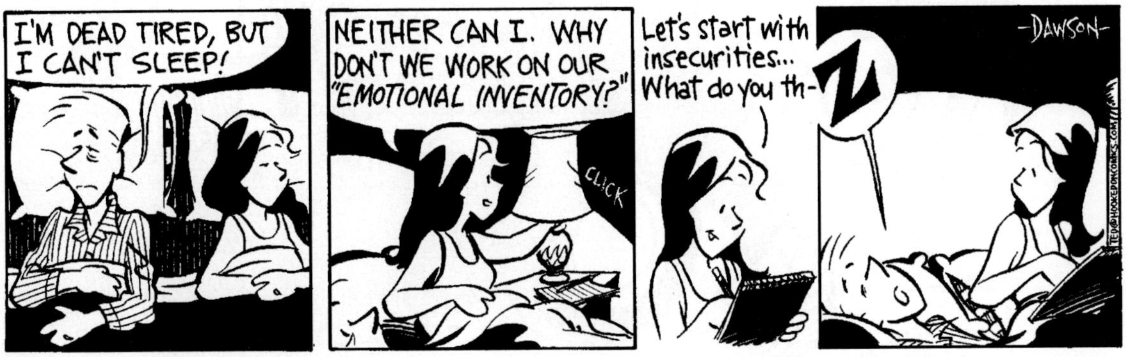
I'M DEAD TIRED, BUT I CAN'T SLEEP!
NEITHER CAN I. WHY DON'T WE WORK ON OUR "EMOTIONAL INVENTORY?"
CLICK
Let's start with insecurities... What do you th-
Z
-DAWSON-

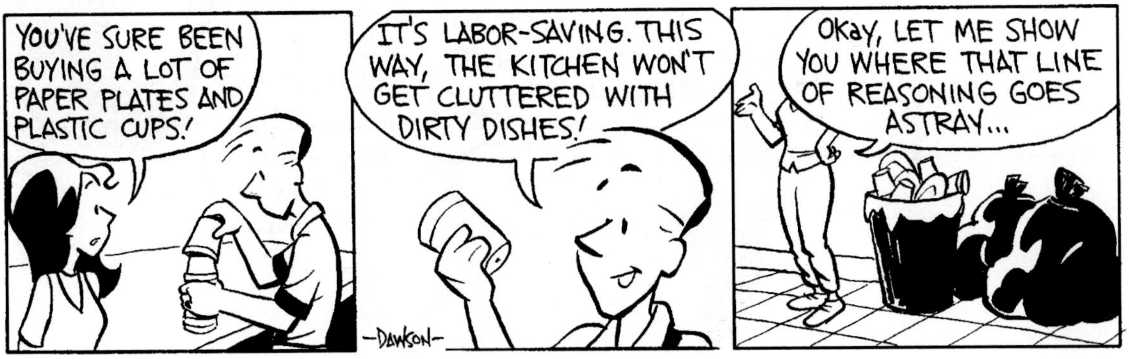
YOU'VE SURE BEEN BUYING A LOT OF PAPER PLATES AND PLASTIC CUPS!
IT'S LABOR-SAVING. THIS WAY, THE KITCHEN WON'T GET CLUTTERED WITH DIRTY DISHES!
-DAWSON-
OKay, LET ME SHOW YOU WHERE THAT LINE OF REASONING GOES ASTRAY...

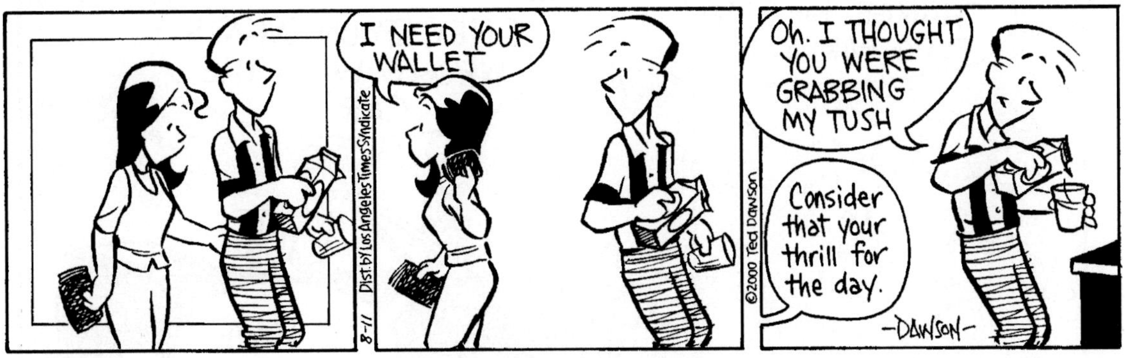
8-11
Dist. by Los Angeles Times Syndicate
I NEED YOUR WALLET
©2000 Ted Dawson
Oh. I THOUGHT YOU WERE GRABBING MY TUSH
Consider that your thrill for the day.
-DAWSON-

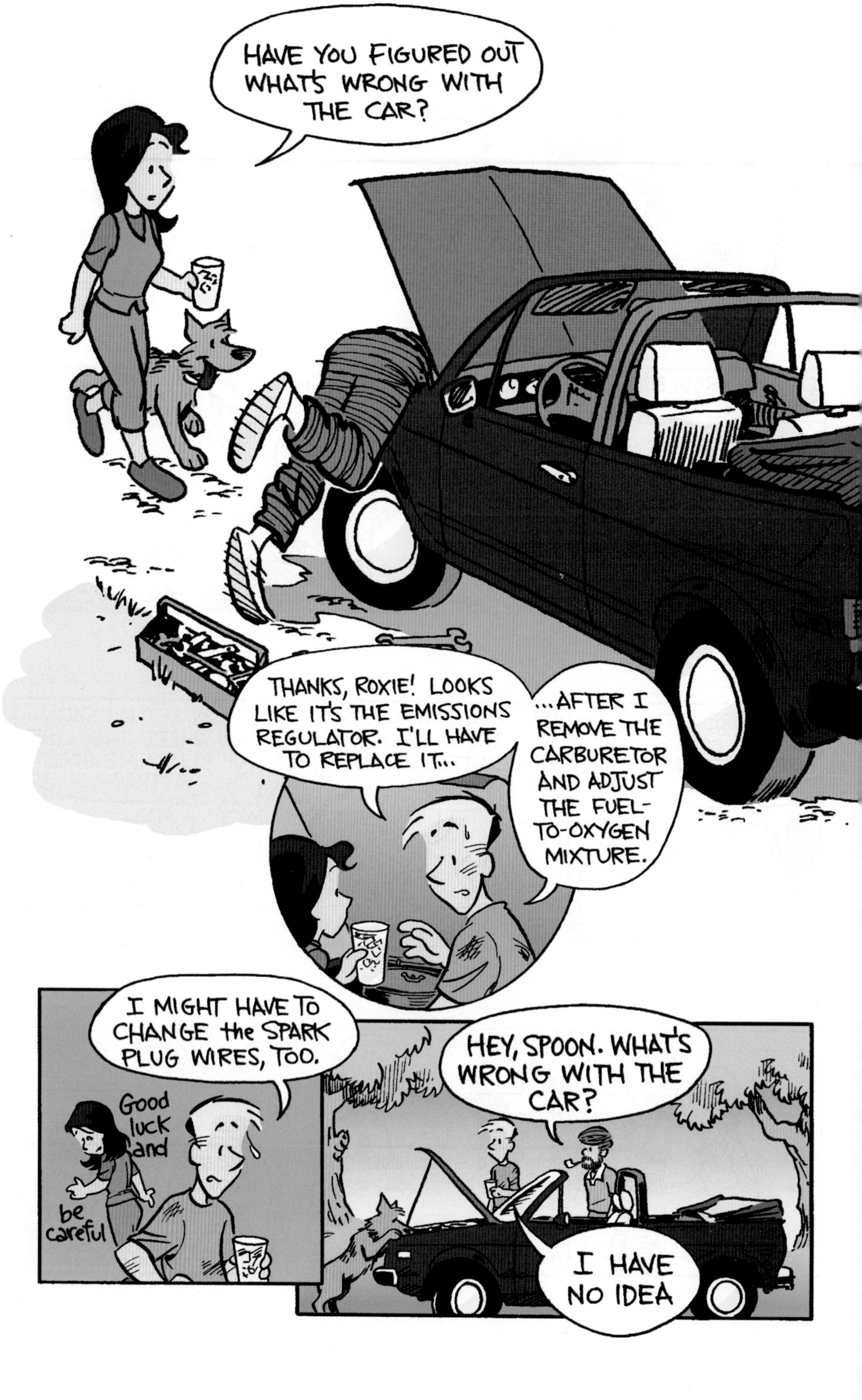
HAVE YOU FIGURED OUT WHAT'S WRONG WITH THE CAR?
THANKS, ROXIE! LOOKS LIKE IT'S THE EMISSIONS REGULATOR. I'LL HAVE TO REPLACE IT...
...AFTER I REMOVE THE CARBURETOR AND ADJUST THE FUEL-TO-OXYGEN MIXTURE.
I MIGHT HAVE TO CHANGE the SPARK PLUG WIRES, TOO.
Good luck and
be careful
HEY, SPOON. WHAT'S WRONG WITH THE CAR?
I HAVE NO IDEA

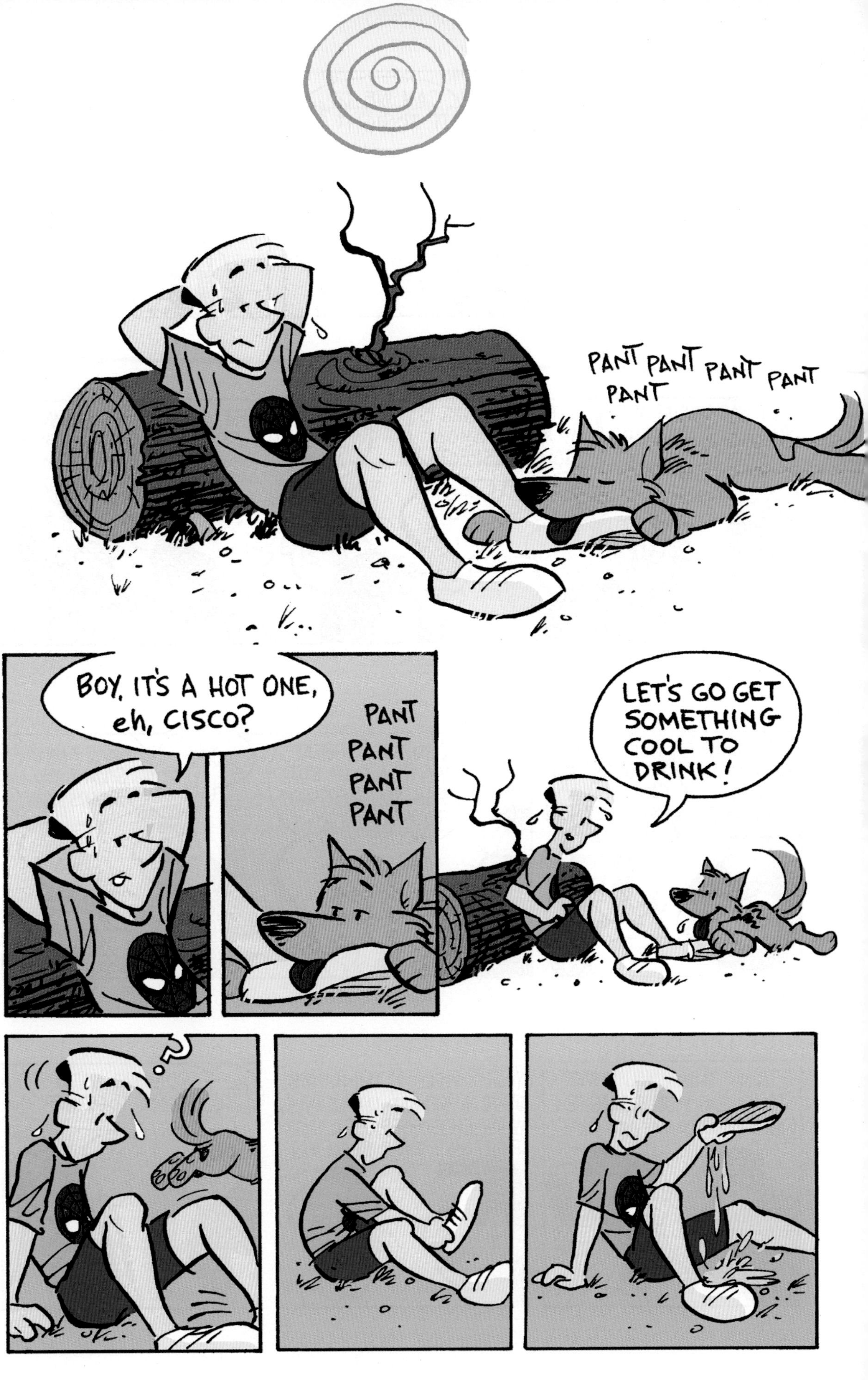
PANT PANT PANT PANT
PANT
BOY, IT'S A HOT ONE, eh, CISCO?
PANT
PANT
PANT
PANT
LET'S GO GET SOMETHING COOL TO DRINK!

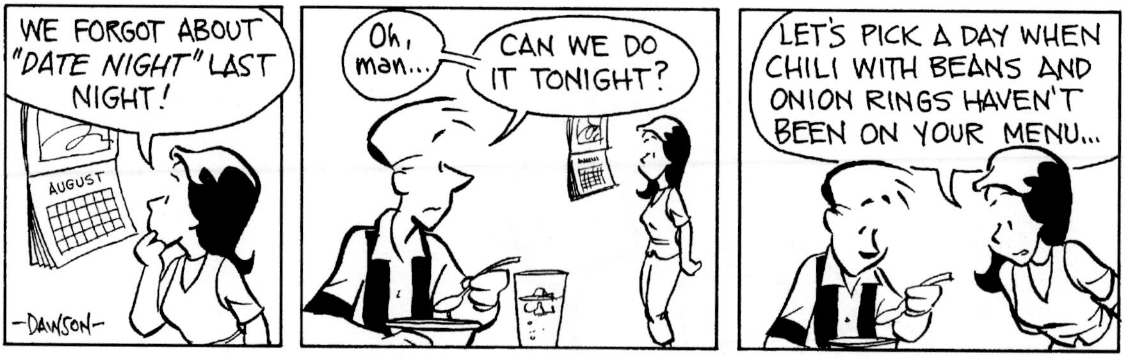
WE FORGOT ABOUT "DATE NIGHT" LAST NIGHT!
AUGUST
-DAWSON-
Oh, man...
CAN WE DO IT TONIGHT?
LET'S PICK A DAY WHEN CHILI WITH BEANS AND ONION RINGS HAVEN'T BEEN ON YOUR MENU...

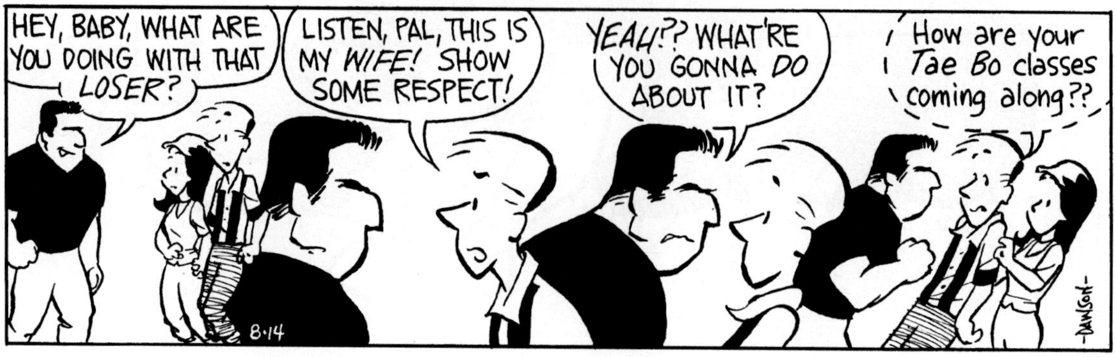
HEY, BABY, WHAT ARE YOU DOING WITH THAT LOSER?
LISTEN, PAL, THIS IS MY WIFE! SHOW SOME RESPECT!
8·14
YEAH?? WHAT'RE YOU GONNA DO ABOUT IT?
How are your Tae Bo classes coming along??
-DAWSON-

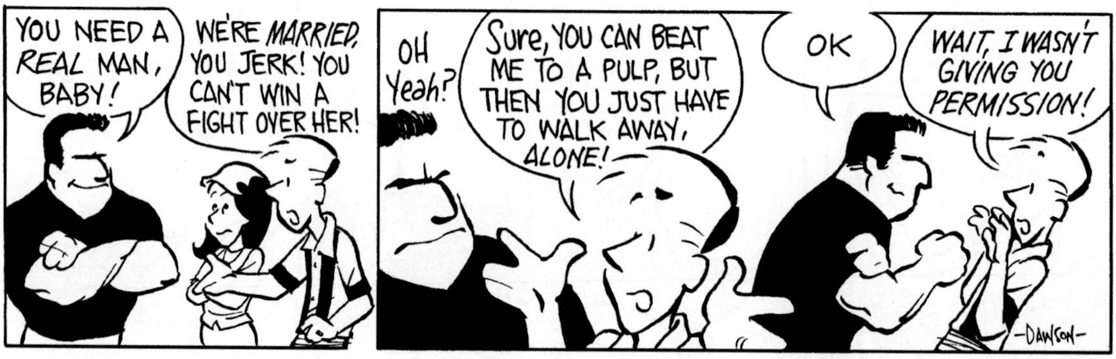
YOU NEED A REAL MAN, BABY!
WE'RE MARRIED, YOU JERK! YOU CAN'T WIN A FIGHT OVER HER!
OH Yeah?
Sure, YOU CAN BEAT ME TO A PULP, BUT THEN YOU JUST HAVE TO WALK AWAY, ALONE!
OK
WAIT, I WASN'T GIVING YOU PERMISSION!
-DAWSON-

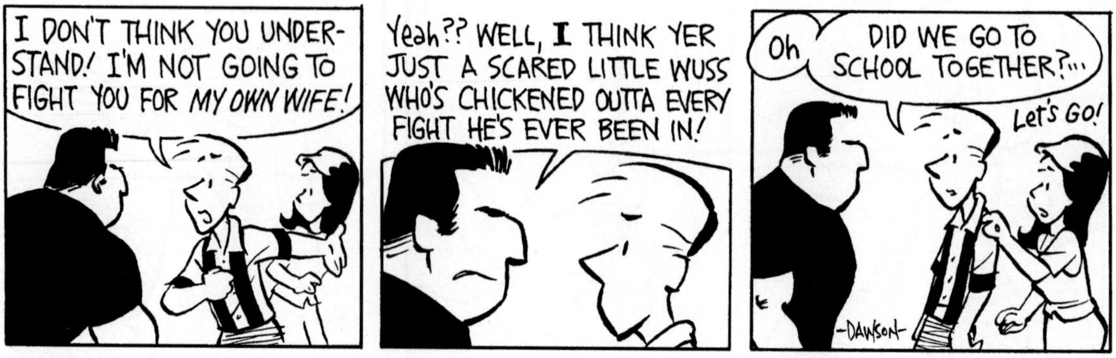
I DON'T THINK YOU UNDERSTAND! I'M NOT GOING TO FIGHT YOU FOR MY OWN WIFE!
Yeah?? WELL, I THINK YER JUST A SCARED LITTLE WUSS WHO'S CHICKENED OUTTA EVERY FIGHT HE'S EVER BEEN IN!
Oh
DID WE GO TO SCHOOL TOGETHER?...
Let's GO!
-DAWSON-

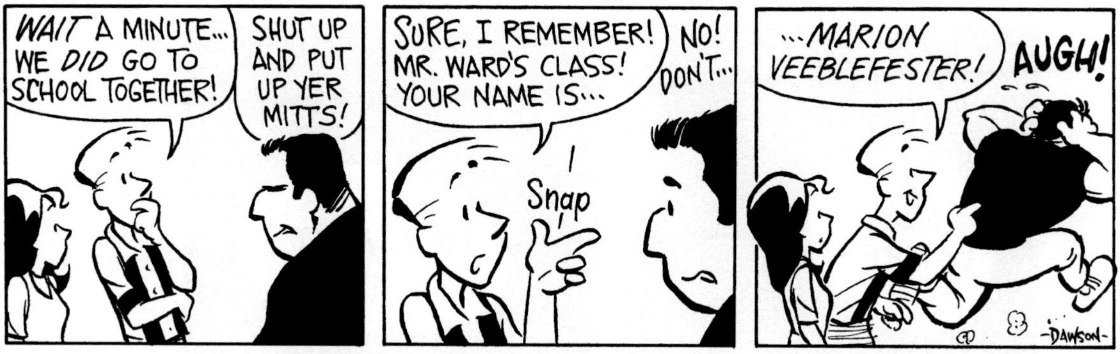
WAIT A MINUTE... WE DID GO TO SCHOOL TOGETHER!
SHUT UP AND PUT UP YER MITTS!
SURE, I REMEMBER! MR. WARD'S CLASS! YOUR NAME IS...
NO! DON'T...
Snap
...MARION VEEBLEFESTER!
AUGH!
-DAWSON-

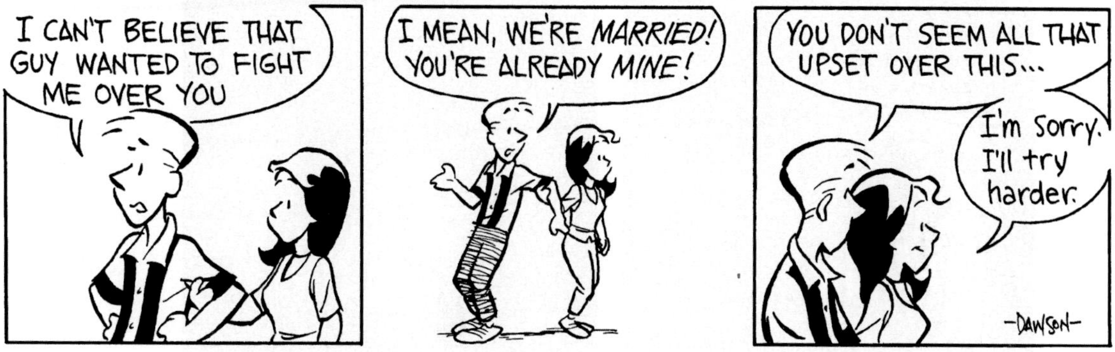
I CAN'T BELIEVE THAT GUY WANTED TO FIGHT ME OVER YOU
I MEAN, WE'RE MARRIED! YOU'RE ALREADY MINE!
YOU DON'T SEEM ALL THAT UPSET OVER THIS...
I'm sorry. I'll try harder.
-DAWSON-

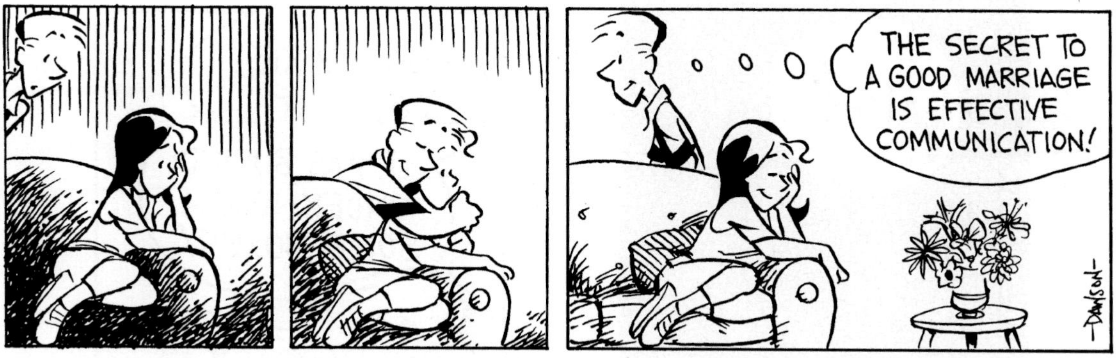
THE SECRET TO A GOOD MARRIAGE IS EFFECTIVE COMMUNICATION!
-DAWSON-

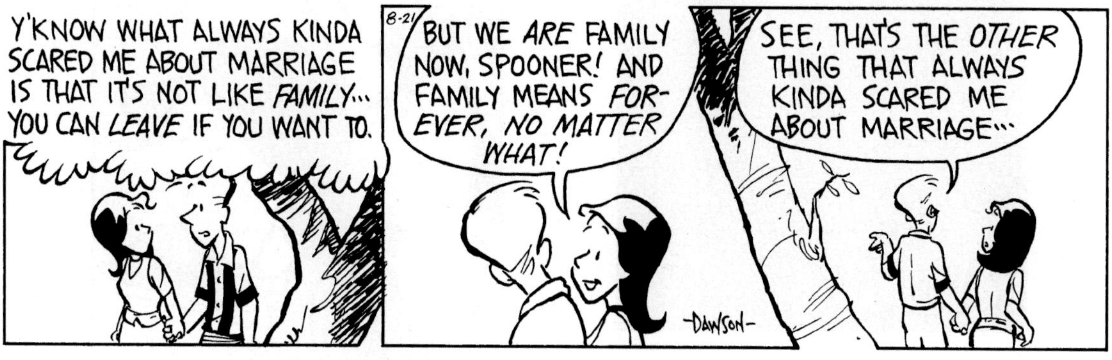
Y'KNOW WHAT ALWAYS KINDA SCARED ME ABOUT MARRIAGE IS THAT IT'S NOT LIKE FAMILY... YOU CAN LEAVE IF YOU WANT TO.
8-21
BUT WE ARE FAMILY NOW, SPOONER! AND FAMILY MEANS FOR-EVER, NO MATTER WHAT!
-DAWSON-
SEE, THAT'S THE OTHER THING THAT ALWAYS KINDA SCARED ME ABOUT MARRIAGE...

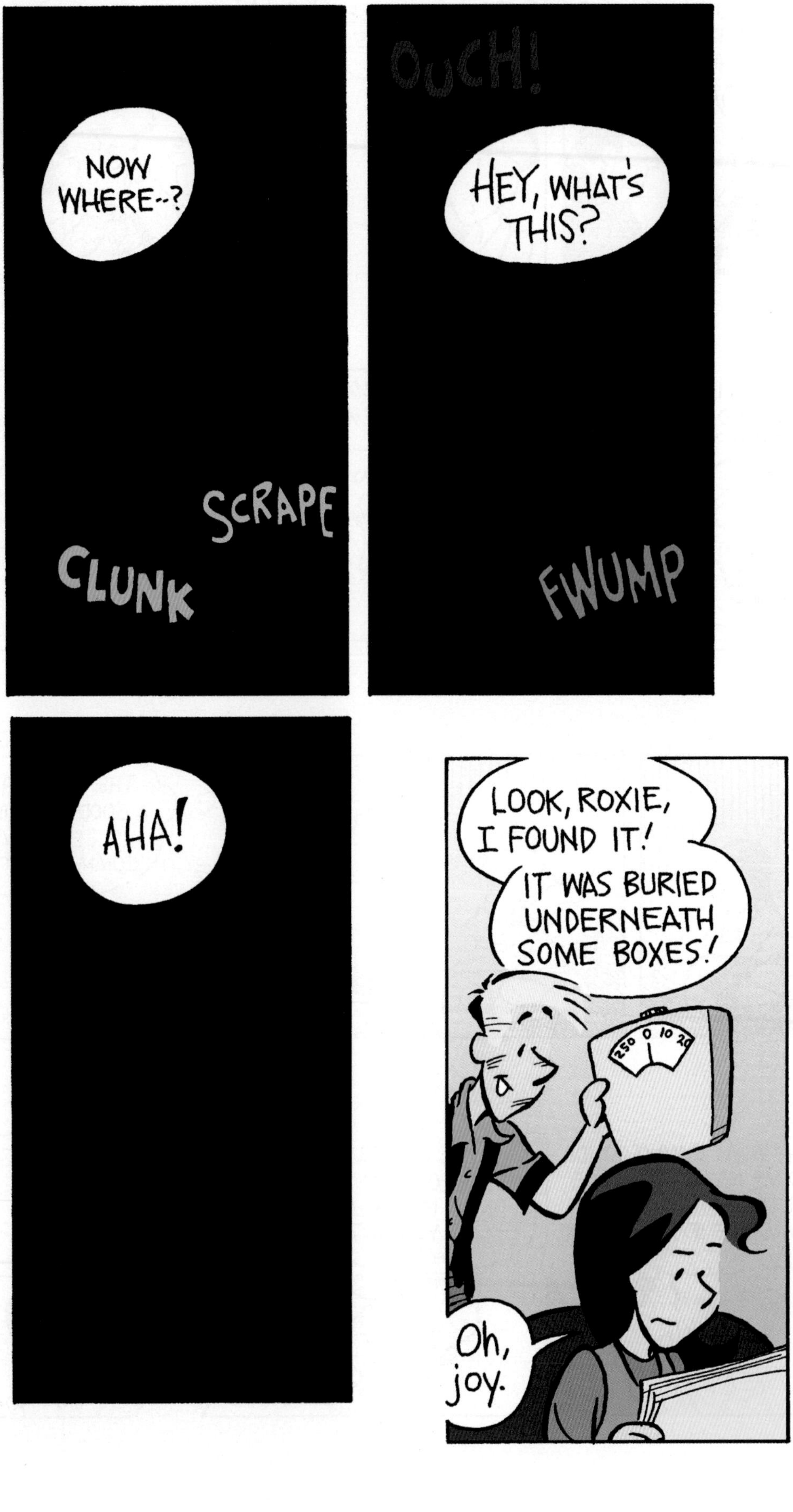
NOW WHERE--?
SCRAPE
CLUNK
OUCH!
HEY, WHAT'S THIS?
FWUMP
AHA!
LOOK, ROXIE, I FOUND IT!
IT WAS BURIED UNDERNEATH SOME BOXES!
250 0 10 20
Oh, joy.

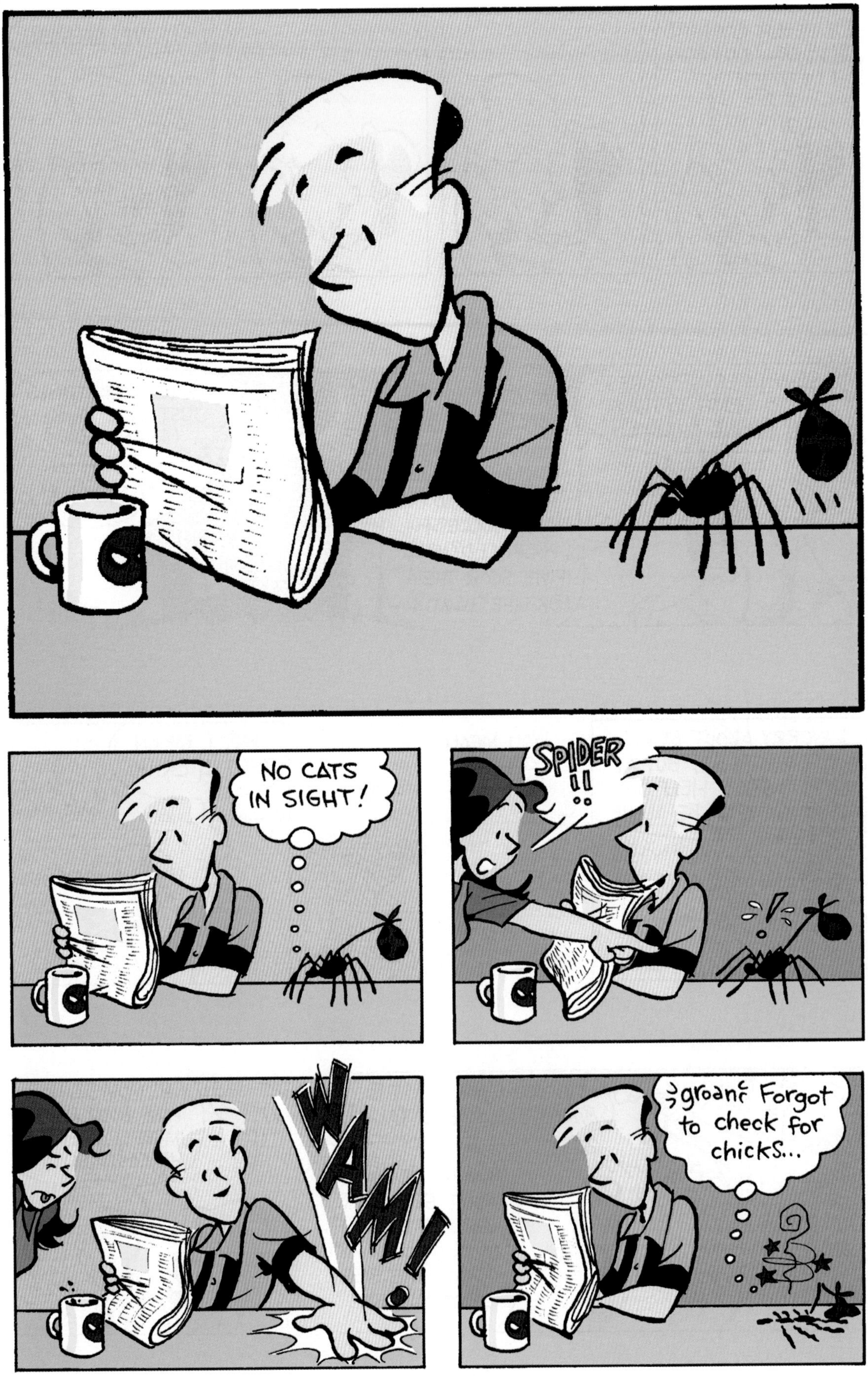
NO CATS IN SIGHT!
SPIDER!!
WAM!
groan Forgot to check for chicks...

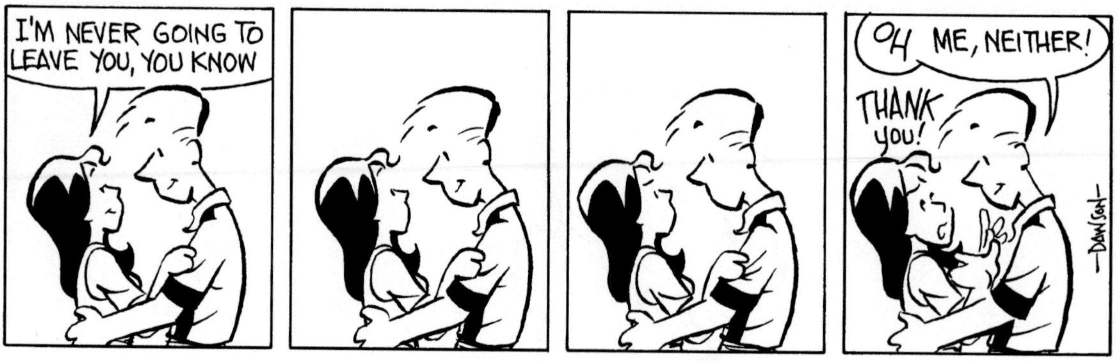
I'M NEVER GOING TO LEAVE YOU, YOU KNOW
OH ME, NEITHER!
THANK YOU!
DAWSON

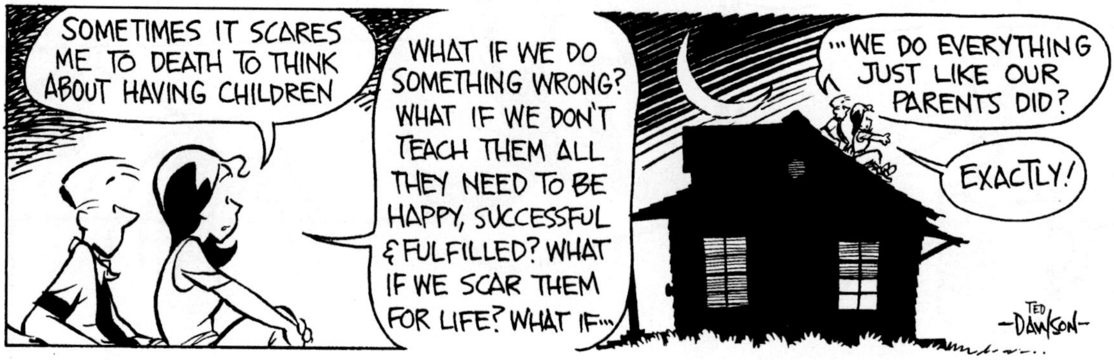
SOMETIMES IT SCARES ME TO DEATH TO THINK ABOUT HAVING CHILDREN
WHAT IF WE DO SOMETHING WRONG? WHAT IF WE DON'T TEACH THEM ALL THEY NEED TO BE HAPPY, SUCCESSFUL & FULFILLED? WHAT IF WE SCAR THEM FOR LIFE? WHAT IF...
...WE DO EVERYTHING JUST LIKE OUR PARENTS DID?
EXACTLY!
TED DAWSON

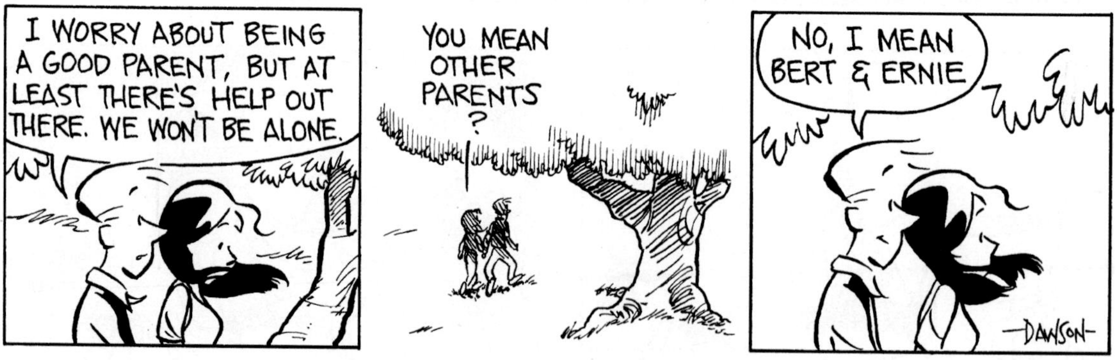
I WORRY ABOUT BEING A GOOD PARENT, BUT AT LEAST THERE'S HELP OUT THERE. WE WON'T BE ALONE.
YOU MEAN OTHER PARENTS ?
NO, I MEAN BERT & ERNIE
DAWSON

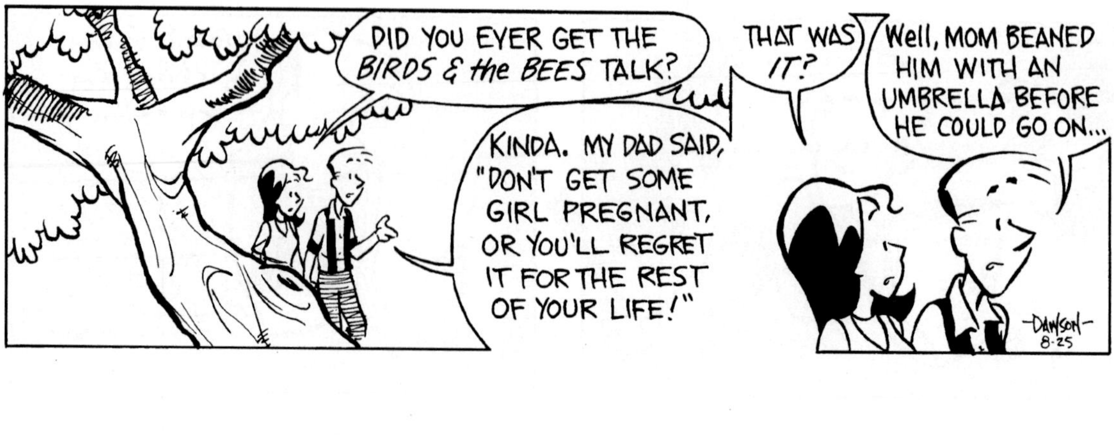
DID YOU EVER GET THE *BIRDS & the BEES* TALK?
KINDA. MY DAD SAID, "DON'T GET SOME GIRL PREGNANT, OR YOU'LL REGRET IT FOR THE REST OF YOUR LIFE!"
THAT WAS *IT*?
Well, MOM BEANED HIM WITH AN UMBRELLA BEFORE HE COULD GO ON...
DAWSON 8·25

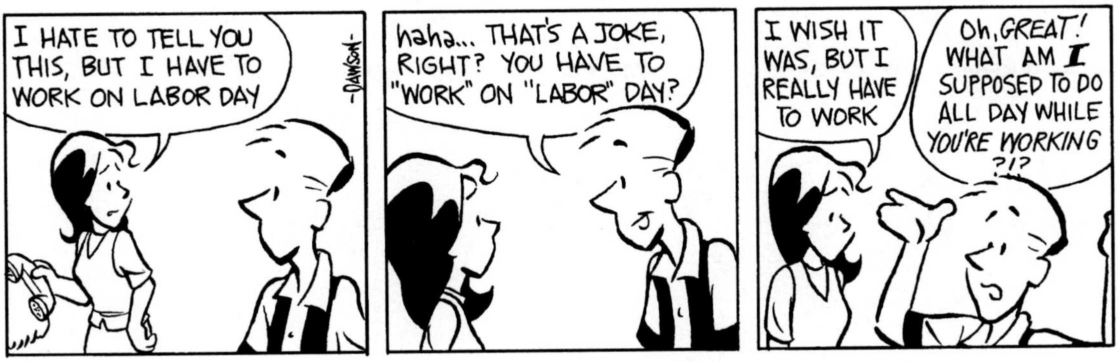

-DAWSON-
I HATE TO TELL YOU THIS, BUT I HAVE TO WORK ON LABOR DAY
haha... THAT'S A JOKE, RIGHT? YOU HAVE TO "WORK" ON "LABOR" DAY?
I WISH IT WAS, BUT I REALLY HAVE TO WORK
Oh, GREAT! WHAT AM I SUPPOSED TO DO ALL DAY WHILE YOU'RE WORKING ?!?

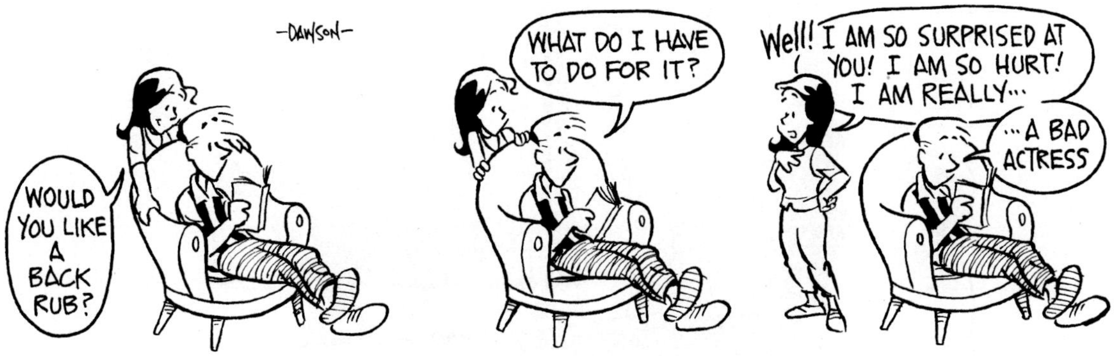

-DAWSON-
WOULD YOU LIKE A BACK RUB?
WHAT DO I HAVE TO DO FOR IT?
Well! I AM SO SURPRISED AT YOU! I AM SO HURT! I AM REALLY...
...A BAD ACTRESS

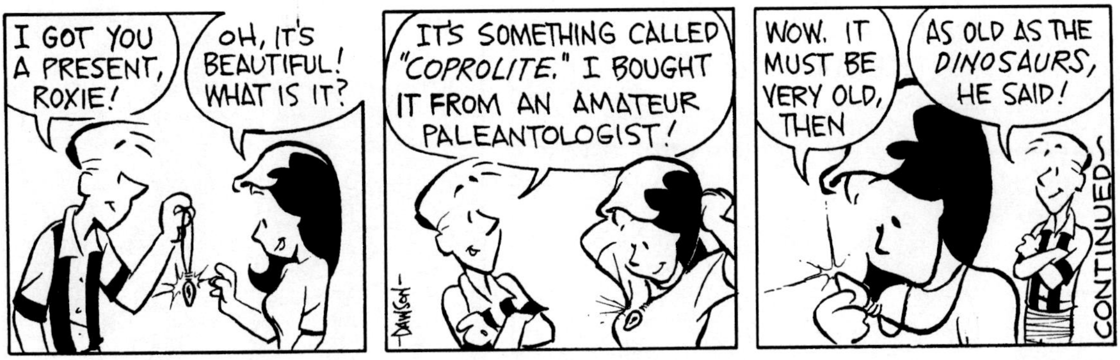

I GOT YOU A PRESENT, ROXIE!
OH, IT'S BEAUTIFUL! WHAT IS IT?
IT'S SOMETHING CALLED "COPROLITE." I BOUGHT IT FROM AN AMATEUR PALEANTOLOGIST!
-DAWSON-
WOW. IT MUST BE VERY OLD, THEN
AS OLD AS THE DINOSAURS, HE SAID!
CONTINUED~

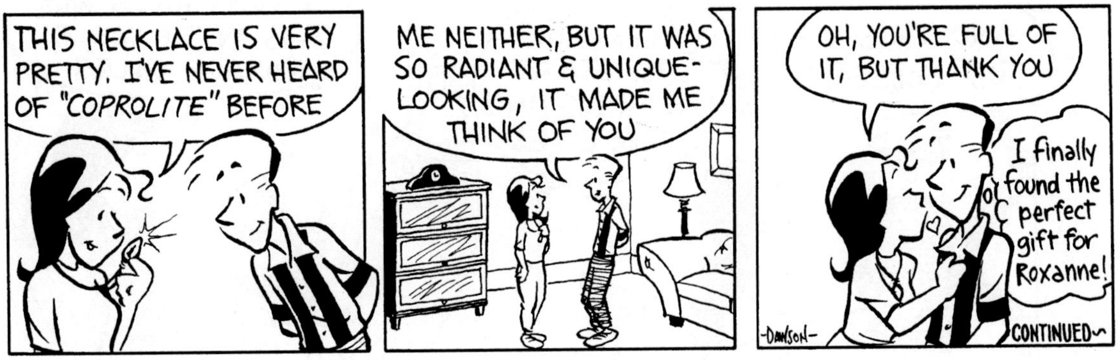

THIS NECKLACE IS VERY PRETTY. I'VE NEVER HEARD OF "COPROLITE" BEFORE
ME NEITHER, BUT IT WAS SO RADIANT & UNIQUE-LOOKING, IT MADE ME THINK OF YOU
OH, YOU'RE FULL OF IT, BUT THANK YOU
I finally found the perfect gift for Roxanne!
-DAWSON-
CONTINUED~

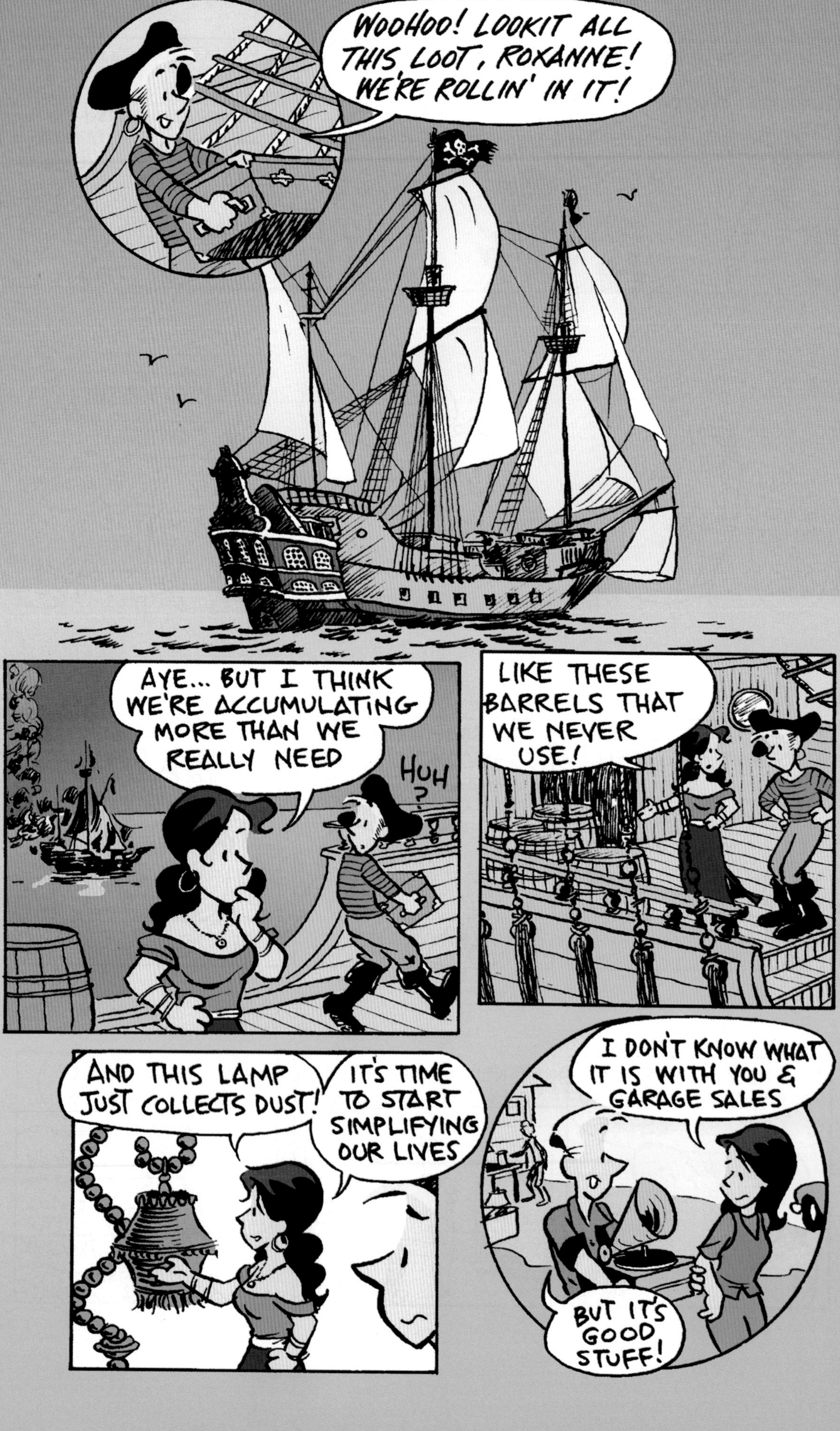
WOOHOO! LOOKIT ALL THIS LOOT, ROXANNE! WE'RE ROLLIN' IN IT!
AYE... BUT I THINK WE'RE ACCUMULATING MORE THAN WE REALLY NEED
HUH?
LIKE THESE BARRELS THAT WE NEVER USE!
AND THIS LAMP JUST COLLECTS DUST!
IT'S TIME TO START SIMPLIFYING OUR LIVES
I DON'T KNOW WHAT IT IS WITH YOU & GARAGE SALES
BUT IT'S GOOD STUFF!

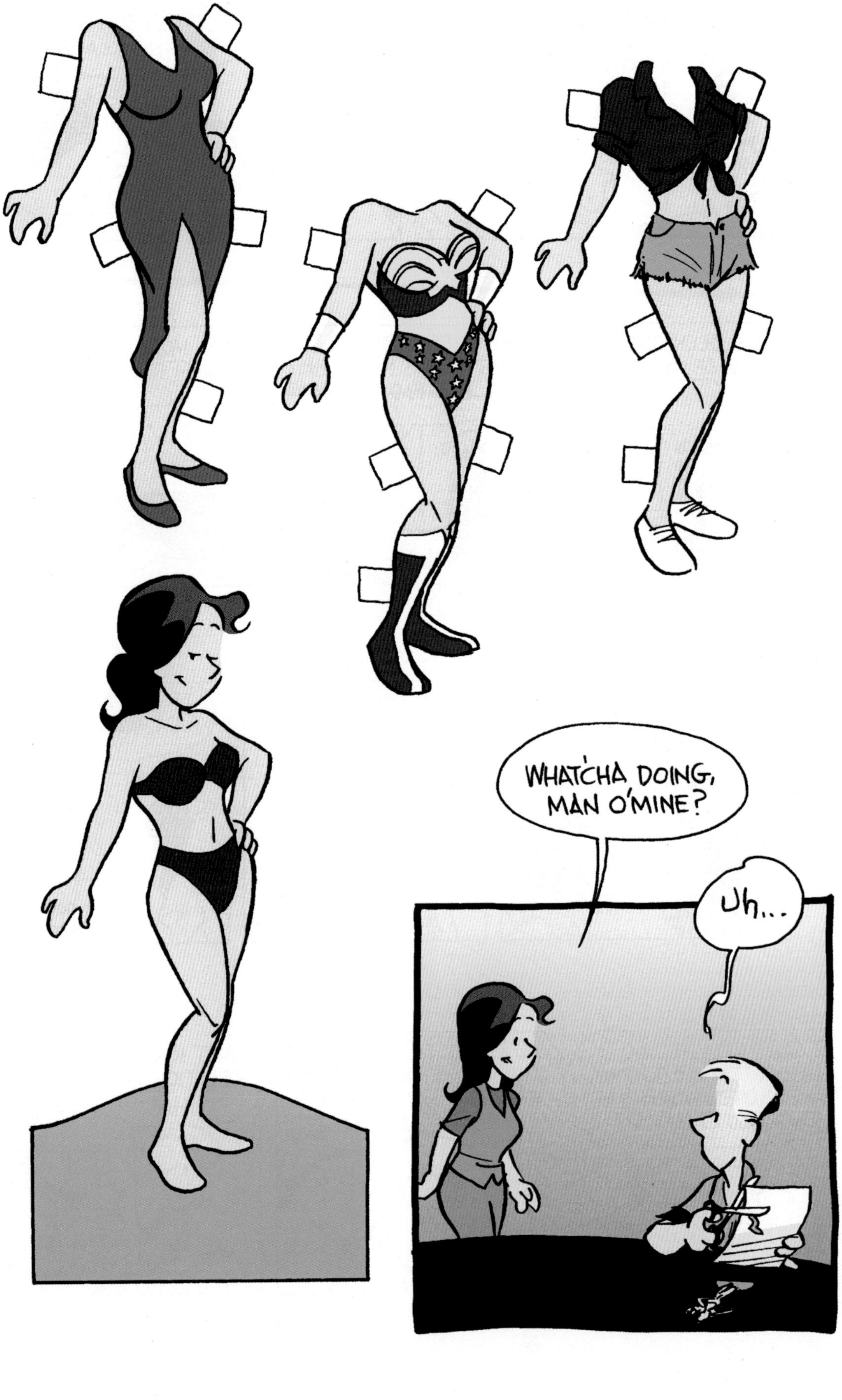
WHATCHA DOING, MAN O'MINE?
Uh...

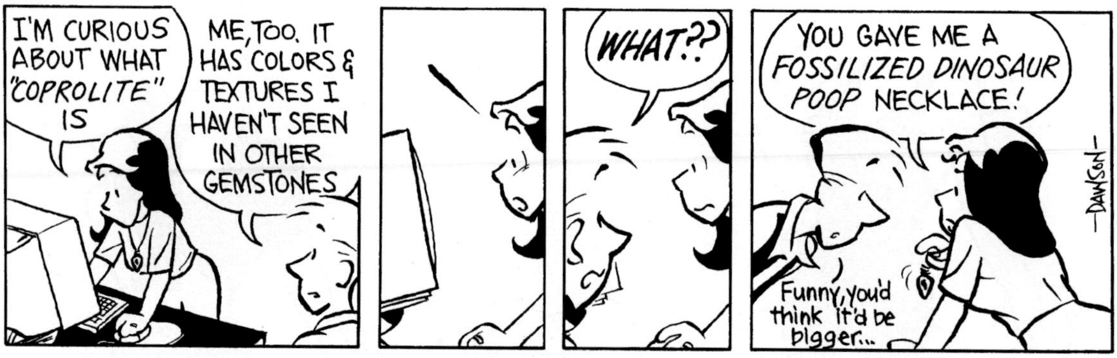
I'M CURIOUS ABOUT WHAT "COPROLITE" IS
ME, TOO. IT HAS COLORS & TEXTURES I HAVEN'T SEEN IN OTHER GEMSTONES
WHAT??
YOU GAVE ME A FOSSILIZED DINOSAUR POOP NECKLACE!
Funny, you'd think it'd be bigger...
-DAWSON-

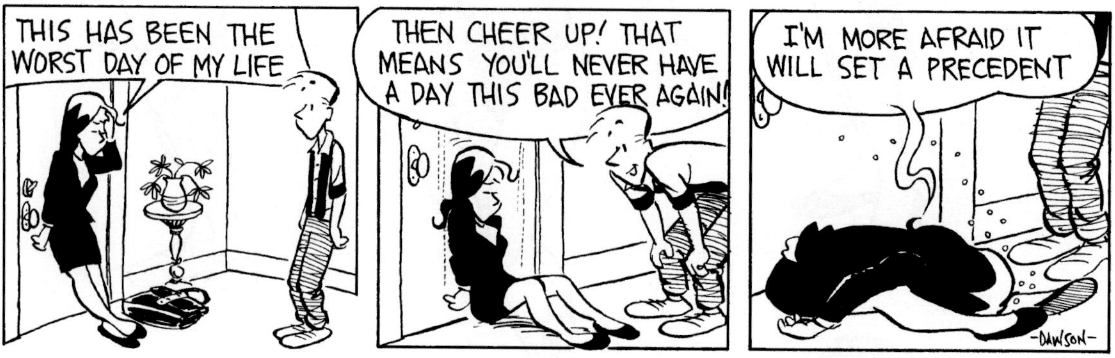
THIS HAS BEEN THE WORST DAY OF MY LIFE
THEN CHEER UP! THAT MEANS YOU'LL NEVER HAVE A DAY THIS BAD EVER AGAIN!
I'M MORE AFRAID IT WILL SET A PRECEDENT
-DAWSON-

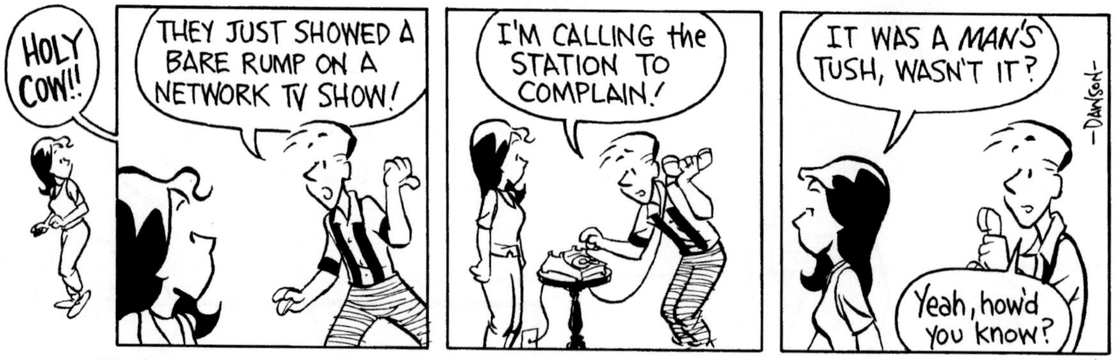
HOLY COW!!
THEY JUST SHOWED A BARE RUMP ON A NETWORK TV SHOW!
I'M CALLING the STATION TO COMPLAIN!
IT WAS A MAN'S TUSH, WASN'T IT?
Yeah, how'd you know?
-DAWSON-

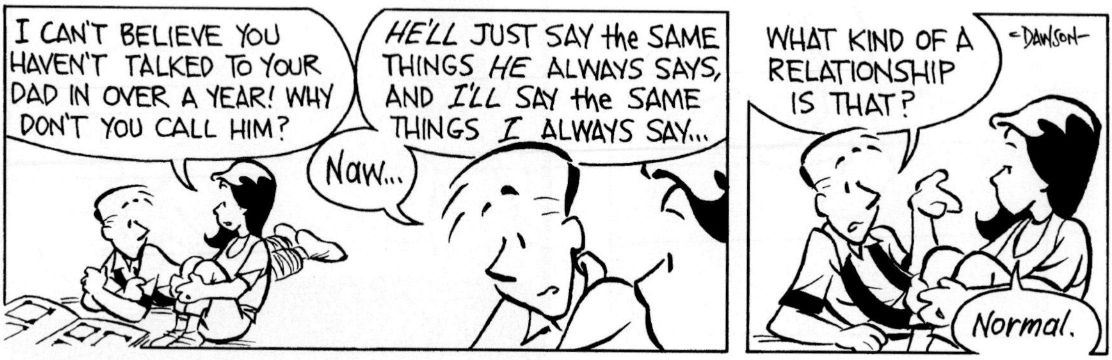
I CAN'T BELIEVE YOU HAVEN'T TALKED TO YOUR DAD IN OVER A YEAR! WHY DON'T YOU CALL HIM?
Naw...
HE'LL JUST SAY the SAME THINGS HE ALWAYS SAYS, AND I'LL SAY the SAME THINGS I ALWAYS SAY...
WHAT KIND OF A RELATIONSHIP IS THAT?
Normal.
-DAWSON-

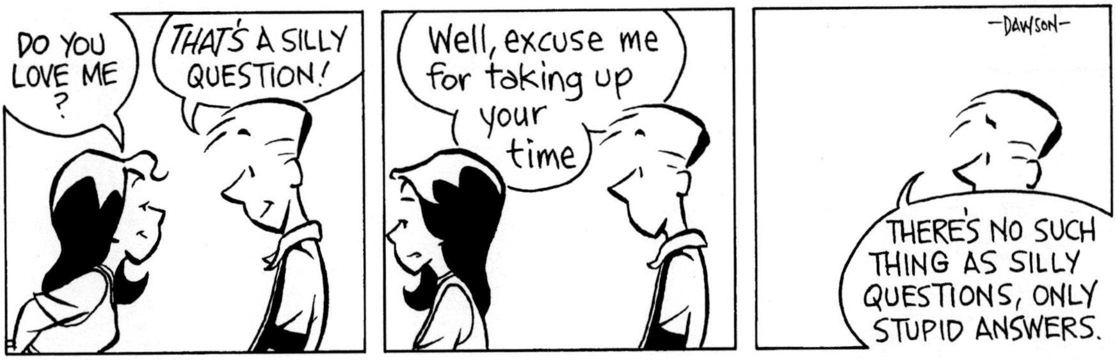
DO YOU LOVE ME ?
THAT'S A SILLY QUESTION!
Well, excuse me for taking up your time
-DAWSON-
THERE'S NO SUCH THING AS SILLY QUESTIONS, ONLY STUPID ANSWERS.

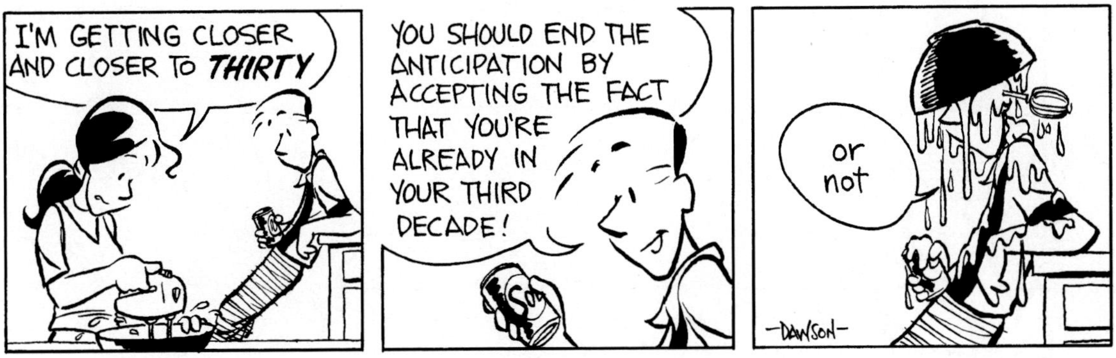
I'M GETTING CLOSER AND CLOSER TO THIRTY
YOU SHOULD END THE ANTICIPATION BY ACCEPTING THE FACT THAT YOU'RE ALREADY IN YOUR THIRD DECADE!
or not
-DAWSON-

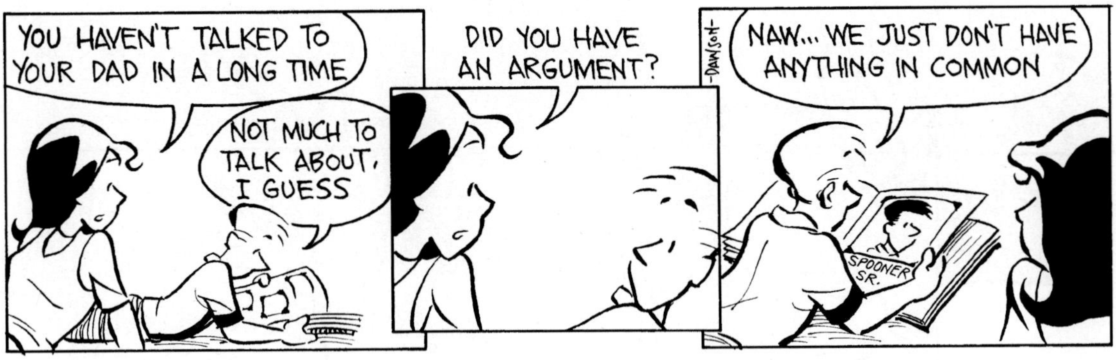
YOU HAVEN'T TALKED TO YOUR DAD IN A LONG TIME
NOT MUCH TO TALK ABOUT, I GUESS
DID YOU HAVE AN ARGUMENT?
-DAWSON-
NAW... WE JUST DON'T HAVE ANYTHING IN COMMON
SPOONER SR.

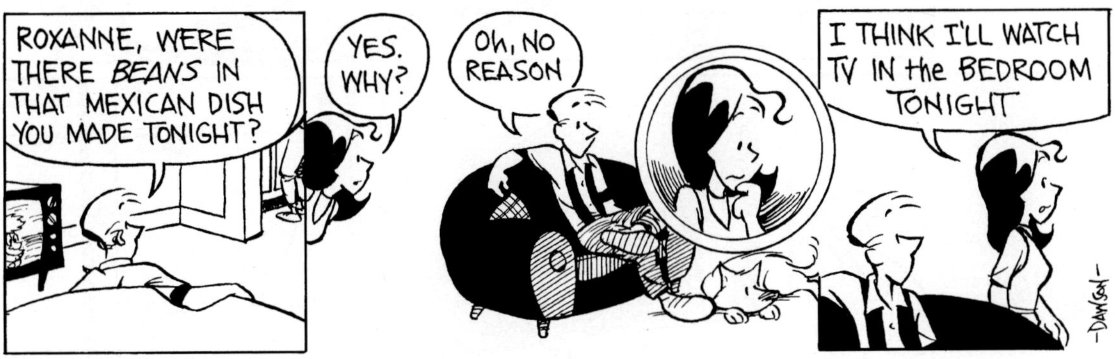
ROXANNE, WERE THERE BEANS IN THAT MEXICAN DISH YOU MADE TONIGHT?
YES. WHY?
Oh, NO REASON
I THINK I'LL WATCH TV IN the BEDROOM TONIGHT
-DAWSON-

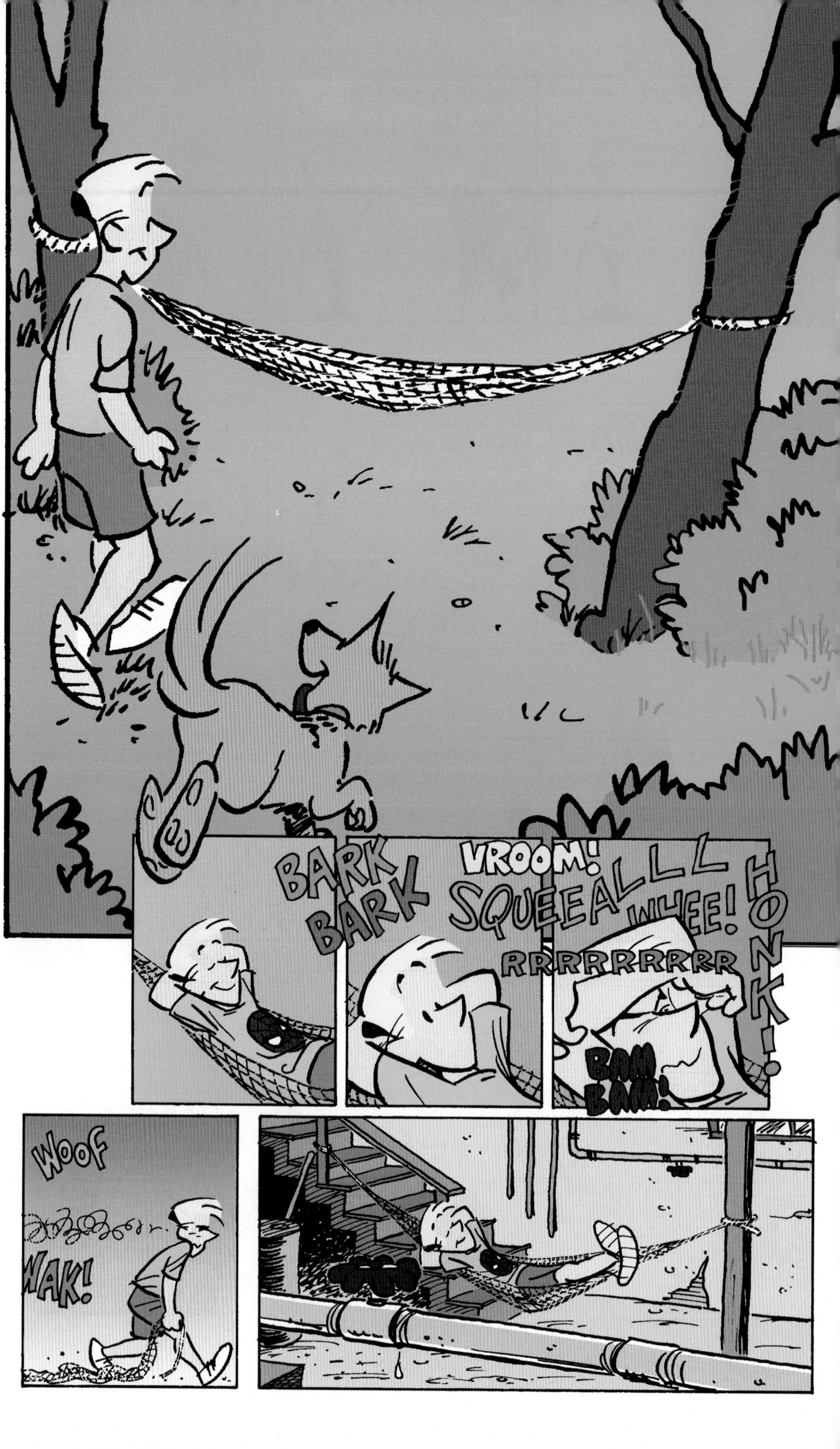
BARK
BARK
VROOM!
SQUEEEALLL
WHEE!
RRRRRRRRRRR
HONK!
BAM
BAM!
WOOF
WAK!

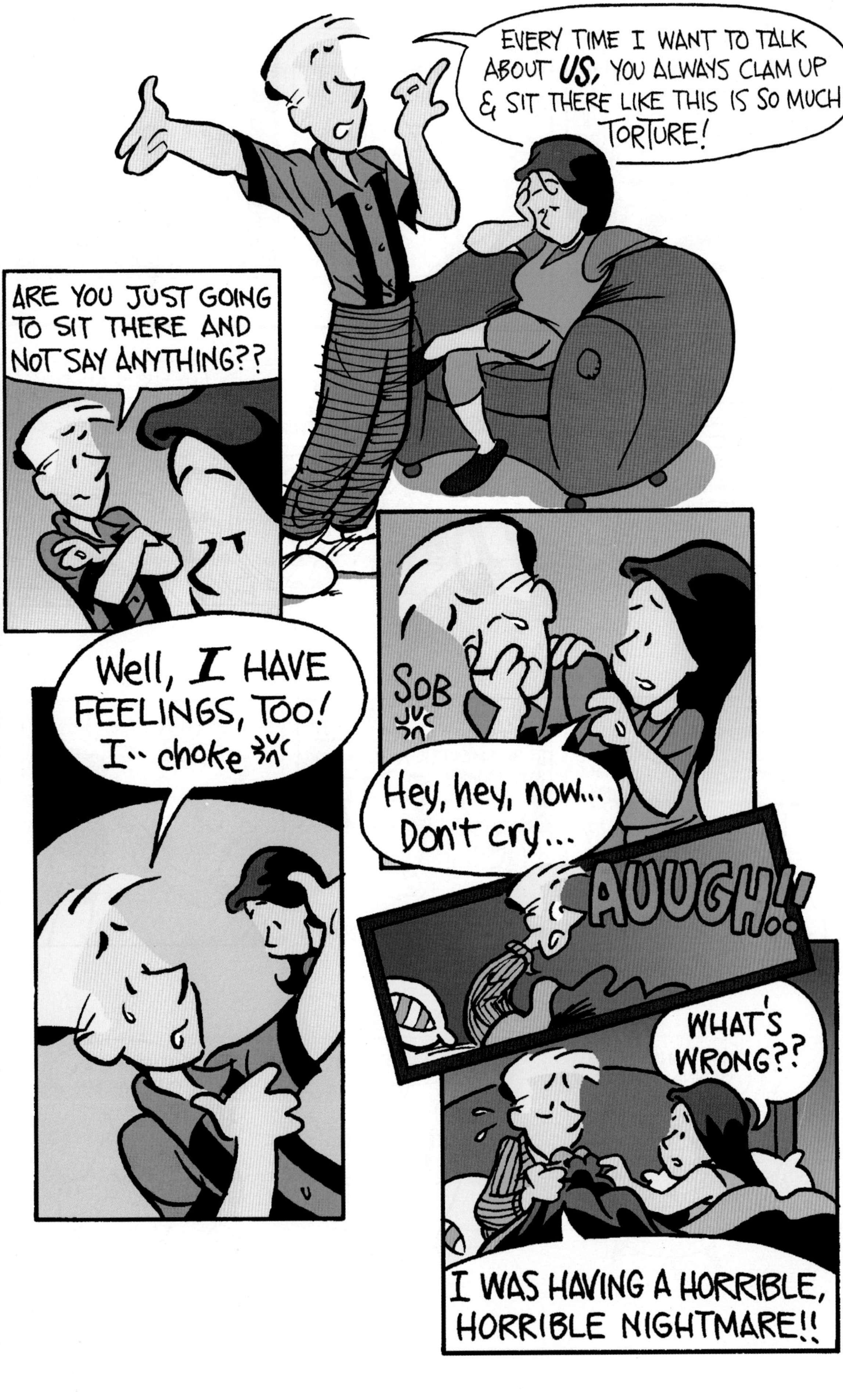
EVERY TIME I WANT TO TALK ABOUT US, YOU ALWAYS CLAM UP & SIT THERE LIKE THIS IS SO MUCH TORTURE!
ARE YOU JUST GOING TO SIT THERE AND NOT SAY ANYTHING??
Well, I HAVE FEELINGS, TOO! I·· choke
SOB
Hey, hey, now... Don't cry...
AUUGH!!
WHAT'S WRONG??
I WAS HAVING A HORRIBLE, HORRIBLE NIGHTMARE!!

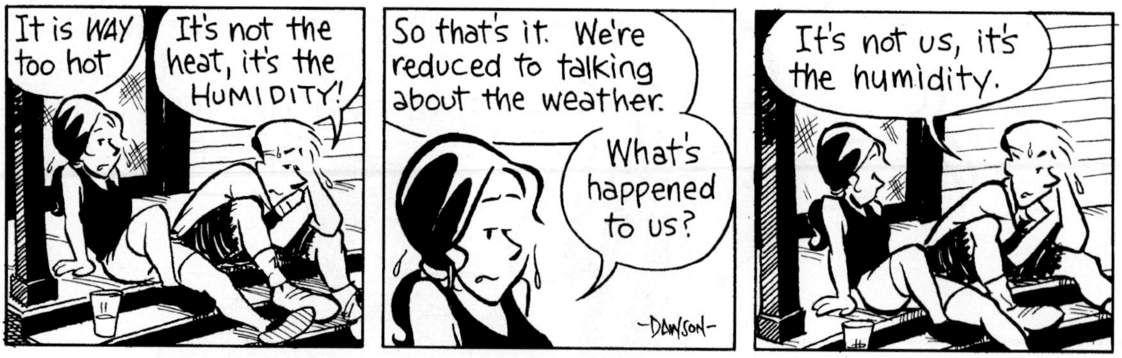
It is WAY too hot
It's not the heat, it's the HUMIDITY!
So that's it. We're reduced to talking about the weather.
What's happened to us?
-DAWSON-
It's not us, it's the humidity.

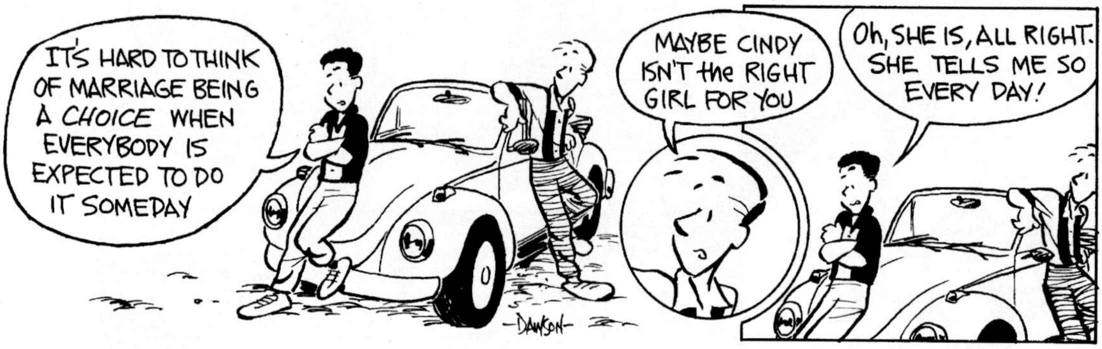
IT'S HARD TO THINK OF MARRIAGE BEING A CHOICE WHEN EVERYBODY IS EXPECTED TO DO IT SOMEDAY
-DAWSON-
MAYBE CINDY ISN'T the RIGHT GIRL FOR YOU
Oh, SHE IS, ALL RIGHT. SHE TELLS ME SO EVERY DAY!

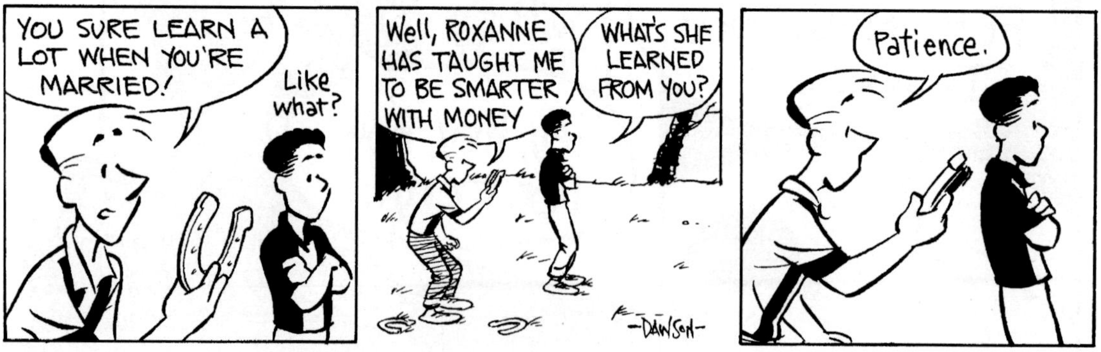
YOU SURE LEARN A LOT WHEN YOU'RE MARRIED!
Like what?
Well, ROXANNE HAS TAUGHT ME TO BE SMARTER WITH MONEY
WHAT'S SHE LEARNED FROM YOU?
-DAWSON-
Patience.

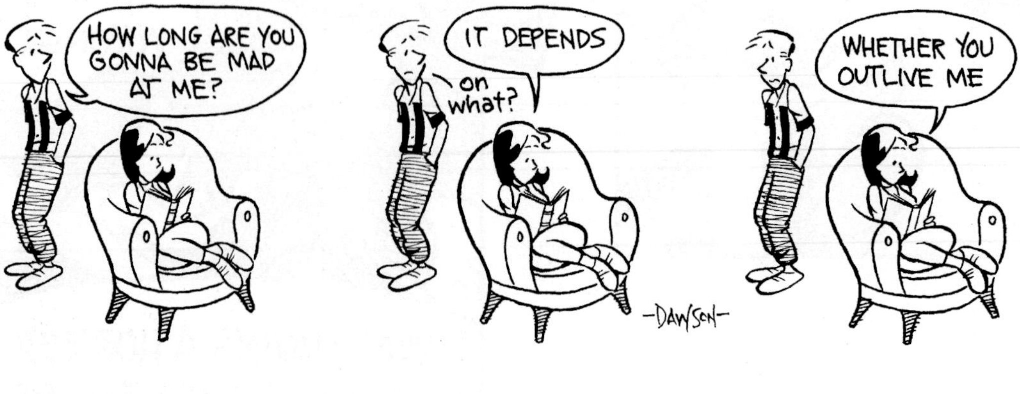
HOW LONG ARE YOU GONNA BE MAD AT ME?
IT DEPENDS
on what?
-DAWSON-
WHETHER YOU OUTLIVE ME

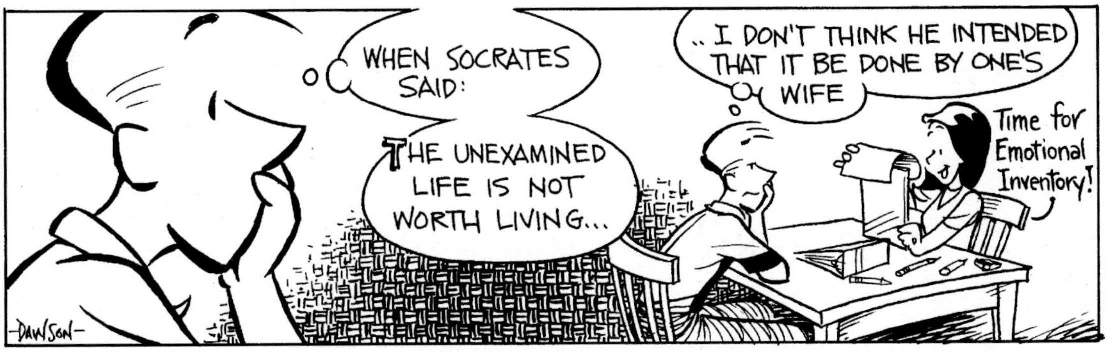
WHEN SOCRATES SAID:
THE UNEXAMINED LIFE IS NOT WORTH LIVING...
.. I DON'T THINK HE INTENDED THAT IT BE DONE BY ONE'S WIFE
Time for Emotional Inventory!
-DAWSON-

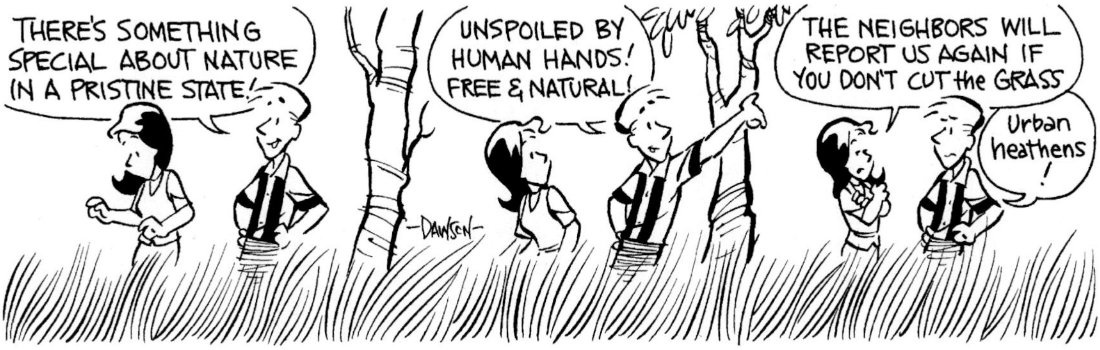
THERE'S SOMETHING SPECIAL ABOUT NATURE IN A PRISTINE STATE!
UNSPOILED BY HUMAN HANDS! FREE & NATURAL!
-DAWSON-
THE NEIGHBORS WILL REPORT US AGAIN IF YOU DON'T CUT the GRASS
Urban heathens!

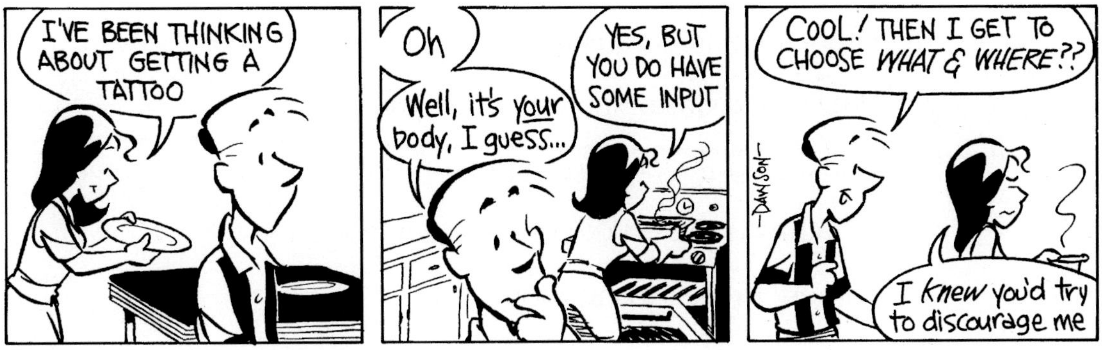
I'VE BEEN THINKING ABOUT GETTING A TATTOO
Oh
Well, it's your body, I guess...
YES, BUT YOU DO HAVE SOME INPUT
-DAWSON-
COOL! THEN I GET TO CHOOSE WHAT & WHERE??
I knew you'd try to discourage me

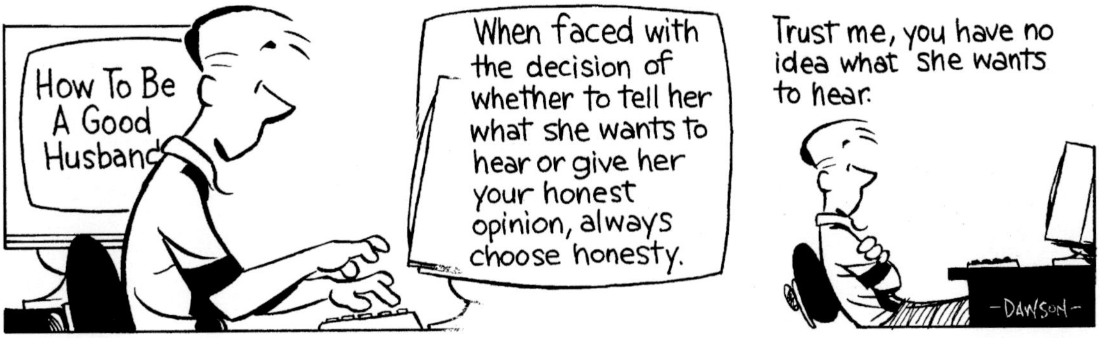
How To Be A Good Husband
When faced with the decision of whether to tell her what she wants to hear or give her your honest opinion, always choose honesty.
Trust me, you have no idea what she wants to hear.
-DAWSON-

Thanks...

You wouldn't be reading this if it weren't for Robbin, Ethan and Sara Rose Dawson, Scott Christian Sava, Mike Kunkel, Sarah Gillespie, Anita Tobias, Amy Lago, Guy Gilchrist, David Waisglass and Stu Rees. Thanks also to all the great folks who have been supportive over the years... Jeff Dawson, Steve Dawson, Ronda Silver, Wilva Silver, Stacy Curtis, Pat Byrnes, Wiley, Stephanie Piro, Darrin Bell, Grant Miehm, Wes Hargis, Chris Crosby, Paul Giambarba, Sandra Lundy, Mark Pett, Ashley, and every single person out there who has accused me of having a hidden camera in their living room.